NO MOPES ALLOWED

A Small Town Police Chief Rants and Babbles
about Hugs and High Fives, Meth Busts,
Internet Celebrity and Other Adventures . . .

CHIEF DAVID A. OLIVER

GRAY & COMPANY, PUBLISHERS
CLEVELAND

The author will donate all of his earnings from this book to The Chief Oliver Foundation, a not-for-profit organization that distributes funds to Brimfield Police Department charitable programs and assists juvenile survivors of sexual assault.

Gray & Company, Publishers
www.grayco.com

ISBN: 978-1-938441-46-2

Printed in the U.S.A.
1

To my wife . . .

Lisa, this book is dedicated to you. You are, without question, the driving force and compass in my life. You remodeled me. When others in my life walked away, you stood fast and walked with me through some tough times. I will always love and appreciate you for being my true love and wife.

To Adam, Emily, Andrew and Anna . . .

A dad could not have better children. You each are your own person and I am so proud of all of you. You will forever be in my heart. I love you.

Special thanks to Andrew Lauer . . . you have been my best friend since we were five years old. Thanks for catching all of those passes and my wicked knuckle-ball. I love you, brother.

Contents

Officers preparing for the arrival of 84 children to our Back-to-School Shop-with-a-Cop.

NO MOPES ALLOWED

Akron Beacon Journal / Phil Masturzo

Introduction

If you're new to the Brimfield Police Department experience, you may have several questions, including "What is this book about, anyway?"

That's easy. This book is an Academy Award-winning movie, in book form—an introduction to an overnight Internet Sensation. Okay, I say that with tongue firmly in cheek. Really, this is a snapshot of two years or so in the life of the Brimfield Police Department, as experienced by a worldwide audience on our Facebook page.

The book includes some of my favorite rants, babbles and other written outbursts . . . along with shift updates (reporting on notable or unusual arrests), community interactions and letters to mopes, which are always fun. You can also find my Top 40 favorite quotes. The order of the postings may not always be chronological; however, it is a great example of our daily flow and what we see, hear and sometimes . . . smell. Yikes.

Comments posted on Facebook by others are not included in the book, likely because it would have taken years to get thousands of people to sign release forms. Plus, that would have required a whole series of books, because of the number of comments and messages we get daily. We also forego our daily weather reports and updates, because we did not want you to actually spend years getting through this story.

As you progress through the book, on the edge of your seat with anticipation, you will travel the road that led us to Internet Sensation status—including receipt of marriage proposals and hugs from numerous ladies. Okay, that was a stretch. The last third or so of the book does recount the rocket-like rise in popularity of our Facebook page and, as a result of that, our being recognized as hip people.

I have to warn you if you have never had the misfortune of reading anything I have written: I am not an author. I am a police officer. A cop. More specifically, I am the chief of police for the Brimfield Police Department, located in Portage County, Ohio.

I have been in law enforcement since 1994. Actually, I've been in law enforcement since I was five years old. It was the first time I remember seeing the television show "Adam-12." Yeah . . . I've been a cop since that day. Andy, (my best friend) and I used to run through the small roads of Burton City, Ohio, arresting bad guys and having shoot-outs. I didn't like criminals much then either. So I worked the first 20 years in law enforcement without really being an officer . . . or getting paid. Four decades later (gasp!) I am the police chief for one of the best police departments around . . . and an Internet sensation. Land Sakes!

The "Internet sensation" joke started with someone in the media making reference to me and the BPD Facebook page.

I will admit at this point and in writing . . . the direction the page has gone is downright odd. I constantly remind people who check in and "like" the page that it is a police department page. We are sometimes not kind to criminals. We aren't mean in the sense of being nasty . . . we just give them no quarter. I firmly believe that everyone should acknowledge and accepting their own responsibility for where they are standing in life. I am the poster child for that little concept.

Meanwhile, I keep posting every day, and tens of thousands of our friends from all 50 states and at least 29 countries keep stopping by for a cup of coffee and a conversation. When we hit 50,000 "likes" I was absolutely humbled. At 80,000 I was astonished. A 16-officer police department, serving a population of 10,500 people . . . and Number 3 in the nation for municipal police departments in Facebook popularity . . . behind New York City and Boston. Yikes.

I hope you enjoy reading this book and finding out how all that happened. Thanks for being here.

Some Personal Background

I was born in Lima Memorial Hospital, in Lima, Ohio, in 1967. The family home was in Cridersville, outside of Lima. It was farm country. Lots of John Deere tractors and corn. We moved to Burton City around 1971. Burton City is close to Orrville. More farms, more corn. There was a lot of turmoil in my childhood. We were the working poor. I was around four years old, so I guess I was the unemployable poor. I am not the product of either of my mother's marriages, and that is the end of that story. My mother and adoptive father both worked in factories and money was tight. Money was more of a nonexistent. As a child, I had heard of this thing called money . . . but don't remember ever seeing any. Now, back to the turmoil. By the way . . . you are in for some fun. I have well-documented issues with staying focused. This will be no different.

We did lots of moving around in my elementary years. I changed schools six times (four different schools) through the sixth grade. It didn't make for establishing lifelong friends, with the exception of Andy. We met when we were about four and have stayed together since. We may go some time without talking, but we are like brothers. All of the moving around didn't help form good habits, like perseverance or commitment. It also developed my strong disdain for landlords, which took me years to overcome. I believed most to be mean for making us move around so much. I had not grasped the concept of rent at that juncture. I attended elementary schools in Orrville, Doylestown and Forest Park before the family settled in Akron in the middle of my sixth grade year. The only constant I had during that time—the only people who stayed with me—were those who could be found on the pages of books purchased for me during school book fairs. I also frequented school and public libraries. To this day I am still a reader. I'll read a dictionary if no other book is around.

After settling in Akron I attended Leggett Elementary, Reidinger Middle and then Central-Hower High School. In middle school two good male figures kept me focused and limited my shenanigans: Mr.

Caito and Mr. Koly. In high school, Ms. Zager and Ms. Elderkin were simply awesome. I owe those four huge thanks.

I truly believe that the mixing of country and city living gives me an edge as a police officer; that and my passion for talking, which gave me a little less of an edge in school. I was always the comedian, likely to keep the negative focus away from me. I usually wore old clothes and often the same ones every day. The blue jeans from my seventh grade year were worn in the eighth grade . . . after some bottoms were sewn onto the legs, to compensate for the summer growth spurt. I do not reveal this for sympathy, but for the purpose of your understanding as to why community programs our police department sponsors, like the Back-to-School Shop-With-a-Cop, are very personal to me.

After high school I worked various jobs until landing with the Brimfield Police Department. I made the decision to attend the police academy in 1994 and was hired by Chief Dennis Holodak in December of that year. Denny is retired now and I see him from time to time around town. I often remind him that he hired me. He was a community-oriented police officer. I spent almost two years in uniform before being assigned to a multi-jurisdictional narcotics task force as an undercover drug agent. I represented the Brimfield Police Department in that capacity for five years . . . and it was a blast.

THE DRUG DAYS

In August of 1996, I was told I was being assigned to the Western Portage Drug Task Force. While I would still be paid by the Brimfield Police Department, I was to report to the drug task force and work undercover as a narcotics agent. Bob Burgess was the chief of police at the time and told me he believed because of my background, I was best suited to do that job. I believed I was also because of my experience dealing with all sorts of people.

So I began becoming "invisible" during my last month in uniform. I assisted in some investigations but slowed down dramatically in making arrests. I hated that time period, because I like making arrests and otherwise upsetting bad guys. In September of 1996, I reported to the secret and undisclosed location from which the task force operated. The WPDTF was a multi-jurisdictional drug unit, comprised of officers from various police departments in Portage County. During any time period we operated with four to eight investigators. This was one of the most fun and fulfilling time periods of my career. I absolutely learned so much during my five years there. The exposure to other officers, supervisors and methods of investigations furthered my knowledge and career in an immeasurable way. The drug unit was a collection of characters that words do not do justice. We did not call anyone by their given name because we did everything we could to protect our identity. I had become the Bruce Wayne of the Brimfield Police Department.

The unit had a collection of mostly eccentric officers who were known by nicknames such as "Daddy," "Frag," "Repo," "Pinky" and our commander, "Gumby." The nicknames were used constantly, because we did not want to be in public or on a drug raid and call each other by our real names. Doing so could lead the bad guys to our department or worse . . . our homes. I earned my drug-unit nickname on the first day I reported there for work. The agents were all heading out to ram a door and serve a search warrant. I jumped in the back seat of one of the vehicles, really pumped up and ready for action. What I did not realize is that I sat down on the lunch of one of the seasoned investigators, who gasped. He then exclaimed, "You just smooshed my lunch." From then on, I was "Smoosh" . . . whether I liked it or not. To this day, the elected county prosecutor still refers to me as Smoosh.

The drug business is one of the most dangerous assignments to draw, because of the overwhelming desire these mopes have to protect their profits. We had to constantly be aware of where we were seen, how we were dressed and who we spoke with. I almost never went to the Brimfield Police Department. In fact, if someone called there for me, they were politely told I no longer worked there. That kind of made it difficult to buy a car or house. It seemed to anyone who checked that I was very unemployed.

During the first few months, I watched and learned. I also began to grow my hair. I had worn a flattop while working in uniform . . . and that haircut is not remotely in style, let alone for someone in the drug world. My hair got longer, my beard grew and I got some piercings . . . both of my ears and later my eyebrow. After a month or so, I did my first undercover drug buy . . . an ounce of marijuana at a library parking lot. A picture of me was promptly taken by the rest of the crew . . . and I was on my way to some good years "working dope."

Gumby was a lieutenant with another police department in the county and was my direct supervisor while assigned to the WPDTF. Without question, he was the best boss I have had in my career. He was the first I had ever had with a college degree. But more than that, he was the first I was exposed to who was a leader and not a supervisor. He was the one who taught me "surround yourself with good people and then stay out of their way and let them work." I was very close to him for the entire time I spent there. I was also close to "Daddy," who is one of the best friends I have had, along with the best undercover person I have ever seen. He was an expert mimic, wore all sorts of crazy clothing and often that clothing smelled like he had not bathed in a month. When I was undercover for that period of time, many officers, prosecutors and others commented about my ability and looks as an undercover officer. I will offer that Daddy was simply the best I have ever seen, anywhere. He is also a spectacular investigator who pays strict attention to detail. If I were ever a criminal, I would not want him investigating me.

For a long period of time, I did most of the undercover buys for the WPDTF. I loved working undercover. I have heard and read the assignment being described as dangerous or stressful. I never experienced those feelings. I was always armed when I was buying drugs and never had any issues handling myself physically, if needed. I have the gift of gab and usually talked my way out of about any situation. I wore Harley-Davidson apparel, including a biker vest or sometimes these God-awful cut-off camo shorts with a raggedy T-shirt. My hair was wild and all over the place, and my goatee appeared as though something could be living in it. Those attributes, along with a pierced eyebrow, put most drug dealers at ease. We used lots of other tricks, which I will not disclose, to keep our officers undercover. Although it was fun, there were some hairy situations . . .

During one drug buy, we were targeting a house which had been called in several times as a drug house. We did our homework and discovered there were some pretty nasty characters hanging out there. Daddy found an informant who could take me in, so we gave it a try. When the informant and I arrived at the location, we knocked and the head mope came out to the porch. He immediately began berating the informant over some money owed over a prior drug deal. Great, I thought. They exchanged some words, and I decided

That's me, with 400 pounds of marijuana.

That's 77 kilos of marijuana. I'm on the left, with Chief Dave Thomas and prosecutor Vic Vigluicci.

2 KILO BUST./COCAINE TALLMADGE RD. VIA L.A..

I loved working undercover.

12 lbs of Anthony's Dope

Being sworn in as Brimfield police chief by Prosecutor Vigluicci in March 2004.

to end the operation so we left. Daddy and I talked about it later, and we decided that I would go back alone and attempt to make nice with the bad guy.

A couple of days later, I went back by myself. I met with the ring-leader again, on his front porch. I began talking with him, trying to put him at ease. I told him I was a bouncer at a strip club and that the informant was not to be trusted and I believed the informant was attempting to be intimately involved with some of my strippers. The response I got was not what I expected . . . "Why the hell would he do that? He's gay." Great. So much for knowing what the heck I am talking about! I spun it back around, and within a day I was buying cocaine, prescription pills and LSD out of the house. After going back for what would be the last time, we ordered the SWAT Team to hit the location. That decision was made after discovering the mope in charge was giving crack cocaine to minor females and then enticing them into sex acts. It was a pleasure to put six of the residents or visitors of that house in the state "bed and breakfast."

I am very anti-drug. It is very tough to work undercover—or really any other form of law enforcement—and like drugs. The effects drugs have on a person, family and society are immeasurable. I have personally witnessed lives unravel rather quickly due to addiction. I understand the American Medical Association has classified addiction as a disease; however, the theft, prostitution and scores of other crimes and victims associated with addiction cause a large amount of collateral damage to innocent people. I often post about addiction, drug sales and use on our page.

I was once in a crack house waiting on a supplier to show up. The female who was going to sell me the crack had a law degree and had practiced law for a period of time. On that day, she was in a see-through nightgown and looked a wreck. At one point during the conversation she fell to her knees and started combing through the carpet. I realized she had seen a piece of white lint or other small fiber . . . and believed to be a crack rock. She was a mess. The dealer finally showed up and I was surprised to learn it was someone who knew me very well and usually carried a gun. I went to a back bedroom, telling the female that I did not want to "meet any new faces." He sold to me through her. She "bumped" some of my package for her own use; however, they were both arrested a week or so later after a few more buys. That was the third time I had dealt with that particular supplier . . . he just kept getting released from jail.

One of the best cases I worked while undercover was also the most complex. We kept hearing the same name associated with bringing large amounts of marijuana into the county. By large amounts, I mean 400-600 pounds every month or so. This guy had an organization under him and usually kept himself insulated from anything other than the large amount of cash he was making. He had a connection in Arizona, who was getting the dope straight from a cartel in Mexico. They would pay a "mule" to bring the supply north . . . and they paid the mule a lot. One trip east with 400 pounds of marijuana could bring $10,000 for the driver. Yikes. The product would be brought into town and the driver would check into a hotel room in our community. A local "mule" would come to the hotel and pick the vehicle up from the parking lot. The weed would then be taken to any of several safe locations to split it amongst the underlings in the organization. I spent a lot of time initially putting this information together. I spoke with officers and investigators I could trust to try to find any info I could on the known players. Gumby, Daddy and I conducted lots of surveillance on the mopes. Ultimately, I reached the point in the case where I needed big help . . . and I called on the feds. My first call and meeting was with the Drug Enforcement Administration (DEA). I figured the DEA worked dope. I had worked with them before . . . it would be a cinch. Boy, was I wrong. I could not sell the case, and I can sell almost anything, according to Mrs. Chief. The DEA bosses asked if there were murders associated with the case, if there was cocaine involved and if there was the potential to seize cash and property. How was I supposed to know any of that at this point in the investigation? I talked and talked to no end. I decided to call the Akron office of the FBI to see if I could go that direction. The agent in charge during that time was one of the best leaders I have ever seen . . . for a fed. He wanted to make cases and catch bad guys. He gave me a new FBI agent, who had been a cop prior to becoming a fed . . . and it worked like a charm. We spent weeks doing surveillance, interviews and investigating. Ultimately we exhausted all other investigative options and were granted a wiretap by a federal judge. Once the wiretap was in place, I was deputized as a federal agent and the case took off.

We spent the better part of six months running the wire and watching bad guys. In the end, we indicted and arrested 18 people in three states and charged them with conspiracy to deliver 1,000 pounds of marijuana. We seized hundreds and hundreds of pounds of the drug, over a million dollars in cash and several properties. The case was a success for all involved, except the mopes.

Many people have argued with me about marijuana and have told me often it should be legalized and taxed. Right. I want the federal government to be drug dealers, primarily because of the success they have had with the post office and Social Security. Marijuana is a drug, period.

Sometimes what I say or write can be construed as being harsh. I do not intend it to be that way. I do intend on conveying my definite sense of right and wrong and also my convictions. Acting within the law and with civility is very important to me . . . I know of no other way, save for the occasional rant about criminals.

My time in undercover work came to an end in September of 2001. At the end of that assignment and still to this day, I reflect on that part of my career and know that some good was done. I was personally involved in hundreds of felony drug cases, most as the lead or undercover agent. In those five years I bought cocaine, crack, heroin, LSD, meth, ecstasy, mushrooms, marijuana, prescription drugs, guns, stolen items and food stamps. I worked undercover with the DEA, FBI, postal inspectors, HUD and the Secret Service . . . along with numerous local agencies. I was promoted to sergeant and returned to uniform duties on September 11, 2001.

BACK TO NAVY BLUE

After being promoted to sergeant, I returned to the navy blue war on crime. It was a very odd feeling putting on the uniform again. I had not been in a police uniform in five years. I also had to start shaving regularly, which was awfully sad, considering the nice beard I had cultivated. I'm sure there was something living in that beard at one point. Yikes.

My first day back in uniform was September 11, 2001. We all know about that day.

As I got acclimated to responding to calls again, I also had to learn all about leading the crew I had. I was assigned to a swing shift, which was 7 a.m. to 3 p.m. I supervised both afternoon and midnight shifts. During this time we hired Chris Adkins and David Knarr as part-time officers. The three of us spent lots of time together working at night and generally disrupting criminals. We hammered the hotel areas and started seizing lots of drugs. The years spent undercover were very instrumental in these efforts. I also became very close with Adkins and Knarr. They both displayed the kind of work ethic I am attracted to, which is hard-charging and doing things correctly.

As time moved on, there were changes at the top within the police department. Dave Thomas, who was the chief at the time, announced he was leaving to go full-time in the military. Dave is one heck of a man. He is a military guy, through and through. The job opening for chief was posted and I applied.

The person who was made interim chief was a part-time detective for the department. He had retired from another agency and joined ours as a part-time detective. The board of trustees at the time just had no idea about police work and chain of command. You never, under any circumstances, put a part-time officer without rank in charge of a police department. I was livid.

I must also say, during this time. I was not a popular guy with at least one of the elected people in the township. I'm not sure if it is the fact that I arrested one of his friends, resulting in the elected person showing up at the department demanding I release the person . . . or the fact that three months later, I stopped the politician and had the audacity to give him field sobriety tests. By the way, on the first issue . . . I kicked the elected person out of the department. That's always a good career move. "Hey, boss . . . get out of the building, we're working."

The job was posted and the interim chief was put in charge of the hiring process. Two internal candidates (another sergeant and I) and several outside candidates applied. The officers at the time submitted a letter, signed by all of them, stating they wanted me as chief. I was floored. To have that support from all of the officers meant a tremendous amount to me.

The day for the testing arrived. Interviews and assessment centers are right in my wheelhouse. I have always liked pressure and I love to talk. Shocking, I know. We went through the assessment and I felt I nailed it.

The elected people during that time thought differently. After the whole process . . . they picked the interim chief to be the full-time chief. I was seven shades of frustrated with that decision. When the announcement came during a public meeting, I was floored. How do you hire someone for a job the person had not even applied for?

After the meeting, one of the trustees approached me to discuss the matter. I was not in a conversational mood. He wanted to discuss his rationale and I just let him have it. I told him he was sneaky, lacked honor and should hang his head in shame. Boy, I was just trying to further my career, huh?

The new chief took over and I continued to work nights. I spoke with one of the elected people who flat-out told me he did not like me and I would never be chief. It was the same one I had ejected from the department. I came really close to leaving the Brimfield Police Department during this time. I did not want anything to do with politicians who lacked common sense and honor.

BECOMING CHIEF

A few years passed, the elected people changed, and the chief was set to retire. So I gave it another shot.

Mike Kostensky came on board as an elected official. Mike is a squared-away guy and a great boss. He is honest and tries to always do what is honorable. I thought I at least had a chance. I was correct.

On March 8th, 2004, I was sworn in as the fifth chief of police for the Brimfield Police Department. I tried to hit the ground in a sprint. I immediately filled the open position by recommending the hire of Chris Adkins as a full-time officer. Dave Knarr and I had talked about implementing a K-9 unit, and Dave was ready with the info. He was a full-time officer by now also. We added K-9 Ace a few months later and we were moving.

Within a year of becoming chief, we worked four homicides. We had no homicides for ten years prior to that point. The first was a very brutal drug-related killing with a hatchet. We worked that case non-stop for three days and caught the suspect in Cleveland, with the assistance of the CPD narcotics unit. The suspect is spending life in prison.

The next homicides were by far the worst experiences of not just my career . . . but also my life. On January 21, 2005 I was at home watching a movie with my family. I received a call from dispatch advising that a subject had possibly killed his live-in girlfriend and her seven-year-old son. I got dressed and started for work. During that time, I was advised that Dave Knarr was on a street close to the original address for a subject with an AR-15 who had held some people hostage for a few minutes and then left the area. I just knew the two were connected.

I responded to the first address and was told it was confirmed . . . the woman and her son were dead, shot multiple times at close range with the AR-15. Shortly after, Dave Knarr called on the radio advising that he and other officers from surrounding agencies, who had responded to assist, were under fire. The shooter had left his house with the AR-15, a nine-millimeter pistol and over four hundred rounds of ammo. He was also dressed in head-to-toe camouflage. This was just a horrible night. The subject eventually broke into a house and took a beautiful and innocent college student hostage. The SWAT team set up on the residence and began negotiating with this monster. He agreed to a two-hour "cooling off" period, after which he promised to let the hostage go.

Shortly afterwards, he hung the phone up and executed her. We had no idea she had been killed. He had been shooting at us all-night and continued to shoot all night, even after the agreement. We attempted to call him back numerous times . . . to no avail. As daylight approached, I was very concerned about neighboring houses being in full view and also for the safety of officers who were posted around the house. I made the decision to send the SWAT team in. The team made entry and found the coward hiding in the bathroom. He was arrested, prosecuted and is awaiting a lethal injection. I will attend when he meets his maker and I hope my face is the last thing he sees on this earth.

I developed a great disdain for some defense attorney types during this time. The stories concocted to try to get this guy out of being responsible for these reprehensible crimes were just . . . ignorant. I was shocked at some of the scenarios and excuses I heard. All were lies and shameful.

After the homicides, things simmered some. Dave Knarr was promoted to sergeant and new officers joined us, while some left. A few left with medical issues, some left because our character did not line up and some just could not work with me or the crew we were assembling. I look for character when I hire. We can teach police work; I do not have time to teach honor and integrity. As the 2000s moved on, Chris Adkins and Matt McCarty were both promoted to sergeant. We added great officers like Bill Atha, Jerry Dumont and others. We were slowly building a great team. I also finished my four-year and master's degrees during this time. My master's is in business management and leadership and one of my major papers was on "branding your organization." That's what I have been attempting to do since becoming chief.

As I put the principles of branding in place, I wanted to get the word out to our community about the changes in the department and the great officers and programs we had. Our reputation within the community had not been great. As I researched the different methods, one thing stood out . . . the move of our population or "customer base" towards technology.

One of the ideas I kept hearing about was social media. Facebook was a big gathering place for so many people. I surfed around the site and saw numerous business "pages." There were also police departments in the mix; however, most were "just the facts, ma'am" in content. "We encountered someone who needed to be arrested, so we arrested them" stories. I just wanted to add more. I believed that civilians needed to see what we see and experience some of the highs and lows. I am also sort of a clown and like humor, so I figured I would write things from that perspective.

In 2010 we launched the page . . . and the rest is history, I guess. The page added "likes" at a slow pace for the first year or so. I kept writing and telling stories and the page just kept growing. In the year between summer of 2012 and summer of 2013, we added thousands of "likes," surpassing 80,000+ in the summer of 2013. It was really catching on.

The emails and message poured in from all over the world. After some review, we determined we had people in all 50 states and 29 countries who read the page regularly. Did I already say the emails and messages kept pouring in? That may be an understatement. We had put Brimfield and the Brimfield Police Department on the map . . . in a big way. I talked to a local Realtor who told me she gets constant calls from people who are looking to relocate to Brimfield because of the department and were looking for a place where they would feel safe.

That is the best compliment a police chief or officer can get.

MY NAME

As I got older (I guess I am still getting that way), my unorganized childhood kept creeping back into my thoughts. One of the issues that had bothered me most was that I did not have the last name of my father. I believe in lots of "old fashioned" things—or so I am told. One of those is that "You are who you are." I always took that to heart. Yet I kept feeling that I could never be who I was unless I identified with the man who played at least half the part in bringing me into this world. Silly to some, perhaps. Not to me.

In October 2011, after establishing communications with my father's side of the family, and careful consideration and hours of talks with my own family, I changed my last name to the family name: Oliver.

My dad was long gone, but I know he is proud. I did not have a chance to know him well, but what I remember and what I have been told by others is that he was a great guy. He fought in World War II with the 645th Tank Destroyer Battalion and saw action in Africa, Italy and Europe. He spent 605 days in combat, 515 of them on the front lines. He was in many, many battles in that war, and earned the Bronze Star, Purple Heart and Croix de Guerre (a French citation for bravery). As a First Sergeant he prepared most of the written reports from battles. I sure hope he had the same disdain for paperwork as his son.

If you have never had a name change, you are lucky. I feel bad for women who change their names when they marry. There was so much to change—bank accounts, insurance, licenses and numerous other identifiers. And this was just not one name change; my wife and two younger children changed, too. They did so in support of me and never blinked an eye. It was an emotional decision for me, for many reasons. Afterward, I felt as though I could drop the baggage from childhood and walk. And that's what I did.

After the change I was still the same person with the same convictions and beliefs—just with a different last name. And now it seems as though it has always been this way. I did get numerous questions concerning the impact to my "professional career," which I find amusing. I am not elected, don't ever care to be, and I am usually just called "Chief" anyway. Name recognition does not motivate me. Catching criminals does.

Welcome to Brimfield

Brimfield is located in Portage County, Ohio, about eight miles east of the city of Akron. We are close to several larger cities in northeast Ohio, including Cleveland, Canton and Youngstown . . . all of which are less than 40 minutes away. Interstate 76 runs east and west though the township almost directly through the middle of the community. That stretch of highway brings mopes through the area regularly. Part of our mission is to make sure they do not impact the community during their visit. My officers are pretty darn good at the mission.

The residents of Brimfield are great to work for. There is a nice socioeconomic mix. The officers who work here must be prepared to deal with residents who are upper-class and live in $400,000-plus homes . . . and then respond to a call in subsidized housing. One thing I have learned is that no matter where you come from, everyone has largely the same concerns. Most want to feel safe to live, work and move around without being impacted by knuckleheads.

When I started as a new officer at the department, Brimfield was largely still farms and open land. That has certainly changed in the last 20 years or so. Some of the old farms and open spaces have been replaced by a shopping center and housing developments. The building of homes and new businesses continues. For the last several years, Brimfield was at or near the top in housing starts in Portage County.

Here's some more information about Brimfield that might serve as a useful introduction to the stories that follow in this book . . .

• Brimfield was founded in 1816. We have the founding year on our shoulder patches. It had a few other names, including Thorndyke and Swamptown. If you ever chase a mope through some of the swampy areas of town, you will understand. It's sort of a black muck and that muck has captured several nice police boots . . .

• Brimfield is a township. Township government is one of the oldest forms of government in the United States. Early in the settlement of our country, townships were formed by land companies in accordance with (then) recently formed statutes. Some were formed as 25 square miles (five wide, five in length), some 36 square miles.

• Brimfield used to be 25 square miles. It's about 23 square miles now. Some neighboring cities annexed some of the land years ago . . .

we have dogs now, so those cities stay on their own side of the fence. We are just kidding . . . really.

• We have a population of about 10,500. We are governed by three elected trustees and an elected fiscal officer.

• Townships cannot enact criminal ordinances like an incorporated (city) community can. Trustees may not establish criminal penalties for speed, OVI . . . or even murder. Township police departments operate solely under the Ohio Revised Code and any charges brought must be a violation of that state law. Additionally, most townships have a mix of roads belonging to the township, county and state. Brimfield is no exception . . . we have numerous roads belonging to the county, the township and also two state roadways.

• Interstate 76 runs east to west through town. Bigger cities located within a short drive are Cleveland, Akron, Canton and Youngstown. Akron and Youngstown are on I-76, with Brimfield in the middle . . . sort of. We are closer to Akron than Youngstown.

• State Highway 43 (SR43) runs north to south through town. At the intersection of I-76 and SR43 we have several businesses, including three gas stations, six hotels, a McDonald's, Wendy's, Pizza Hut . . . and other restaurants. We have older farms and new housing . . . so quite the mix of people.

• I-76 has another on-off ramp access in Brimfield, which is at Tallmadge Road. That is where the Cascades Shopping Center is located . . . Walmart, Lowe's and other stores can be found there.

• Several nice universities are close by, including Kent State, Akron and NEOMED . . . which is where doctors are hatched . . . errr . . . educated.

• Our schools, the Field Local Schools, are rated Excellent With Distinction by the State of Ohio. That is the highest rating possible.

• The Brimfield Police Department is located here. They are Internet sensations. Their Facebook is third in the country in "likes" for municipal departments, behind New York City, Boston and Philadelphia . . . in spite of their police chief, who is surly and introverted. The BPD is adored by women, children, dogs and an occasional llama. They bathe regularly, have fresh breath and smell nice.

Come and see us, anytime.

BPD Basics

The Brimfield Police Department has 16 full-time officers, including me. Our command staff is composed of a chief (me), Captain Adkins and three sergeants: Sgt. Knarr, Sgt. McCarty and Sgt. Dumont. Each sergeant is assigned to his own shift. I believe in having a leader on each shift, to help with day-to day operations and accountability. All three sergeants do a great job and bring a lot to the table.

One of the unusual aspects of the Brimfield Police Department is the number of K-9 officers we have—four. Our dogs are Havoc (utility/drugs), Joker (utility/drugs), Drogen (utility/drugs) and Nitro (utility/explosives). Using simple math, you can see that one-fourth of our officers have a furry four-legged partner. I tease my staff regularly about teaching the dogs to drive and not needing human officers. K-9 officers are absolutely invaluable to police work. Indispensable. These officers can track, find drugs, detect explosives, recover evidence, apprehend criminals and locate missing people. A department should not be without at least one K-9. If you have never seen a dog at work, you are missing one of the great tools associated with police work.

The Brimfield Police Department building has a temporary holding facility. We usually keep arrestees long enough to book, process and interview if needed. At the end of our process, we either transport to the county jail or release the person on bond.

I'm not sure why I started referring to the county jail and the state prison as the "bed and breakfast." I just used it one day on the page and it caught on. Numerous people talk about it when they meet us. I find that people really do enjoy humor.

Not everyone we arrest ends up at the bed and breakfast. Many people arrested for misdemeanors have the legal right to post bond, unless there is violence or there are multiple offenses included.

I have often told people Brimfield sure has changed since I started working here. When I became a Brimfield officer, we were handling around 5,000 calls for service per year and making 300+ or so physical arrests.

Boy, have times changed. Since 2010 we have averaged about 14,000 calls for service per year. In 2011 and 2012 we averaged close to 1,000 physical arrests. The fortunate thing for the community is that we rarely arrest anyone who lives here. It happens, but not nearly as much as the transient motorist, warrant or drug arrest at one of the hotels, or someone who comes through town looking to steal or otherwise make someone a victim.

Our officers conduct a large amount of traffic stops and write lots of warnings. I am a huge believer in officer presence being a downer for the criminally predisposed. That being said, if you get a ticket in Brimfield, you probably deserve it. Most are for excessive speed, driving under suspension and operating a vehicle while impaired (OVI). Other than those and a handful of other offenses, I much prefer my officers to be looking for criminals. We use traffic stops to accomplish that mission and I am happy to say the officer here are very good at it. The numbers of meth labs, meth, heroin, stolen items and fugitives are pretty steady in our jurisdiction. The goal, as I relay it to my staff, is to catch them before they make it into the neighborhoods.

A Year (or Two) In the Life of the Brimfield Police Department . . .

With Chief's Rants and Babbles,
Letters to Mopes, Police Activity
Reports, Favorite Quotes
and More

Kindergarten field trip. *Akron Beacon Journal / Phil Masturzo*

Eight years

I will soon complete my eighth year as chief of police here. There is a reason for telling you that; I will get to it. Yesterday I worked some of the afternoon shift with Sgt. McCarty and his crew. Honestly, I need to get out of the office and just do police work sometimes. I stopped a vehicle at I-76 and Tallmadge Road, on the entrance ramp. One of the rear passengers was acting weird . . . "I can't remember my date of birth" weird. He told me he may have some warrants and then gave me his real name and identifiers. I handed the info to Sgt. McCarty and kept talking. The passenger then began quickly putting baggies of meth in his mouth in an attempt to swallow and destroy the evidence. As I was hanging out of the rear of the vehicle, through the open window, struggling with this person, it dawned on me why I got into this profession. It was to make a difference.

In spite of the obvious dangers associated with eating five grams of meth, this person chose to attempt that instead of facing the consequences of having it. He likely didn't think it through, which is usually why users are users. Yet it is our job to protect people from themselves, as well as others, at times. He was able to swallow a one bag. We got the rest. He had a detour to the hospital and then to the bed and breakfast.

Being a police officer is like no other profession. In a lot of cases, people see us when they would rather not—at crashes, when speeding, committing crimes or fighting with a spouse or significant other . . . and when riding around with meth and the chemicals to make more. We choose this job to make a difference. Any officer who works it for any other reason (pay, job security) discredits what we, who are "the police," are trying to accomplish. I cannot believe it has been eight years. It seems like it was yesterday that I was sporting eyebrow and earrings, wearing a beautiful goatee and buying crack while working undercover.

At many milestones in our lives we reflect on the path we have taken and review our actions. To be very honest, there is very little I would change in my administration of the police department. Some believe me to be hard-headed and to have a big mouth. They are correct. When I am firm, it is never for personal gain. I am firm for right over wrong—that will never change. When someone comes to your houses and your community, and chooses to commit a crime and make you victims, they will be called out. When people complain about me keeping the public informed, they will hear it, too. I know no other way.

This is not a one-man show.

To my bosses, particularly Mike Kostensky, thanks for having faith in me eight years ago. It was a risk for you, I know. I had big ideas and no money, but we did OK. John Dalziel, the Township Fiscal Officer, is another who helps us tremendously and works for this community tirelessly and without fanfare.

When I started as chief, I was determined to surround myself with the best officers I could find. We are selective when hiring here. We have parted ways with lots of officers who could not fulfill the mission of "making a difference." Now, as the team moves forward, we are starting to see results. We will be building an addition on the headquarters (thank God), we will be evaluated for accreditation this year, and our officers are more thoroughly trained than they have ever been. Our arrest numbers are through the roof, and we had a nearly 100% conviction rate in 2011. We also have developed a FB following and interaction with the community that still boggles my mind.

This community is proud of the officers and staff here—and should be. I have never been around a finer group of police officers. They walk into work every day ready to fight crime and kiss babies. When their assigned vehicle hits the streets, they are on watch. They write great reports, win their court cases and make it very tough on the criminal element. They also attend community and charity events and just have great hearts.

Thanks to the community for supporting us. We have a very special relationship and I adore it. Call on us when you need us—and we will do the same. We strive to make a difference every day.

Here's to another few years, at least.

"We don't give our criminals much punishment,
but we sure give 'em plenty of publicity."

—Will Rogers

Who is a mope?

We often get asked one question by our new Facebook friends: "What is a mope?" We prefer to define WHO is a mope, as evidenced by the following list, which may not cover all mopery:

- A mope is someone who leeches off of society and usually breaks the law. Mopes also lack character.
- Mopes can be from any economic class. Bernie Madoff was a very rich guy. He stole lots of money from investors. Bernie is a mope.
- If you sell or use drugs, you are a mope. Drug traffickers prey on the addicted. The addicted prey on society to feed their habits. Mopes.
- If you break into houses or cars that are not yours and take things that are not yours, to either keep them or sell them, you are a mope.
- Thieves of any kind are mopes. See #2.
- Deadbeat dads . . . mopes.
- If you drive while drunk, you are a mope, simply because of all of the warnings not to. You are also selfish.
- Suspended drivers . . . there are a lot of reasons the BMV or courts suspend licenses. Being suspended does not make you a mope. Sometimes bad things happen to good people. If you DRIVE when your license is suspended, you are a mope. If you crash into us, we pay the bill, because you are uninsured. Even if you have insurance, they will not pay, because you are not valid. That is at least mope-ish.
- A person who commits any criminal act in the presence of a child . . . mope to the 10th degree.
- Any person who makes a victim of children or senior citizens . . . BIG mope.
- Sexual predators . . . creepy mopes. We know, because if they live here, we visit them.
- Once a mope, NOT ALWAYS a mope. People change. I have seen it with my own eyes.

While I am not into "name calling" like a child, I do firmly believe in the mope concept. I also believe in calling it like it is. There is no need in society to act contrary to the laws that keep us safe and keep order in our great country. While there is no "need" to act like a mope, many do, simply because it is easier than putting in an honest day's work. It is the opinion of this chief, located in a small corner of a great big world, that we need to, as a society, become a little more intolerant of people who commit crimes for a living. When we start yelling about it being unacceptable, people will take notice and the practice will shift; either by putting people in jail, funding drug treatment or behavioral changes by the criminals.

The more we tolerate crime, the more crime we will have.

ATTENTION RESIDENTS . . . This is an APB. We repeat . . . an APB. It's an All Pig Bulletin. If you have a black potbelly pig, make sure you still have it. Some nice residents recovered one at Old Forge and Congress Lake last night. If it belongs to you, message us. We are hearing it was quite the "round up" catching this little piggie last night. There is no confirmation the little piggie was on his way to the market or had roast beef.

DID YOU KNOW . . . ? The Brimfield Police Department does NOT use ANY tax dollars to purchase police vehicles? All vehicles purchased are done so using criminal proceeds, including forfeited money, property (mostly from drug dealers and repeat OVI offenders) and impound fees.

DID YOU KNOW . . . ? Ohio law mandates that the county sheriff "check on" registered sex offenders once per year. Registered sex offenders living in Brimfield are visited by our officers at least once per month . . . just to make sure they are "okay."

MIDNIGHTS . . . If you reside near the 1500 block of Old Forge and have a damaged mailbox, we are aware of the situation(s). A drunk driver hit a few of them trying to get away from our midnight shift officers. The drunk driver was arrested. Nice job to midnight officers; two OVI arrests last night.

"It is much easier to become a father than to be one."

—Kent Nerburn

Racial profiling

Often, police officers are hit with the "race card." I am not one to deny the past racial tensions in our country, and the world for that matter. I do, at times, reach my limits with law enforcement being labeled as "racists" by those who would benefit if we truly were racist.

Law enforcement is a tricky job. When a suspect refuses to comply or it seems as though he (or she) is going for a weapon, or won't show his hands, a police officer has less than two seconds to decide what force to use . . . out of about five or six options. For most officers, that scenario is far less irritating than being called a racist when we stop or take enforcement action on any skin color other than our own. This is not limited to white officers. I have African-American friends in law enforcement who also suffer from being labeled "racists," by other skin colors and sometimes their own.

So . . . on with the babble today. Again, I am the mouthpiece for this department and my officers. I don't speak for other chiefs or officers. I do not speak for my bosses, and they are generally happy when I don't. At the Brimfield Police Department, we do not racially profile. I personally don't know officers who do. We enforce a set of laws legislated by the General Assembly of Ohio. It is called the Ohio Revised Code. For example, 4511.19 of the ORC says it is illegal to operate a vehicle while impaired by drugs or alcohol. Nowhere in the code does it delineate skin color, height, weight or any other trait. As a matter of fact, if you ask a Brimfield officer what would happen if he or she stopped someone based on race, every one of them would answer "The chief would fire me." So, if you are white, and Officer Lee Allen (African-American) or Officer Dumont (Asian) stops or otherwise deals with you, do not march down here and whine to me about being stopped because you are (insert race). If I stop you and our skin is different and you accuse me of racism, you will be laughed at with my trademark hearty and obnoxious laugh, and then you will receive a long "woodshed"- type lecture on where I come from. I know what is in my heart and the hearts of my officers—and it's not a racial divide.

Ignorance comes in every color, shape and size . . . as do criminals.

Good morning, drunken and arrested person...

Boy, I bet you have a headache today. Sorry about your choices. We really try to give most people an opportunity to NOT be arrested. You didn't get the hint. After reviewing your arrest, I would like to point out a few things which are weak links in your chain of intelligence. Take heed...

• When an officer says "You are being disorderly, stop your behavior" (yelling, cursing, peeing), you should stop whatever you are currently doing. It's like one of my favorite childhood games, freeze tag. It is the BPD catch phrase, similar to Nike saying "Just Do It." Ours is "Just Stop It."

• We appreciate you referring to us as "bubble gum cops" because we are "nice to children on Facebook." We disagree with your assessment that we "cannot arrest" you because we are "bubble gum cops" because we are nice to kids. You got arrested and went to the bed and breakfast. This morning I will be slapping high fives with children. Your hypothesis was proven to be invalid.

• Requesting officers to "call my dude, the chief" at 3:30 a.m. is also an incorrect thought process. "Dude" was the name of Dean Martin's character in the great John Wayne movie "Rio Bravo." I would appreciate a call from Dean Martin or John Wayne at 3:30 a.m. You and I are not "dudes" in the sense that "dudes" means "boys," "pals" or "BFFs." The old Chief-ism "Don't Poke the Bear" fits nicely here.

• I'm sorry we could not provide you with socks while you stayed in our holding cell, so you would not "catch athlete's foot." Life is about preparation. Grandmothers all over the world suggest you wear fresh, clean underwear in case of an accident and a hospital trip. Your lot in life may be to have fresh, clean socks in the case of a drunken arrest. Life lesson: Wear shoes when you drink.

• We know you may be from "The Brim," as you put it; however, people from "The Brim" do not act like you did. All of those types left

MORE...

town years ago. We are a quiet, intelligent, thoughtful and decent people, and we aren't even sure what "The Brim" is. ANY way ... we hope this helps. We also hope your headache is subsiding. Enjoy the oatmeal. If you return to "The Brim," please act like you have some fetchin' up.

—Chief

OVERHEARD AT THE BPD . . . Female arrested at Walmart for shoplifting. The conversation goes something like this . . .

Officer Pettit: "Stand-up, you are under arrest."

Female: "I'm getting arrested?"

Chief: "Don't come to Brimfield and steal. Yes, we arrest you here for stealing."

Female: "Okay, just to let you know, I'm crazy . . . so I won't remember putting the items in my bag and stealing them."

DAYSHIFT TODAY . . . Officers Rafferty and Petitt apprehended a Tier 2 sex offender who had failed to report his address and was hiding out on Meloy Road. The offender's prior victim was a 7-year-old child. We explained to him that after he is released from prison, we would like him to find another place to live. Great job, Officers Rafferty and Petitt.

OVERHEARD AT THE BPD . . .

Irate visitor to BPD: "You didn't have to tow the truck!"

Chief: "If you don't want us to your truck towed, don't drive around with meth in it."

Irate Guy: "Well, yeah, the meth was mine . . . but I was borrowing the truck!"

FACEBOOK . . . To celebrate making it to 500 people who "like" us we will be building an Ark. The Ark will have lights and a siren . . . because we are sure it will continue to rain.

DAYSHIFT . . . Sgt. Knarr and K-9 Havoc with a traffic stop of a vehicle leaving an area hotel and arrest of two subjects . . . SIX (6!) crack pipes recovered, along with other crack-related items. SHE says they are "friend's." HE says she is a prostitute from Akron. WE said they are no longer welcome in Brimfield.

The OVI checkpoint

We will be hosting another OVI checkpoint soon. I know . . . some of you don't like them. I apologize in advance. However, how about not driving drunk?

I recognize that some people have issues with sobriety checkpoints. I am fully prepared to listen to the sarcastic comments of "show me your papers, please" and to be called a Nazi or be compared with the old Soviet Union. Yet those people fail to contrast while making comparisons. Totalitarian governments conduct checkpoints to combat anti-government beliefs; we check cars to get drunks off of the road and educate the motoring public. There is no comparison worthy of discussion, and a bunch of differences.

My detractors say, "I don't deserve to be messed with when I am driving legally."

We aren't messing with you. If you do not want a delay, avoid the area.

I do not approve checkpoints to be held in this community to fly in the face of those of you who dislike them and think they are a violation of rights. As a matter of fact, I am a huge advocate of all of our rights. My stance remains that driving is a privilege, and many abuse that privilege by driving impaired and causing property damage, injuries and deaths. Checkpoints are well publicized, marked with flashing lights and signs . . . and we STILL average 10 OVI arrests when we have one.

Some have told me they believe these to be "unconstitutional." I understand the theory. But these cases have gone through numerous appeals and scrutiny by high courts all over the nation. There are very specific rules we have to follow when conducting a checkpoint. We have to notify the public pretty much all week before the event; we have to provide well lighted "detours" around the checkpoint; and we have to notify motorists of a "checkpoint ahead" on the roadway. So, if you are driving drunk, you have all the advantages in the world. The cards are stacked against us.

Checkpoints are a tool I would rather not use, but believe I have to because of the need. Kind of like my lawn mower. People who drive drunk injure and kill. While I am in charge here, we will use all the legal tools we can to intervene.

I did not take the job as Chief of Police because I wanted to be popular and wanted chicks to dig me. I took the job because I believe this team can make a difference. I have about a zero tolerance for nonsense when it comes to lawbreakers. You do the crime, you get the bracelets.

AFTERNOON SHIFT . . . Officers Diehl and Gyoker responded to a residence for the report of an unwanted guest inside of a house. The intruder was . . . a duck. Officer Gyoker advised that the duck appeared to be acting alone and that Diehl wanted to waterboard the duck to obtain information on any additional suspects.

OVERHEARD AT THE BPD . . .

Conversation from a traffic stop today . . .

Subject: "Every time I come to Brimfield I get stopped by you guys!"

Chief: "Could have anything to do with the marijuana, pipe, scale and magazine full of bullets in your car?"

Subject: "Yeah, I guess . . . "

MIDNIGHT SHIFT LAST NIGHT . . . Officers also responded to numerous calls (busy night). One was a call for a bat in a house . . . and a wife locked in the bathroom, because of the bat. Both were set free. Nice job, mids . . . at least it wasn't the duck again!

AROUND THE DEPARTMENT . . . There are a couple township residents here right now washing police cars. They are not washing the cars because they got in trouble. They are Steelers fans and MAY have lost a bet with the chief. The bet MAY have been on the Super Bowl. Although we wondered if Steelers fans were capable of working, they seem to be doing a good job. As usual, the chief says "GO BROWNS."

DAYSHIFT . . . Meth lab, part II . . . After securing the meth lab and bad guy last night, Officers Gyoker and Dumont noticed a suspicious person in the hotel lot. Officers determined she was with the meth cook. That led to a search of her room . . . and another meth lab! We would have posted this sooner . . . we were all sleeping, after a very long day and night!

More on the upcoming OVI checkpoint

We (and the State Patrol and other agencies to be determined) are STILL hosting an OVI checkpoint tonight. If you drive drunk here we will arrest you, regardless of who you are, where you work or who your relatives are.

You will wear handcuffs, have your car towed and receive a free photo-shoot. That photo-shoot is nothing like Olan Mills, by the way. You will be brought to the Brimfield Police Department and put in one of our holding cells. It has a NICE new solid steel combination toilet/drinking fountain/sink. You will be offered a breath test. If you refuse, you will lose the privilege of driving for one year. If you test over the legal amount . . . 90day license suspension. After booking we will see if you are eligible for bail. If not, it is off to the county bed and breakfast. Try the oatmeal.

It is likely to cost you, your parents or someone else lots of cash. You may even have to call or visit a pawnshop and sell the Xbox or the big screen.

Since it is the weekend, you will have a minimum of $50 in impound fees, $125+ in towing and loads of embarrassment. Embarrassment "is an emotional state of intense discomfort with oneself, experienced upon having a socially unacceptable act or condition witnessed by or revealed to others. Usually some amount of loss of honor or dignity is involved, but how much and the type depends on the embarrassing situation. It is similar to shame, except that shame may be experienced for an act known only to oneself."

Great. You will likely feel shame too, which is not a great feeling. Before the impound and towing fees are paid, it is time to go to court. You will have to catch a ride, since we have notified you that you are under a license suspension from the time of arrest . . . and we have your car. When you get to court, it will seem busy, because there are others there who are feeling embarrassment and shame. The judge will set a court date and notify you of a bunch of things that will come at you at record speed. In court, people associated with the case, like attorneys, police and jurors will see the video of your stop and field tests. They will see you intoxicated and attempting to do divided-attention tasks. You will look silly and be embarrassed.

In the end, you will likely attend a three-day school, during which you will watch videos of innocent victims (and the rare OVI driver who actually gets hurt) being cut out of vehicles. You will see parents and brothers, sisters and others crying over the senseless loss of loved ones. Oh . . . and you will also spend three days in the county bed and breakfast.

You will pay nearly $5,000 when it is all done—attorney fees, fines, the OVI school. GEEZ, where will the money come from? We told you we will always tell you the truth. If you drive drunk in Brimfield tonight or any night, we will arrest you. We are out looking for you and we are tired of the pain and heartache you cause. Get a ride if you are drunk. The designated driver concept started years ago . . . don't be an idiot.

AROUND THE DEPARTMENT . . . In the last 14 days officers from the BPD have handled five death calls. None have been homicides. We have had a fatal vehicle crash, an overdose, a health-related death and two non-locals—self inflicted— at the hotels. Officers are getting a little jumpy when dispatch calls us on the radio.

OVERHEARD AT THE BPD . . . The line of the weekend was by some of our kids at Brimfest: "Hey Chief . . . there's a drunk hobo passed out in the bushes over there." We have not heard the word "hobo" in quite some time. The intoxicated person was given a ride out of the area by a sober driver, in a police car.

FACEBOOK . . . We cannot believe there are 800 people following us . . . there is certainly no pressure to make sure we are heading in the right direction . . .

DAYSHIFT . . . Just when we thought it was too quiet . . . Officers Atha and Pettit (dayshift dynamic duo) traffic-stopped a vehicle and recovered a heroin needle. A subsequent search of a residence resulted in the seizure of heroin, needles, heroin paraphernalia and a marijuana grow in a hidden area in the garage. No weed found at the grow; however, the suspect does have some great digital photos of what used to be several plants. All of this took place with a nine-month-old baby in the house. Arrest made, children's services involved and the bad guy gets to go to the quaint bed and breakfast in the country.

OVI checkpoint, part II

Here's a reminder about the upcoming OVI checkpoint, since we know there are many of the "criminal" element who check our page daily (we know these things). As I stated earlier in the week, the BPD and the State Patrol are hosting an OVI checkpoint this weekend. There will be like a million cops in Brimfield. Maybe two million. And lots of drug dogs. Tell your friends.

We are hosting this because we want to educate drivers and also get drunks from behind the wheel into the comfort of our holding cell. It isn't plush, but we treat you with hospitality. So, education and enforcement are the ideas . . . but mostly enforcement.

If you are one of the golden ticket holders who spends St. Patrick's Day getting hammered and, when liquid intelligence settles in, you are CONVINCED you can drive and choose to do so, here are some things to remember . . .

1) We are not causing you to "lose your job" by "giving" you an OVI. We didn't give it to you, it was earned.

2) We are sorry your wife/husband/girl/boy/domestic partner will be leaving you because you earned an OVI. Again, that's not on us.

3) We are not #$%* or %^#$ . . . or other nasty names. We are children, husbands, wives, fathers and mothers who are trying to prevent others from being your victims.

4) Don't whine to us about the judge. She will likely put you in jail, but since you will be unemployed and spouse-less, it should impact only you.

5) Lastly . . . do NOT hit, spit or vomit on us. If you are going to drink, have the ability to do so without acting like an ass. "Hold your liquor," I believe it is called.

It may be easier to not drink and drive in our community. I just wanted to give you the heads-up if you make the CHOICE to do so.

MIDNIGHTS . . . It must be close to Halloween. Officers were called to the historic cemetery on Mogadore Road last night (LATE) for suspicious people. The subjects were taking photographs of headstones, to determine if ghosts could be seen in the background of the photos. Officers gave them directions to several haunted houses in the region and sent them on their way.

What really matters

My neighbor is in his late 80s. He served in the Navy in a submarine during World War II. I love him. We have spent a lot of time during the last five years, just talking. That generation of people was likely our best ever. A whole bunch of 18-21 year olds signed up for service after the attack on Pearl Harbor and deployed in foreign lands under conditions that history books cannot recreate. At 18 years old, I'm not sure if I was tying my own shoes yet.

My neighbor's health is failing. He has beaten cancer three times and now has it again. He is down to a percentage of one lung and has some trouble breathing. Last week the ambulance rolled up in front of his house. I went over and walked into the house to see my friend on the cot, wearing an oxygen mask and being worked on by the medics. In the middle of all of that commotion, he saw me. He took the time to sit up, take off his mask and introduce me to all of the medics as his "buddy" who watches out for him. Talk about being humbled by someone. Here is a gentleman who has some bad things going on, yet wants to make sure everyone knows ME. He is back from the hospital now. We spoke when he got back home. He told me he only had pneumonia and will be fine. My response was I believed he could have been pregnant and was glad it was only pneumonia. He laughed. If you know a World War II vet, thank him or her. The debt we owe them can never be repaid.

We have passed the 500 mark in our "senior program" here at the BPD. We now have over 500 people enrolled in the program. We keep in touch with them and host several breakfasts during the year, to honor them for the dues they have paid. As the police chief and as a department, we look out for our seniors, children and ladies. If you commit crimes against any of these groups, particularly, we will do everything we can to send you to a state-sponsored retreat for many, many years. Have a great day.

AFTERNOON SHIFT . . . Yesterday, two Steelers fans were at a local saloon here celebrating and attempted to "high five" each other . . . they missed. Both fell off of their stools and one cut his head open; he was treated by the squad and is okay. Go Browns!

Dear Mope,

I'm sorry you acted in a way resulting in our arresting you. Self-control is paramount in life. I cannot say I am disappointed that you will not be returning to Brimfield because, as you say, I am a "[expletive deleted]." Professionally speaking, I wish you would be gone from here.

I have some other thoughts about our encounter:

• When police arrive on scene and you and another person are on top of a third person, beating him, it is not self-defense.

• Yes, you have a right to free speech. It's unfortunate for those who are within earshot. Yikes, you cuss a lot. Also, you seem to have my name confused. My first name is not "Mother," and the last name you used wrong, also.

• Who wakes up at 12:30 in the afternoon? I may have an idea about the reason behind your employment status.

• I'm sorry you are not going to vote for me. I would have more regret if I ran for office, ever. I am appointed to this position. I will keep your "no" vote in mind if I ever run for office . . . which will be never.

• You do not pay my salary. You do not work or own a home. Harsh, yet true.

• When we say, "You are under arrest," you saying, "No I'm not" is not the proper response. We are here doing paperwork; you are at the bed and breakfast. I guess you were under arrest.

• Last, I am happy your "friend" left you "lots of money" and you will be using that money for hiring an attorney to sue me. There are a few mopes ahead of you in the litigation queue, so be patient. Getting sued is one of the costs of doing police work. If we are wrong, we admit it. In this case, you acted like a mope and got the bracelets . . .

Good luck in the future,

—Chief

Saying thank you

Good Morning . . . I tend to post long-winded messages on our FB page. If you have ever talked with me, you know this is totally within my character. This one will likely be no different.

We started working on the FB page in January of 2011. I was looking for a platform to communicate with our residents and keep them updated in as close to real-time as possible. I honestly figured if we could at least get 250 people to check our page regularly, we would be successful. When I contemplated what would be written on the "wall" in the form of updates, I decided to just be myself and let it fly. As you know, I am not generally shy or at a lack for words.

When we passed 1,000 "likes" I was shocked. You folks and I bantered back and forth about it—I was just amazed. In the late fall of last year I posed a poll question, asking when you thought we would hit 2,000 likes. I believed it would be late in 2012. It was a month later. It is now the 10th of April and we are just shy of 3,000 likes. Amazed is not the word or feeling I want to convey; the word and feeling is deep, deep gratitude.

Police work and being an officer is a very gratifying job, but let's face it, we are not usually the most popular of people. One of the goals of this page was to show people who we are and what we believe to be the truth from our perspective. Operating that way apparently has struck a nerve with a lot of people. I started thinking about all of this yesterday. I was stopped on three different occasions, while out and about, and complimented on our page. The three individuals were not from Brimfield; however they wanted to take the time to tell us how much they liked the page.

So, as we move forward please know we are grateful and thank you humbly for your continued support. If you don't support us, we are grateful for your opposition. It keeps us on our toes. We will continue to communicate openly.

For those of you who do not live here, thanks for virtually stopping by. And to our 80+ out of country friends . . . we are honored.

Almost 3,000 . . . really?

Domestic violence

For most of my career I have dealt with men who repeatedly hit women. I guarantee you I am not alone. Every officer I have ever met can tell stories about men who are drinkers, control freaks or just bullies and assault their spouse or mate. In addition to physical abuse, there are countless threats made every day amounting to psychological abuse. All of us have been in some sort of relationship. We have all said things to our significant others we wish we hadn't said. In my younger and less mature days, I was the king of running my mouth. Some of us may have slammed doors, punched a wall or otherwise threw a hissy. These are NOT the things I am speaking of.

I know that women hit men, too, and there is also same-sex couple violence . . . so don't bog down the computer with messages about me being "not fair." I'm a fair guy; however I am also practical. A large majority of our domestic violence cases (and cases from all over) involve men beating women, and it has to stop.

I have noticed with many repeat domestics over 17+ years that things get more and more violent.

See, there are stages of the domestic violence cycle. It starts with a "honeymoon" phase, when the man is cuddly (or at least social) and professes his love for the victim. That falls by the wayside and we go to a tension-building phase. It is exactly how it sounds. The victim walks on eggshells, trying to not make the bully become the hulk. It does NOT work . . . ever. Something triggers the abuser and that leads to the next stage—the battering incident. He lashes out and strikes. After that, he apologizes and we are back to the fairy tale. You believe it will all be okay and he has changed—that's the remorseful and re-bonding period. The problem is this; as time goes by, the re-bonding period gets shorter and shorter. You get a bunch of tension and then a sock in the nose. He stops apologizing, because you are getting what you deserve. And then we go back through the cycle.

The honeymoon, or "I'm a nice guy" phase gets shorter each time. The first time he hit you was the hardest for him. He felt horrible and guilty after it. Over time he becomes comfortable and normal being nasty and violent. Eventually, things are always tense or physical . . . the cuddly is gone.

If you are reading this and it describes you, get out of this relationship. He will not change, no matter how many times he says he will.

Get out and don't look back. If you have children, take them. Do not rationalize that you don't have the money, the children need their father, he has a good heart, he is just angry or one of the million other excuses for why he hits you. There are no excuses; there is just control. It's about control. If you or someone you know is the victim of this nonsense, get help. It is not a way to live. It is NOT your fault. Do not let an abuser keep you from living a happy and healthy life. You are not supposed to be hit by someone who "loves" you. It is not normal or natural, nor is it because of his "rough childhood." It is because he seeks to control you, period.

If you are a victim or know one, call us or your local police. We will put you in touch with someone who can assist you. It will be rough at first and you will second-guess yourself. When the dust settles and your head clears, you will know it is right.

No one should live life being abused.

AFTERNOON SHIFT . . . Sgt. McCarty arrested a subject for OVI offense number FIVE after a traffic crash on Edson near Meloy. The subject also possessed painkillers (no prescription). His passenger had a warrant for child endangering, possessed heroin needles and painkillers (again, no prescription) and attempted to hide the drugs . . . in the back of Sgt. McCarty's police vehicle. Both are now on a weekend retreat . . . at the bed and breakfast. Great job afternoon shift!

MIDNIGHTS . . . Halloween time. Loud party complaint resulted in the arrests of: Chuck Norris (who officers said more closely resembles McLovin), William Wallace (Braveheart), a priest, a flapper, a secretary, and a "Reno 911" cop.

College students under 21: It is best, if you are going to party, not to let the party get out of control. No urinating in the middle of the street for neighbors to see . . . no music that can be heard from BUFFALO . . . Remember: the object of the game if you are breaking the law is to LAY LOW.

---

*"If you don't get enough time-outs as a child,
you get them as a grownup."*

—Andrew Bonifacio

On being a police chief

Police chiefs generally do not have great job security. I answer to three elected trustees. It takes two of the three to vote to remove me ... and then I will be fishing, until someone else needs a chief. I took this job knowing that, because I truly believed I could make a difference in the community and inside the walls of the police department. So far, we are making some progress.

One of the downsides of the job is the close work with elected people, from all levels of the government. I have a definite opinion on most politicians; however, since there are women and children present, I will yield. Suffice it to say, many I have met are impacted by the power of the position and end up making decisions based on keeping that power instead of doing what is right. Therein rests the problem with me and my officers. It's the Immovable Object and Unstoppable Force theory. Both cannot logically exist in the same universe. So here's what you need to know ...

Regardless of job security, paychecks or any perceived power I have here, I will make decisions based on ethics and what is right, period. If any elected official, office-holder or public servant misuses tax dollars, I will take action. If anyone violates ethics laws, I will report them. If they hire family members, take trips to conferences and use tax dollars inappropriately, I will speak up. Friends won't have any advantage over others in securing contracts or being vendors on my watch. If I end up unemployed, I will leave with pride. General Patton once said "Do your duty as you see it and damn the consequences." Yep.

I will also offer that for the most part I have worked with good elected people here. Mike Kostensky is nuttier than me, which is fun to watch. When I have wild ideas, he usually likes them. I have found him to be honest yet outspoken. He is a leader. Fiscal Officer John Dalziel is the best fiscal officer I have ever worked with. As overwhelming as the part-time job is (he works two other full-time jobs as a business owner) he is an honest and truthful guardian of your tax dollars. Sue Fields is like my own grandmother. I loved my grandmother. I have worked with lots of others on all levels; some better than others.

So, back to what you need to know. At the Brimfield Police Department, we will do what is right ... always.

Dear Burglar,

You are a tool. I'm not sure when during our time as a society it became acceptable for a person to creep onto someone else's property while they are sleeping and take things the homeowners worked hard to acquire (that means "buy and possess").

Just so you are aware, we were fairly busy last night. We had a vehicle that cartwheeled down I-76, a combative arrestee who had to be hogtied and many other calls. We also had to handle situations at a local hotel that booked three wedding parties, resulting in drunken shenanigans for the better part of two hours.

On a side note, Mr. Burglar, when you get out of prison and find some lucky, senseless girl to marry you, have all of the guests stay in your own hometown. While we appreciate the boost to our own economy, we prefer guests who can handle intoxicating beverages and not act like idiots.

Now, back to you. Brimfield is an interesting community. We have very informed residents who watch for creepers like you. I'll bet you wet yourself when the resident opened the upstairs window and yelled at you. I'll bet you REALLY had the vapors when the husband chased you down the street. Did you hear all of the sirens? I've always wondered what it sounds like on the receiving end of those sirens to someone living the "thug life."

Not unlike the drug dealers and others I have given advice to, I have some pointers for you, because . . . well, you need them:

• The thing inside of a vehicle that looks like a little box and has a couple buttons—that is a garage door opener. When you push that button at 4:00 a.m., the homeowners . . . well, the entire neighborhood looks out their windows.

• In Ohio, entering an attached garage with the purpose of committing a theft offense is a burglary, not a breaking and entering. The difference is about six years at a state-run resort for men. Take soap-on-a-rope.

MORE...

• Ummm...and this is a tough one...you forgot to take your car. I know, in all of the confusion and sirens, one can get a little "sensory overload." We appreciate your running in the general direction of your car. A vehicle with a warm engine, sitting in a driveway where it doesn't belong is...a clue!! We have your car. We need to talk.

• Last, today you will report your car stolen. It's an age-old knucklehead move. It doesn't work. Our detectives are closing cases at record pace using DNA. That option just became available to us. It's like "CSI Brimfield" without the cool sunglasses.

I know the economy is bad. A job might help. If you can't pay the bills with one job, get two. There are plenty of hours in the day for work.

See you soon...

—Chief

IN THE SCHOOLS . . . At a recent mother son/dance at the elementary school, a raffle was held with the winner getting "lunch with the Chief" at a local restaurant of his/her choice. (Really? That was the prize?). Today third-grade student Connor and the Chief went to Beef O'Brady's for burgers and fries. The duo then went to the department, where Connor met K-9 Havoc and may have played with the lights and sirens in a police car, thanks to Detective Lance. Connor then had mug shots taken—the pictures were promptly emailed to his mother. We might have chosen door number two for OUR prize. Just saying . . .

AFTERNOONS . . . Someone has a voodoo doll of Sgt. McCarty, we are convinced of it. Yesterday, someone brought a "shake and bake" meth lab to the department . . . they found it in the front yard of a relative's house on SR43. Lab team brought in AGAIN and the lab was disposed of. McCarty's crew also called to a rental unit to recover some heroin paraphernalia . . . left there by the prior tenant. We are cutting down a tree today, to assist Sgt. McCarty with the paper needed to finish all of his paperwork. Thanks for all of the work officers!

"Life is tough, but it's tougher when you're stupid."

—John Wayne

What I hate about police work

If I could change one thing about the job—and believe me, I am not alone—I would erase death and all of the memories from police work. Police officers see far too much death. I believe the only professionals who see more death than police and firefighters are likely funeral directors. However, they usually don't see it as it unfolds.

In my career I have seen it far too many times; all ages, from newborn to 95. I've seen it at crashes, homicides, suicides and for a bevy of other reasons. I have crawled into upside-down vehicles, held hands with the elderly and hugged more of other people's relatives than my own . . . so, death and I have a relationship.

The catalyst for this particular babble is my neighbor. If you remember, my neighbor is a World War II vet. He served in the Navy as a submariner. Who knows how many Nazi boats went to the bottom of the ocean on his watch. He has been sick. This morning, as I was ready to leave for work, our doorbell rang. I knew immediately it was neighbor-related. My neighbor's wife was at the door and nearly hysterical. My World War II buddy had fallen and was in a bad spot. When I got into the house and went into the room where he was, I saw he was likely hurt. I told his wife to call the medics, got him a pillow and then sat with him. He reached out and we held hands while I talked. He tried to talk—I told him not to, because of a shortness of breath. When I told him I would do the talking he replied "I have a lot to say to you." We both just smiled. The squad took him. We will wait . . .

If you are the loved one of a police officer or medic, talk to them. If you are a police officer or medic, TALK about what you see and experience. I'm not numb to it, by any stretch—I acknowledge it and then let it go. If you have grandparents, visit them. If you know a vet who is getting older, tell them thank you and also tell him the chief says thanks. I would gladly take a bullet for a veteran of World War II, Korea and Vietnam. While I'm on this topic . . . our Vietnam vets were treated in a very foul way when coming home. If you see one, tell him welcome home and thanks for serving. They have all earned it.

Have a great day.

Losing a hero

Many sources estimate we are losing World War II vets at a rate of about 5,000 per day. Most are in their late 80s and early 90s.

Last night at about 9 p.m. we lost another. My neighbor, who you have all read about here, died last night. His wife came to our door, frantic, to get us. Mrs. Chief was the first there . . . I followed a short time later. We both knew as soon as we walked in his room. I phoned the medics to confirm . . . and they did. We waited with his wife until family could arrive.

This man was a gentleman. I never heard him swear or say anything bad about another. As I have said, he was in a submarine for much of the war, firing torpedoes at Nazi boats. We had frequent talks about the war and we also did some Internet research for him on the where-abouts of his old ship. He was as tough as nails— he fell out of a tree at 80 years old. He had climbed it to adjust a bird feeder. He also battled cancer four times, winning three of those battles.

Last night we lost another hero, a man who left here as a kid to fight the biggest war in our history. There were millions of these kids. If you know one, you are blessed.

IN THE SCHOOLS . . . This morning, the Brimfield Police Department and Brim-field Elementary School conducted our regular active threat drills. The drills in-volve police arriving at the school for an active threat (school shooter or other) and locking the school down. During the drill, all classroom doors are secured and all students remain out of view. Officers check doors and also for notifica-tion of anyone needing assistance. As usual, Mrs. Way, the staff and students responded like a well-oiled machine. If you are an elementary parent, talk to your children about today's events.

We are not happy to conduct these drills; however there are people in our society who prey on others. We must offer the training and assistance to allow our chil-dren and adults to operate under these possible conditions.

"If it is not right do not do it; if it is not true do not say it."

—Marcus Aurelius

Integrity

Webster's defines integrity as "firm adherence to a code of especially moral or artistic values: incorruptibility." I love the last word—incorruptibility. The staff at BPD likes the concept of integrity so much, we included it as one of our three guiding principles.

The fuel for this babble is the idea that someone with any sort of power would call or visit a chief of police with the question "What can we do about this ticket?" attempting to get a ticket voided or torn up. I detest that phrase. I have been asked that question often during my tenure as chief and also before. I have been asked by politicians, attorneys, police officers, friends and just about every profession out there. I once had an elected official (he is no longer here) ask me to release an OVI offender from the department and NOT charge him. When I said no, he "hinted" that my job was at risk. My response was simple—I told him unless he would like to sit in the cell beside his friend, he should leave the property. He left.

As I have said here before, we make a lot of traffic stops; however, in comparison to our stops, we write very few tickets. As percentages go, we arrest far more than we ticket, which means my officers are doing good police work—stops resulting in arrests. Over the weekend one of my officers ticketed a woman for driving with a license that has been expired for three months. The driver informed my officer her husband is a police officer. We respect that; however, that does not make her a valid driver. This may not be a stance popular with some police officers and I understand that. If I conducted business here based on popularity, I likely would have been voted off of the island long ago.

So, this morning I received a call from the husband/ officer. He is a patrol officer. I am a chief. I put no stock in either of those ranks, with the exception of the fact I would have NEVER, when I was a patrol officer, called a chief to discuss a ticket. I'm a chief now and still wouldn't do that. After exchanging greetings the dreaded question was popped . . . or kind of stated . . . "I'm calling to see what we can do about this ticket." To summarize my answer, "we" cannot do anything about the ticket. The driver can get valid and appear in court. "We" do not void or "do something" about tickets. If "we" did, how would the courts, the public or MY OFFICERS have any trust in my integrity? Not the answer he wanted . . .

Integrity, to us here, does mean incorruptible. We will not randomly or excessively write tickets—but when we do, you have earned it, no matter who you or your relatives are. No pressure or position will change that.

AFTERNOONS . . . Sgt. McCarty and afternoon shift were at it again yesterday. A traffic stop resulted in K-9 Drogen being asked to tell us if there were drugs in the stopped vehicle. Drogen told us there were. Officers recovered assembled chemicals for the manufacture of meth. The subject was arrested and charged. Oh, yes . . . he happened to be the same person we arrested last week for stealing at Walmart, resisting arrest and possession of meth. He will not be attending Black Friday sales this year . . . or next.

Criminals: Please take the time to read all of the posts on our FB page. Use the various search engines. We are not going to turn away from crime. We will utilize all legal means to catch you and give you "three hots and a cot" for an extended period of time. Anywhere but here, boys and girls. Great job Sgt. McCarty, Officers Dumont and Allen, and of course Drogen. I am ordering extra turkey for Drogen this year.

AFTERNOONS . . . We just arrested a female from Akron for theft from Walmart. Alert loss-prevention there notified us. She stole about $500 worth of merchandise . . . AND she brought her eight-year-old with her. We do not believe that would be an approved home-schooling field trip. Female arrested, distraught child picked up by grandmother. We did not arrest the mother until she was away from the child. We are soft when it comes to kids.

The frequency of parents taking children with them when they commit crimes is baffling to me. Again, folks . . . wisdom (common sense?) from the Chief: Don't commit crimes here; however, if you choose to do so, count on being arrested . . . so for GOD's sake, leave your children with a sitter!

MIDNIGHTS . . . Sgt. Knarr and I worked "Black Friday" at Walmart last night from 8 p.m. to 3 a.m. The place was a zoo, although it did slow down later. The biggest fuss of the night? $9 blenders. Last year it was the $5 Hello Kitty pajamas. Most people were civil, some weren't and had to watch Black Friday from the outside of the store. We ejected four, arrested none and warned a bunch.

Filling the void

People generally distrust federal government right now. Gee, I wonder why. One of the things I aspired to do with this page is separate us from the mess. We are not the government. We are the police department. By definition we are a government agency; however, I am not a politician. This department, as long as I am in this position, will never be swayed by political influence. I think we, as a community and region, need to have constant interaction on the local level. If the big picture is ever going to get fixed, we have to start in our own corner first . . . which is why I am here every day. Brimfield does not have access to all of the national-level programs and funding, so the police department improvises. Who will help our seniors when the feds don't? Well, if no one is filling that void, we will. What about positive interaction with our children? Void filled. I have found over the last eight years, if something needs done, my officers don't stand around and ask who is supposed to do it. They just get moving. Inherently, police departments do not check on seniors, high-five kids, host golf camps or engage in other functions. I don't buy that and never did.

I get asked regularly about running for this office or that office. No thanks. I am humbled by the requests, but still . . . no thanks. I can have more of an impact being a police chief and working than I can by going to meetings and talking about working. Talk is idle. Besides, my story stays the same, no matter who I am talking to. We have something very special here. We could not do it without you. I'm not sure if you have noticed, but we have a partnership.

AFTERNOONS . . . Sgt. McCarty and afternoons were at it again yesterday . . . Thefts from Walmart, three arrested on felony charges—which means they stole over $1,000 worth of items. Two of the three had active arrest warrants from other agencies. We also recovered lots of heroin-related items—needles and such. (There is no feeling like searching someone and finding a used needle).

All three were given complimentary stays at the county bed and breakfast, courtesy of the BPD Travel Agency—relocating criminals for over 20 years!

Dear ... Mother?

We called for you last night ... several times. We were sitting with your teen daughter and her friend. They were absolutely suffering. They had been hanging with a couple mopes for the last two weeks, smoking meth. They met these two on the Internet.

The girls were pretty much under the control of these two. They weren't held by force, but they were given a very addictive drug and shown some attention. I'm sure you had to have seen your daughter during that time because, according to everyone there, she came home for a shower and clothes every couple of days. Did you speak with her? Did you look at her face? We did, for seven hours last night. Those hours were kind of tough for her, because you would not come to get her. You rejected her.

She needed to see you last night. She had been up for two straight days and was "coming down" from a two-day binge. One of my sergeants and others attempted to get you to come to her but we were told "no." You were busy ... it was too late ....

Shame on you. I'm not sure mothers have a "mom card" similar to a "man card" ... but if it exists; I am requesting its immediate revocation.

I know your daughter has not been an angel. She is a very spirited girl. I also know, as a parent of an underage child, if your child calls, you go. I'm not talking about a 25-year-old who keeps getting into trouble. I'm talking about a young teen girl who was strung out and REALLY needed to see her mom.

We talked to her instead. Officer Allen and Officer Putnam spent LOTS of time with her. I found her a big teddy bear ... and then she called ME a big teddy bear. My tough-guy image was shot. We heard about her life, her mistakes and her dreams. We heard about you and your choices. We heard about a "dad who is not in the picture." Oh, by the way ... dad can pound salt, also. Men who have nothing to do with their children are not men. Even a skunk can make a baby.

MORE...

So . . . we hope your date, your night out or your night of restful sleep was good for you. We stayed up all night with your child. She was in a bad place mentally but a good place physically. Today, she is in the care of someone else because we made the decision to separate you from your inherent responsibility. One of the hundreds of foster families who specialize in rebuilding kids and their dreams will begin the slow process of putting her back together. We hope it isn't too late for her . . .

Like it was "too late" when we called you last night.

—Chief

WE CAN'T MAKE THIS STUFF UP . . . So . . . a female enters Walmart and steals two large televisions. On the way out, with the stolen televisions, she stops to check on the status of the pictures she left at the photo store . . . a year ago. The workers cannot find the photos, so the suspect leaves her name and phone number for them to call her—and then pushes the stolen televisions out the door. We called her, but not for the pictures. The televisions have been recovered and charges are pending.

AFTERNOON SHIFT . . . Yes . . . we did pick-up a naked guy this evening in the Pleasant Lakes development. He is not from here, but somehow found his way to us, without clothing. We received numerous calls of a naked male strolling (?) through the neighborhood. No car was found. It appears to Sgt. McCarty and Officer Allen the male is on some sort of drug, possibly bath salts. He and his brand new blanket have relocated to the bed and breakfast, where he will receive a nice orange and white jumpsuit and new pair of slippers—parting gifts from BPD Travel . . . finding criminals (even naked ones) new places to stay for over 20 years!

AFTERNOON SHIFT . . . Well . . . the end of the year is much like the beginning. Officers made a traffic stop on Tallmadge Road. Three individuals from Akron arrested for possession of meth. They had just purchased some items to make more meth. One of the subjects was transported to the hospital—he has had a needle stuck in his arm for two days. All subjects will celebrate the new year by singing Auld Lange Syne at the Portage County Bed and Breakfast. Great job, officers!

Our "wanted people"

Remember when I told you if I made a mistake, I would own it and apologize for it? Stand by for that . . . We have warrants for over 250 people. These are people who have failed to show up for court on a variety of charges. Heroin possession, identity theft, OVI, robbery . . . we have a bunch of people who need to be seen by the judge, and they won't show up for court. So, in my infinite wisdom, I got the idea to post pictures of some of these individuals on our page in order to generate some leads and clear up some of these warrants. I am not the kind of person who posts pictures or names on our page. We will NOT be a tabloid-style page. I get enough grief for being outspoken; I don't need more for something I really don't want to do anyway.

So, with bright idea in mind, I posted the first (and last) three last week. The normal amount of insults and opinions flowed through. We did get some leads, but then something else happened. A juvenile child of one of the "wanted people" contacted me. In posting those pictures I overlooked the one thing I stand for the most . . . the children. You see, even though the adults are wanted and may be in the mope stage of their life, they may have children. Those children are likely on Facebook. I can imagine no worse feeling as a child than seeing mom or dad listed on a police department Facebook page, under "wanted persons."

So, although it is perfectly legal to post pictures of people wanted by police, because it is all public record, it may not be the right thing to do. In this case, while I am in charge, it is most definitely NOT the right course to be on and we won't go that direction. Absolutely regardless of the conduct of a parent, the child should not pay the bill. Children should not suffer because their parents cannot act like adults. Alienating these children from police and other authorities drives them further towards a life which will lead to trouble. I cannot do that. I am supposed to look out for them, and I will. "I am sorry" goes to the children who saw those posts. Look at the example of the life you have been exposed to and break that cycle . . . you can do it.

We do not have to be a product of our environment if we choose not to be.

MIDNIGHTS . . . Sgt. Adkins and K-9 Joker (we don't know which one was driving) made a traffic stop on SR43. Driver was arrested for driving under suspension. When he exited the vehicle, marijuana fell from inside his pants leg and little amounts kept dropping out. We recovered more on station; it was stored in his unmentionables. Yes, we are a dedicated bunch. Great job Sgt. Adkins, Joker and Officer Putnam!

MIDNIGHTS . . . Midnight shift celebrated the New Year in a time-honored BPD fashion—with handcuffs. Five arrests last night; Sgt. Adkins made the first OVI arrest of 2012. Two highly intoxicated subjects were arrested after a fight erupted inside the limo they rented. We have no clue how the royal rumble started in the back of a car; we know it ended with tears and handcuffs. We also had an arrest on a warrant, and Officer Putnam had an arrest for driving under suspension. The first eight hours of 2012—five arrests . . . it seems as though we will have a seamless transition to the New Year. Great job Sgt. Adkins, Officers Putnam, Allen and K-9 Drogen.

WEATHER REPORT . . . Roads are snow-covered and slippery in some places in Brimfield this morning, and it is 20 degrees. Drive a little slower and all will be fine.

AFTERNOON SHIFT . . . Sgt. McCarty and Officer Allen got into another "cluster." The two made two arrests at Walmart for theft, and the case took off from there. Their investigation revealed the subjects, from Pennsylvania, had been "visiting" Walmart stores in PA, Ohio and W.VA., stealing items and then returning them for gift cards and cash refunds. One of the subjects had nine fake identification cards from Nevada. Our investigation tells us the subjects were making about $500 per day at their "job." We have recovered numerous stolen gift cards, stolen merchandise and store receipts. The thieves will be spending some time at the Portage County Bed and Breakfast, where it is cash only for cigarettes and chips. Way to go the extra mile, afternoon shift! Criminals . . . anywhere but here.

"No man in the wrong can stand up against a fellow that's in the right and keeps on a-comin'."

—Motto of the Texas Rangers

Road rage

Some time during the last decade or so, many in society have lost their manners. I cannot diagnose the cause; my brain would catch fire from all of the thinking. This loss of manners is never more evident than when we are driving. When I started in law enforcement 18 years or so ago we responded to very few calls for "road rage." Now it is a normal call for us. We have people who get out of cars and yell at each other. We have had fist fights and punched or kicked vehicles. What is making everyone so angry?

Recently I was driving and had my youngest daughter in the vehicle with me. We were just under the speed limit, behind an older female driver who was more than comfortable driving at that speed. I didn't mind either—it gives me time to look around. Another younger woman was right on my rear bumper . . . and I mean right on it. Had I needed to stop quickly, her vehicle would have been in the bed of my pick-up. The driver in front of me slowed to make a turn, and we all slowed with her, except for the driver behind me—she was checking out her hair in her rear-view mirror. She had to slam on her brakes when the front vehicle stopped to turn. It was then that the cussing began. I could see her through my mirror and she was letting me have it. I was reading lips and she called me everything you could imagine. She was angry. I am still trying to figure out why. I was just the guy in front of her, at the mercy of the person in front of me.

A point I would like to make is this—before you drive angry, think. Ohio is a CCW state. In addition to the legal carrying of weapons (which I support) many of the criminals have them also (which is why I support the GOOD people having them). It takes very little to escalate an altercation into a shooting . . . it happens somewhere every day. Assaults with bats, tire irons and other objects happen too. That's not a snipe on the CCW crowd—it's just a fact. I carry a weapon off-duty, just in case I am out with my family and happen to run into one of the many people who have had extended stays away from home because of me. Do you think the motorist behind me thought about whether or not I was armed before she began screaming profanities at me? I am not bothered by it but it could send someone else into a rage. I am hopeful she does not, at some point, push the wrong button on the wrong person. I'm not sure what happened to us that made us so angry when we drive and so intolerant of each other. I kind of miss the days when people waved at you using ALL of their fingers.

NEW AT THE BPD . . . We would like to welcome the new addition to our special-purpose vehicles . . . our pre-owned, full-size Humvee. It runs great and is in great shape. This beauty comes to us from the LESO program, courtesy of the U.S. military. It was FREE to us. We will use this (if needed) for search and rescue operations, off-road recovery and marijuana eradication. Did I say it was free? We will paint the vehicle using drug-seizure money and donations of materials and labor. It will match our other vehicles when completed. I hope we never have a serious use for it; however, our motto is, better to have it and never need it than to need it and not have it.

AFTERNOON SHIFT . . . We had a very intoxicated male sitting on his guitar amp with his guitar strapped to his back on the side of the road. He was crying. He said that his friend jumped him because he would not pay him for helping him work on a vehicle. We went to the house and were greeted by two other very intoxicated males . . . one of them had a warrant for his arrest. Timing in life is everything.

AFTERNOON SHIFT . . . A male subject pulled his vehicle into a residential driveway and passed out, due to heroin use. Our staff and the med unit responded and he was transported to the hospital. He used the drug in Akron and drove here; thankfully, no one was hurt.

Brimfield and surrounding communities have seen a sharp increase in heroin use over the past two years. The drug is cheaper than ever and is highly addictive. We will continue to make it as uncomfortable as possible for drug dealers and users.

DAYSHIFT . . . Officer Diehl with a traffic stop and arrest of a Tier 1 sex offender from Wayne County. He advised he was in the area for work; he must have forgotten that he needs to be a valid driver . . . oops. He gets to wear the "non-bedazzled" version of silver bracelets—they are not too fashionable, but we like them.

Dear Shoplifters,

When you come to our fine community to steal, please don't.

Next, if you decide to, here's a pointer: When you walk into a store looking like you weigh 100 pounds, and after 15 minutes you look like you weigh 500 . . . we call that a "clue."

It may have been the nine shirts, three bras and the pair of pants you had on UNDER your original clothing—"Just sayin'!"

Two mopes in custody for theft and obstruction; clothes recovered. Mopes have reservations at the county bed and breakfast . . . where the weekend meals are very tasty.

—Chief

WEATHER REPORT . . . Roads are okay and the salt crews are out. We have had no reported crashes yet this morning. During snowy/icy conditions, remember, please, to keep distractions (cell phone, texting, doing the Macarena while driving) to a minimum.

JUST WHEN WE THINK WE'VE SEEN EVERYTHING . . . A resident on Sandy Lake Road came home today to find a burglar in his house. The burglar had some of the resident's possessions in his arms.

Resident: "Who the *#&! are you?!"

Burglar: "I'm the guy who just got caught."

The resident called us and we have the bad guy in custody. He also hit another house today and we have recovered those items. The suspect will likely get an extended stay at a state-sponsored retreat. Great job (and courage) shown by the resident and also great job to the officers on the arrest and follow-up on the additional burglary.

WEATHER REPORT . . . Light snow overnight; nothing to vapor-lock over. SR43 is just wet and our township Public Works Department has been salting since 4 a.m. Some intersections may be slippery. We have all done this before. Think positive; we will all be fishing before we know it.

On the state having its head in its posterior

I am a little miffed at the state right now. The Ohio Lottery Commission has lost its mind. This is my opinion only; it may not be your view or the view of those who thought it was a good idea to make me the chief.

On Friday, I received a mailing, at my home, from the Ohio Lottery. It was a voucher for a lottery ticket. The nice colorful mailer instructed me to take the voucher to my nearest "lottery agent" to determine if I had won $500. If I was not a winner, I could still get a discounted lottery ticket.

I have said it here numerous times . . . We are not the morals police. That being said, our state government, from a law-enforcement perspective, has no business owning liquor stores and running a gambling business. What if I am a gambling "addict"? They mailed a "trigger" for my behavior to my own home! What next . . . is the state going to legalize crack and send me a sample? Why doesn't the state send free samples from the "state liquor stores" to a couple of alcohol rehab centers? It's not as if the police don't have enough to do with all kinds of addicts and crimes committed due to addictions to gambling, drugs, alcohol, sex and sniffing paint, we also have to worry about the state acting like a criminal enterprise. (I wanted to say pimps, but I didn't want to be over the top.)

Meanwhile, people argue about reciting the Pledge of Allegiance, God in schools and heaven forbid we let the BOY SCOUTS meet in a government-owned meeting room, after all there is a separation of "church and state" . . . just not one of state and vice.

The lottery was originally going to solve our school funding issues. Ask the Field Local Schools how that is working out. The government is supposed to represent the people and govern for the greater good, not sell lottery tickets and liquor.

And, just to clear it up . . . I am not a prude. In my younger days, I acted without regard at times. This is strictly an issue of the state government losing its way and making more work for police officers; while telling all of us to do more with less.

Morons.

Sexting

When I was in school, we passed notes to each other. I had a few of my notes captured by teachers and read out loud. That was often embarrassing, but not nearly as embarrassing as what is now floating around in cyberspace.

Adults, young adults and children . . . we have a concern. If the trend continues, we will have a problem. Sexting is the transmission of sexually explicit information via a communications device. In English, it means sending naked or near naked photos or videos to someone via a cell phone or other smart thingy. It is far more common than you think. Oh, I know, I'm being moral again—or perhaps just a prude. I have not led a shielded or privileged life. What I am worried about is not only the behavior, but the journey of pictures and/or videos.

When you make the choice to send a "racy" picture of yourself, you are so far out on the limb you cannot see the rest of the tree. Although you may love and trust the recipient, the old saying about everyone having at least one person they tell a secret to is very true, more so among young males. Most young males are goofy and can't keep secrets. I know, because I was young once (a long time ago). Also, relationships end. Your BF or GF of today may be your arch enemy tomorrow. There is NOTHING like an embarrassing picture or video of you floating around in cyberspace.

Adults, please use some good judgment. We have had a number of women reporting their "exes" are threatening to send or post compromising photos. Parents, we have our work cut out for us. Talk to your kids about pictures and videos which are inappropriate. Set boundaries. I have had more than my share of crying mothers, angry fathers and embarrassed daughters in my office and in this situation. Do not let your children be naïve because the topic is sensitive. Take a look at their phones and text messages if needed. Remember, trust is earned. And for our young ladies who follow us . . . if you get this type of request from someone you are dating or have a relationship with, tell them to get lost, get bent or whatever other vernacular is suitable for you. Be firm and do not give in.

Tell them if they really cared about you and had ANY class, they would never ask.

My sergeants

This may come as a surprise to many of you: I am very, very difficult to work for. Many of you see me joking around, laughing and having fun, which I love to do. I also am sworn to run a police department, which no matter how large or small the department, is a task. Now, back to being hard to work for. My sergeants have a tough job. Not only do they answer calls, write reports and perform other police work, they are also responsible to me for the patrol officers in the department. If an officer acts contrary to policy or rules, the officer answers for it—and so does his or her sergeant. It doesn't happen often; however, when it does, it is not fun. Over and above the disciplinary issues, which are rare, the sergeants check reports (and kick a few back), determine trends and make decisions on numerous situations on a regular basis. The reason I believe I am not easy to work for (besides them telling me) is that I expect excellence and rarely settle for less than superior work.

The sergeants here, unlike times in the past, all have advanced leadership training. All sergeants are graduates of the Supervisor Training and Education Program (STEP) and the Police Executive Leadership College (PELC). Two have college degrees and one (Sgt. Adkins) will graduate in December.

This babble is nothing more than to publically commend and thank my sergeants for tolerating my stubbornness and seeing my vision. I always tell them it's my job to map the course and their job to get the troops moving in that direction, and the sergeants here work tirelessly accomplishing that goal. As residents and supporters of the Brimfield Police Department, I just thought you all should know.

Sergeants Knarr, Adkins and McCarty . . . I thank you.

"It's not the critic that counts, not the man who points out how the strong man stumbles, or where the doer of deeds could have done better. The credit belongs to the man who is actually in the arena."

—Theodore Roosevelt

Our K-9 program

I get some flack about the number of dogs we have working here. A while back one anonymous poster gave me the name "Chief A-dog-in-every-car." I howled at that name, because it was very funny.

I love dogs. We have two in the Oliver house. One is a rescue (she's a small mix), the other is from a breeder (Australian Cattle Dog ... very high strung). I have had dogs since I can remember.

I really like police dogs. They like to work, are intelligent and they work for food and a belly rub. You would be hard pressed to find a better tool in the police tool box. K-9 handlers are usually eccentric and wacky ... which fits right in with how I roll. (I thought I would use some hip vernacular there.)

When I took over as chief, I told Sgt. Knarr (he was a patrol officer at the time) to find us a dog. He did. Shortly after I was sworn in as chief, K-9 Ace joined us. He was a knuckleheaded little fur-ball, running around the department biting uniform pants (while the pants were being worn) and chasing all of us around. He grew quickly and became a dynamic police dog. His life was cut short due to an illness. When we put him down, that small vet's examination room was full of crying cops. A smaller department may have no dogs at all. We now have four police dogs and we will never be without close to that number as long as I am chief. These dogs are invaluable members of this department.

A dog on each shift is truly is like adding another person to the shift. I tease my officers regularly about teaching the dogs to drive and not having human officers . . . I think they worry.

If we didn't have the need to transport arrestees, there would be a dog for every officer who wanted one. Our four-legged officers have recovered countless drugs, found lost children, tracked dangerous suspects and hung around in my office, which is always a solid career move on their part.

Some chiefs don't want the hassle of a K-9 unit. By hassle I mean the training, care and maintenance. Chiefs also at times run into issues with the Fair Labor Standards Act and some headstrong employees and unions. I weigh a risk versus reward with most decisions I make. The bottom line is that we have good officers, who are selfless, and a

K-9 Joker giving Sgt. Knarr a bite.

chief who believes in K-9s. Being a K-9 handler is a great job and also has some drawbacks. When you are assigned a puppy, he is your new companion for the next seven or so years. You go to work—he goes to work. You go home, he's with you, and there is hair EVERYWHERE.

If you have never seen a K-9 unit at work, you are missing some of the best interaction between a dog and his/her partner ever. Sgt. Knarr has K-9 Havoc now. When they walk into a room it is astounding how close attention Havoc pays to every sound or movement Sgt. Knarr makes. He is absolutely tuned in.

When a K-9 unit works, the results are amazing. I have personally seen Havoc, Joker and Drogen find drugs, people or evidence when a human officer did not stand a chance of finding anything. Joker once tracked a bad guy for two miles nonstop . . . through grass, a swamp, through a creek, the woods and then right to the back door of the mope's house. "Knock, Knock." Havoc has found a gun thrown away by a bad guy, a bat used in an assault and thrown away, and once tracked for over two miles across every imaginable surface to find someone who had run from officers because of felony warrants. Drogen and Nitro will not be too far behind these older dogs. They are displaying young brilliance every day.

For the detractors who say we have "too many" dogs or express that we don't need any, I'm sorry for your luck—you currently have a chief who believes otherwise.

We would not be the same department without our hairy dog cops.

Dear Convicted Drug Dealer,

After a few hours of reflection, I want to apologize for Sgt. Knarr and I ruining your life.

You are 100% correct; you are now in a bad situation because of us. I mean, the fact that you just got out of prison on Friday notwithstanding, you might have been going down a different road . . . except for the drugs you had last night.

I understand the police in Summit County caught you with more than three pounds of weed and you are on probation . . . That's a tough break. I probably wouldn't be too happy to face my probation officer, either.

I would like to offer some advice, so you stand less of a chance of police officers ruining your life in the future. Please read carefully:

• Don't park your car on the dark backside of an open business. I know you and the carload of mopes were "chilling and trying to figure out which hotel you were going to stay at"; however, at two in the morning, it looks suspicious.

• When I approach your car and begin talking to you, try telling me the truth. I sincerely hope you don't play poker in addition to selling drugs. Your poker face sucks.

• When K-9 Havoc barks and scratches a car, it is not because he is "hungry" or "playing"; it is because the car has drugs inside. Your situation is the perfect example.

• Another piece of advice: Don't blame the female in the vehicle for your drugs. That wins you ZERO points with the ladies—and we think it is lame.

• Last, it helps if you are not on probation for a gazillion drug charges and your friend isn't on probation for "stuff involving having a gun and stuff." When we have guns and drugs together, in police work, we call that a "clue" . . .

Good luck with your future endeavors and please stay out of Brimfield.

—Chief

Let's legalize drugs

I haven't lost my mind. Since others sometimes live in a fantasy world, I thought I would join them.

Poof; drugs are legal . . .

All of them . . . heroin, crack, cocaine, meth, weed, uppers, downers, everything. Let's also do what the drug legalization folks want to do—we will have the feds regulate the sales, do compliance checks and the feds and state can both tax the sales. Nirvana! It will be just like the other countries who have legalized drugs and had no ill effect, either by an increase in users (bogus) or an increase in crime (another lie). Poof . . . just like that.

According to the National Institute on Drug Abuse, "in 2009, 605,000 Americans age 12 and older had abused heroin at least once in the year prior to being surveyed." That's 605,000, and it is ILLEGAL, and that's just heroin. Now that it's legal, we will bump that number up and round it to a million. I'll use poetic license on that number. Now, we will say a percentage of those who used it once are now addicts. They can go to the state "drug" store and buy a bag or four. How are they paying for it? . . . Anyone? They cannot stay gainfully employed. It's impossible. They are physically sick if they do not have heroin in their veins. Anyone care to let them operate a tow motor? How about make your burger? After all, the social stigma is gone. They are addicted to a legal substance, just like alcohol. How about the meth addict? She has lots of energy . . . she will be great at keeping up with the kids at a daycare, or cleaning your house. Things my come up missing, but that's the "nature of the beast." They need the money to buy the drugs that have nearly doubled in price due to regulations and taxes.

Well, no one wants to let them work, so, we will "subsidize" their habits by giving them a government card. They can take that card to any state "drug store," swipe it and get their fix. The bill goes to government. The government pays the tab, to themselves, with tax dollars. The addicts can also go to the still-existing black market for their drugs; however, it's hit or miss whether that is the time they get the fix that kills them—it's not regulated.

We can substitute any of the listed drugs for the heroin in our scenario. Don't snipe me on the weed, either. It is not like alcohol, contains cancer-causing chemicals and slows reaction time down by large percentages . . . and it is illegal. If we start with legalizing and taxing weed, it will be the crack in the dam that causes the flood.

I don't know about the rest of you, but I don't like the thought. To my fellow officers from departments around the globe—we need to stay constant on arresting drug dealers. They are an enemy to our quality of life. Keep pressing on and let the politicians who have their heads in their hind end catch up.

WEATHER REPORT . . . We are not in the "scare the crap out of you" business. I believe informed people make better choices . . . and fewer visits to ditches while their hands are glued to the steering wheel and life is in slow motion. We have all done the driving-in-the-snow thing before—you are all pros by now.

AFTERNOON SHIFT . . . Great job on the arrest of a subject for his SIXTH OVI offense. This one is a felony . . . hopefully he will spend some time in a state resort for wayward bad people . . . We are not callous, hard-hearted people at the BPD. We actually are very nice—as long as you do not endanger the lives of those who live, work or visit here. When that happens, we do everything we can, legally, to remove you from the presence of law-abiding people.

DAYSHIFT . . . When it rains . . . Dayshift is on their third arrest today. The first was a driving under suspension; Officer Pettit used his bedazzled bracelets for that one. Next, the officers were called to Lowe's for a male who appeared to be sleeping in his vehicle. He had just smoked crack . . . we recovered a pipe with crack in it. Handcuffs, again. While we were at Lowe's, three subjects attempted to steal a rather large television. They also assaulted security and THEN almost hit them with a car. We have one of them in custody and will have warrants for two more . . . The way the year is headed so far, the bed and breakfast should buy more salmon patties and gravy.

"It is not our job to protect the people from the consequences of their political choices."

—Chief Justice John Roberts, U.S. Supreme Court

Guns

It may come as surprise to many of you: I like guns. When I was growing up, there were guns in my house. There were likely guns in my friend's houses. We played with toy guns too. These were REAL toy guns . . . they shot caps and didn't have the mandatory orange tips. One of the most stressful situations of my childhood was a result of running out of caps during a gun battle with bad guys. I can't remember if I was "Starsky" or "Hutch." I do know I ran out of ammo.

Some of you love guns; some of you hate guns . . . and I understand. Having responded to at least two children wounded or killed as a result of gunshots, I get why people have issues with firearms. My issue isn't with guns . . . my issue is with dunces who happen to have guns.

We are a township here. Lots of our residents have guns. Many of those lots of residents shoot guns on their property. When people first move here, we get called because of "shots fired" or "my neighbor is shooting." We also get asked "What day is trash day?," but that question is not relevant to this topic. What I have come to realize is these are the pains of a growing community. People from more developed areas (Stow, Cuyahoga Falls and Akron) move here and suddenly believe they have arrived in the middle of an outdoor firing range. They are correct, to an extent . . . the difference is, many of the folks here were raised around guns, know how to shoot and do so safely. Now, we occasionally have a burr in the saddle, like the dimwits who sit on their porches plunking away at birds and squirrels, and we deal with those. For the most part, people are responsible. Here are a few reminders . . .

Please don't do a bunch of shooting at night time. It freaks out your neighbors and my night shift ends up with the hair on the back of their neck standing up while looking for you out in the back forty. Please have proper back-stop. Please, please do not fire up into the air. Bullets always come down . . .

What it is reduced to is having consideration for those around you. Lack of that consideration results in injuries and deaths.

Most of us do a great job with that . . . some need just a little work.

What happens when you are arrested?

We get asked that question often, so we will try a general overview of the process. A Brimfield officer stops a vehicle for driving left of center. The officer also noticed the driver is driving 30 mph in a posted 45mph zone. The officer approaches the vehicle and begins speaking with the driver. The officer notices the driver's eyes are "glassy" and "watery" and also smells the odor of an alcoholic beverage coming from the inside of the vehicle. After asking for license, registration and proof of insurance, the officer notices the person has obvious confusion and trouble removing the items from his wallet and glove box. His speech is also slurred.

The officer asks the subject to step from his vehicle and notices the subject stumbles when walking back towards the police vehicle. The officer can still smell the alcoholic beverage and it is coming from the person's breath. For the sake of brevity, let's just say field tests are completed and the subject performs very poorly on the tests . . . YAHTZEE . . . we are arresting a drunk driver.

The subject is told he is under arrest and placed in handcuffs. There are dangerous situations for officers and this is certainly one of them. Many people fight during this time. We will say it goes without incident. The subject is handcuffed and read his rights (Miranda) and placed in the rear of the vehicle. Officers do an inventory of the contents and condition of the vehicle. We list any items of value and any damage, mostly for our protection. There's nothing like someone saying the cops took their Elvis Greatest Hits 8-track tape.

Officers call for a tow truck ($130+) and the vehicle is taken to our impound lot ($25 per calendar day). The subject is taken to the PD, where he is read a form called the BMV2255. That form advises the subject that he is under arrest; and also of the consequences of a refusal of a breath test and the consequences for testing above the legal limit. The theme from "Jeopardy" begins to play as the subject decides whether or not to "take the test." We will say he takes it and tests a .201% BAC (Blood Alcohol Content). By state law, his license is now suspended. We go through the rest of the booking process (read: lots of paperwork), take three mug shots, issue tickets and may release him on a bond . . . depending on his demeanor. Believe it or not, some behavior results in a trip to the bed and breakfast. He is given a court date within five days and appears. He pleads not guilty and it is set for trial. If he hasn't hired an attorney yet, he will need to . . . and it is not cheap. All told, if it goes to trial (we don't plead OVI cases down), the subject will have spent over $5,000 in attorney fees, fines, court costs, tow/impound fees and license reinstatement costs. Insurance will also cost a lot more now, and so will the yellow plates assigned to his vehicle because of the high BAC test.

If he drives ANY vehicle for a living, he may lose his job. Is it worth it?

NEW AT THE BPD . . . As many of you know, we are in the process of building/renovating our police building. I want to bring you up to date on the project.

We are currently under budget of the total cost of $1.5 million dollars. That is a lot of money—we know that. I have a good history and practice of being stingy with tax dollars and that has not changed with this project.

The need was overwhelming. My officers and staff were using the same restroom as arrested people; we eat lunch (when time permits) at the same table that we process evidence on . . . it's the only table in the department. Two years ago I confiscated the officer locker room area and converted it to an evidence room, because of the amount of items we recover or seize. I also had a garage bay converted into a records room because our calls spiked from 8,000 to 14,000 and stayed at that level.

We will be using JEDD money, from our Joint Economic Development District agreements with Tallmadge and Kent, to pay the note. These agreements tax workers and development in the districts and prevent Kent or Tallmadge from "taking us over" through annexation. NO levy money will be used for the building. We use levy money to operate the department, period. As long as I am chief, levy money will be used to pay officers and buy equipment to provide services . . . not for bells and whistles.

I have the plans hanging in my office. If any of you would like to stop by for a cup of coffee and see them, you are always welcome. I love to talk.

"The only place success comes before work is in the dictionary."

—Vince Lombardi

AFTERNOONS . . . Sgt. McCarty and Officer Dumont are up to police work again . . . two in custody from another theft at Walmart. These two had felony warrants and were also in possession of a stolen truck from Florida, and other stolen items in the truck.

In addition to that, we have captured the two OTHER subjects from the TV theft today. Thanks to a "friend" of ours they were spotted and held for us by the Ravenna Police Department. It's a regular ol' round-up tonight.

Update: The two just arrested in the stolen truck also had assembled the chemicals to manufacture meth. Sgt. McCarty and Officer Dumont also recovered meth from them. We are like America's Top 40 . . . the hits just keep coming.

AFTERNOONS . . . Update . . . I love my officers. We now have close to the complete story of the stolen truck/meth incident yesterday.

Sgt. McCarty and Officer Dumont were called to Walmart for a theft. The subjects were stealing various items, including those used to make meth. Many officers would have made the arrests (or even written a summons) and moved on . . . not my officers.

McCarty and Dumont recognize a couple of the items as meth ingredients and wonder, "What vehicle in this lot belongs to these two mopes?" So, they have the GREAT loss prevention crew at Walmart rewind the tape and find a very nice F-350 Super Duty. Another clue. This truck is a beauty . . . all lettered up, company name on the doors . . . too nice, actually. The bad guys deny knowing anything about the truck—although that would have worked a lot better if the KEY WAS NOT IN HIS POCKET.

The truck was stolen from Florida. When it was stolen, it was hooked up to a trailer hauling a NASCAR Sprint Truck belonging to Mike "the Gun Slinger" Skinner. All vehicles have been recovered, along with thousands of dollars in stolen tools. We also have checkbooks, purses and other items stolen from states between here and Florida.

My officers call it the "Brimfield Triangle" . . . criminals come here and disappear (for 10-15 years).

"You can't get rid of poverty by giving people money."

—P.J. O'Rourke

Dear Father or Mother Meth Cooks,

You have lost your mind. What in hell were you thinking when you made the decision to cook meth with your child in the house? You have violated the most basic principle of being a parent: the safety of your child. I am fed up with watching this behavior and also with being concerned about the long-term effects of what you have exposed YOUR child to.

I know you understand the dangers of making meth because you turn on exhaust fans and wear a mask while mixing the chemicals. Meanwhile, your 13-year-old or 8- year-old or 3-year-old sleeps in the bed upstairs, or on the couch or next to you in the hotel room while you mix toxic chemicals with pseudoephedrine so you can get high and escape a reality that YOU created.

Making a decision to cook meth with your child nearby indicates you can no longer take care of your child. You are not making proper decisions to ensure the health, safety and future of someone you brought into this world. This does not mean you do not love your child; however, it does mean you have decided to place your own wants and desires ahead of someone whose very life depends on you placing his or hers first. In language you will likely understand: You suck as a parent.

If you cannot overcome your addiction, if you cannot stop cooking meth with your child present, I have an offer for you. It is an unusual one at best. Bring your child to me at the police department. You don't even need to bring extra clothing—just the child. I will contact the proper people and help find the child a safe place to live, a place where he or she can breathe without developing lung cancer and won't be subjected to other abuse and neglect. If you love your child as much as you say you do, swallow your pride and show up here.

You know deep down it is the only way to break the cycle.

—Chief

What we do

Yesterday, after posting the story about Officer Pettit and the pilot light caper, I read the comments and thought about us lighting a senior citizen's pilot light. I didn't agree with a couple of the comments; however, the posters were correct. It is the often-cited scenario when both parties have a valid point.

Police officers, by definition, are not HVAC professionals. We also are not animal wardens, psychologists or marriage counselors. We do not get paid to buy a gallon of milk for a shut-in senior or shovel snow from sidewalks and driveways. We do not get paid to host senior breakfasts, Safety School or golf camps. Attending youth baseball games is not in our job description, nor is stopping by an elementary school student's house because he is SO excited to show you his pet turtle. Kissing cows? Nope. Nowhere in the job description. That same job description does not contain the verbiage for sitting with an 88 year-old Army veteran who stormed the beaches at Normandy and after 70+ years has found comfort in talking about it. The gentleman with the pilot light out was in a tight spot financially or likely would have had it fixed three days prior to telling us about it. What we do is protect the public . . . and serve them. The aforementioned things are my definition of service. The cool thing is, since I'm the chief, I supply the definition of how we serve. Whoever comes after me may decide it is too much to do.

So, all of those things are within my definition of service—as are scores of other things we do or have done because of our relationship with our residents. We were by no means trying to honk off the HVAC guys in our friend's world; just like we are not trying to make milkmen and marriage counselors snap. I hire the officers in Brimfield—the Trustees actually legally hire them, but have never done so against my recommendation. When I hire, I hire servants. I can teach a person to catch bad guys. I can't teach them to have compassion and heart. Lastly, I will never make a decision, or allow one to be made on my watch, based on whether or not we may be sued. I trust officers with lots of guns and cars that go really fast—two of the biggest liabilities in police work. There are times we have to drive fast, pull our weapons, deploy a TASER or use a K-9 to find drugs or a fleeing suspect. I have been sued, as your police chief, approximately 14 times. When you can sue McDonald's for spilling coffee on yourself, just imagine the target on police officers.

If I worried about lawsuits, I would have all of my officers on bikes, carrying squirt guns.

DAYSHIFT . . . Let's talk Walmart . . . Dayshift had our SIXTH arrest there in the last two days today. A wanna-be sneak removed an Internet router from the shelf, walked around the store and then returned it for a gift card. He was arrested for theft.

Folks, Walmart is NOT an issue for us. We are sending a message. Many jurisdictions issue a ticket for theft and release the person from the scene. Thieves are expecting to come in and steal . . . and get a ticket. Most don't appear for court anyway, so it's just a loss of a half-hour for them and they are "back to work."

I made the decision, after about two seconds of thought: We will not ticket someone who has the gumption to walk into a store in this community and steal. Stealing is dishonest and illegal and causes all of us to pay more for what we work to buy. So, if you steal here, you will wear handcuffs, get your car towed and post a bond. If you can't post, phone a friend for money for your jail account, because that is where you will be. And tell your friends not to come here to commit crimes; we have ZERO tolerance for it. Also, a big thank-you to the Walmart staff; they like catching people almost as much as we do.

WEATHER REPORT . . . We haven't received any calls yet . . . Please do not be alarmed by the bright orange object in the sky; it is the sun and will likely disappear again before long.

AFTERNOON SHIFT YESTERDAY . . . Sgt. McCarty and Officer Dumont were at it again. A traffic stop resulted in the arrest of a female who had four felony warrants and also a bunch of needles and heroin. She pulled the old "heart attack" routine, which we are professionals at handling. After she figured out we were going to stay with her for the entire hospital visit she experienced a miracle and the heart attack stopped . . . we may be better than aspirin. She is at the bed and breakfast now, in a new orange and white jumpsuit with complimentary shoes. Great job, afternoon shift!

Safety School

As we get close to August, I get really pumped up for our Safety School Program. We conduct lots of great programs at the BPD, and I love to participate in all of them. Safety School is at the top of the list.

Starting the last week of July, we hold two separate weeks of the program. We take 50 children per week, from 9 a.m. to noon. We hold it at the Victory Baptist Temple on SR43. The church has been kind enough to donate the facilities and classrooms for the two weeks and the chapel for graduation. When the week begins on Monday, some of the kids are more than apprehensive about leaving mom/dad for the day to hang with cops. By Wednesday, most of them are up early, wearing their T-shirts and ready to go to Safety School.

Some of the most memorable times of my police career have been at safety school, like when Zach picked up the wrong microphone in the police vehicle and when ordering a "bad guy" to "freeze and put up his hands." Instead of being on the loudspeaker, he sent those orders out countywide, on the police band, causing a captain from a neighboring department to spill coffee all over his desk. It was pretty loud. I'm sure most officers nearly vapored out when that shrieking voice came across the air, breaking what had been a quiet silence . . . and it was hysterical when the Captain advised me over the air to "tell that child he owes me a cup of coffee."

During those two weeks the children learn about police work; meet officers and K-9 units; learn about seat belts; riding the bus; stranger danger; bicycle safety; vehicle safety and also learn a song for graduation. Each child is assigned to a team, with a coordinating color T-shirt. The fire department helps us out, as does the Portage County Dive Team for water safety. The week ends with a great graduation ceremony attended by parents, relatives and friends.

It is our way to help the children and parents prepare for the separation that takes place a few short weeks later when the children start kindergarten . . . and give the kids some guidance along the way.

Andy Griffith

Mayberry is a fictional town in North Carolina. The Sheriff there is Andy Taylor. His deputy is Barney Fife. Those two have been woven into our social quilt since the early 1960s, when the show debuted with the episode titled "The New Housekeeper."

Andy was a widower, raising his son, Opie, with the help of his Aunt Bea. The cast of characters in the show and in Mayberry may go down as the most eclectic group living anywhere on the planet. Otis, the town drunk, arrested himself regularly, and released himself after sobering up. The Darling Family gave us some of the best blue-grass music, with Briscoe Darling playing (and sometimes drinking from) the moonshine jug. Ernest T. Bass threw rocks, tried to enlist in the Army and went back to school—all to find a girlfriend. Floyd the barber ran a numbers game for a short while . . . and had no idea his shop was being used as a front for organized crime.

Although the show began before I was born, it has never been off of the air. Since the first episode, some station in some city has played reruns. I watched. I watched Opie kill a mother bird and then raise the baby birds until they could fly. He did so because his father was teaching him a lesson about life, as he did so many times. I watched as Barney bumbled his way through catching dangerous criminals and saving lives—usually with the unknown help of Andy. If you never heard Barney sing or watched him train in judo, recite the Declaration of Independence or "make moves" on Thelma Lou, you have missed some great laughs. I have watched them all.

Andy Griffith helped design a show that contained no nudity, sex, swearing, killings or other things commonly found in today's television, and it has stood the test of time. There have been real-life experiences which influenced my choice to become a police officer; however, there were no greater fictional influences on that choice than the way Andy "sheriffed." He did so with compassion and a genuine love for right and wrong. He was slow to anger, yet quick to action. He would get on a knee to look children in the eyes to speak with them, he was a gentleman with the ladies and looked out for old folks.

He did all of that . . . and I watched. Rest in Peace, Sheriff Taylor.

What America means to me

I believe we live in the greatest country in the world. When I am done typing this, I can get into my truck and drive ocean to ocean. Mrs. Chief would love the break. I can listen to talk radio as the hosts bash the government. I can turn on various news channels and watch people "occupy" various locations. Because my personal values do not mesh with the occupiers, I can speak my opinion about most of them needing to occupy a place in the workforce, and I do not have to worry about any government repercussions. However unpopular it is or may become, I can attend church, believe in God and read the Bible. I can sing loud if I choose . . . although that could be construed as disturbing the peace.

As a citizen of this country, I have responsibilities. I have rights; however, I must be responsible and understand my rights end when they infringe upon your rights. I have a right to shoot guns. That right will come to a screeching halt when a stray round interrupts your July 4th barbeque. I have a responsibility to shoot safely. Believe it or not, it is my right to expect other citizens to be productive citizens. It is my right to believe we should not have four consecutive generations receiving government assistance in the way of food stamps and discounted housing. It is your right to disagree with me, so long as you do it in a civil manner. I can believe drugs are a cancer to our way of life. You can believe otherwise and give me the "protected free speech" middle finger, as long as you do so within the guidelines of the Supreme Court's free speech ruling. It is my responsibility to NOT punch you in the face when you give me the one finger salute . . . But I can think it.

In my very humble opinion, some (not all) of those among us place rights over responsibilities as citizens. It is kind of like the government has become their parents . . . and they are 16. They need a car, some money, a prom dress, car insurance, cell phone, cool clothes and the credit card. The responsibilities, such as cleaning the room, doing dishes and mowing the lawn? No thanks. They would rather NOT . . . at least not now. This transcends into police work more than you could ever imagine. Thefts, drugs, violent crimes and lots of other issues law enforcement deals with comes from believing there are only "rights" and no responsibilities—and, for some, if the two conflict, rights always are placed first.

I believe, as citizens of this great country, we have responsibilities. Thanks for reading and Happy Independence Day.

DAY SHIFT TODAY . . . A prostitute was arrested at a local hotel, after offering her "services" and accepting money from . . . an undercover officer. We HATE when that happens.

Officers recovered . . . ummmm . . . "criminal tools" (we will call them male birth control) and a used meth needle, spoon and syringe. We also have a nice list with phone numbers and how much she charged each one over the last three days. Although often considered a "victimless crime," prostitution brings other crimes with it, including drug trafficking and abuse and other quality-of-life issues.

Criminals: We know you read our page; we have lots of informational sources and you all know our reputation. We will pursue you relentlessly, day and night.

OVERHEARD AT THE BPD . . .

Phone conversation between the Chief and Mrs. Chief:

Chief: "I'm going to be a little late today."

Mrs. Chief: "Okay. Is everything all right?"

Chief: "Yeah, we're just going to visit a prostitute."

Mrs. Chief: "Oh, okay. Good luck."

Only in this business.

DAYSHIFT . . . Officer Pettit with a traffic stop and the arrest of a subject for a drug offense. The stop was well within 1,000 feet of Brimfield Elementary . . . the subject was charged with possession with intent to distribute methamphetamine (packaged for sale) and possession of drugs. Officers recovered over two grams of meth, oxycodone, Valium, digital scales, empty zip baggies and $1,150 in cash. The bad guy gets a trip to the Gray Bar Hotel, which includes meals and recreation time . . . see ya!

Dear Weed Smoker,

I understand that marijuana is not considered the "crime of the century." I also understand that some people believe it should be legalized. I am not in that group. It is still illegal.

For no other reason than the fact that weed is illegal, please take the following advice:

• Do not call us to report that your weed has been stolen from your hotel room.

• That also applies to your grinder and weed pipe.

• Chalk that situation up as a loss and move on.

Calling the police to report your weed has been stolen . . . Seriously? You are a walking billboard for the fact that smoking weed kills brain cells.

If you can't stop using drugs, stop coming to this community.

Best regards,

—Chief

DAYSHIFT TODAY . . . Officers handled at least 10 traffic crashes, along with assisting with the cluster of a crash on I-76 involving at least 30 vehicles. Officers also arrested a drunk driver who drove off the road and deep into a field. The person was taken to the county bed and breakfast and is in time-out at least until Monday. Afternoon shift is still handling disabled vehicles and crashes. Officer Pettit knows he has feet, but cannot verify it because he has not been able to feel them for the last four hours.

"My father used to play with my brother and me in the yard. Mother would come out and say, 'You're tearing up the grass.' 'We're not raising grass,' Dad would reply. 'We're raising boys.'"

—Harmon Killebrew

Sex crimes

We get our share of sexually related crimes at the BPD. If you speak with any police officer working at any department, these crimes will likely rank right up there with the worst to deal with. I like people. I like protecting them. I am old school (or so I am told) when it comes to crimes in general . . . and worse when the crimes involve women and children. Those folks fall into a special class for me. I am not a chauvinist by any stretch of the imagination. Mrs. Chief would not tolerate it. I do, however believe in being a gentleman. I also believe in protecting those who others perceive to be "easy targets."

Sex crimes involving women and children make the hair on the back of neck stand up. These crimes are mostly NOT the result of desire, but of anger. When a rape is committed, it is not because the man has desire—it is 100% about control, revenge or anger. Yes, even a "date rape" scenario boils down to control or anger. It may shock some of you (that is totally sarcastic, by the way) but I tend to be a conservative guy. Not specifically politically, but as a general statement. I believe in hard work and a paycheck, helping your neighbor and opening doors for strangers. Actually, I have never met a stranger. Despite that conservative outlook, I don't care what a person wears, how they act or what they say. We all have that freedom. I do not believe any woman ever "asks" to be assaulted. I do not believe it is how she dresses, talks or even that she gets really intoxicated at times. Those are signs of something else, but not signs of wanting to be a victim.

Somewhere along the line people began getting an idea that if a woman dresses provocatively or drinks alcohol with a purpose, she somehow shares the blame if bad things happen. Hogwash. I have interviewed scores of sex crime suspects. Not one of them ever said "look how she dresses" or "she was SO drunk" . . . until a defense attorney got involved. These perpetrators are mean and angry. They hate women, even if they are attracted to them. They may even be married with children, yet hate women for whatever reason.

Pedophiles are some of the worst and they can't be fixed. It is a specific abnormality. You can counsel, talk and put them in more focus groups than you can count . . . at the end of it all, they are attracted to children. When we work case involving those mopes, the intention is to present a flawless case, so the prosecutors can win it and we can get them removed from society, hopefully for life. Again, this is NOT a sex-based crime, but one of control and dominance . . . with the most defenseless victims.

If you are a victim, or know of or suspect a child victim—report it. Do not wait and do not worry. If it happened here, we will carry the burden so you don't have to. Justice does exist.

NEW AT THE BPD . . . Building update: The advertisement for the addition to our police department was placed in papers yesterday. I don't think I have been this excited since I caught my first fish. We have a 30-day window for general contractors to review plans and submit a bid. We are under budget so far and I will keep it that way. We find it easier to negotiate with people when we have TASERS. (That was chief humor . . . or was it?)

IN THE SCHOOLS . . . Good luck and Godspeed to our middle-school students who are leaving for Washington, D.C. today. In spite of some of the people we have elected to work there, there is a lot of history and "coolness" in our nation's capitol.

IN THE SCHOOLS . . . I think by now you all understand how important the children in this community are to us. We spend a lot of time at our schools interacting with "our kids." This morning, we were given quite the surprise when we were asked to attend an assembly at Brimfield Elementary. For the school's "Act of Random Kindness" week, the students donated nearly 400 stuffed animals to the police department. We give these stuffed animals away to kids during calls for traffic crashes and other incidents during which we may find a child who needs some uplifting. We are honored and humbled by "our kids" and we love them all. We will continue to serve and protect them with the fiercest efforts.

DID THIS REALLY JUST HAPPEN . . . ? Officers were called to the plaza for what we can only describe as an illegal dumping incident. The caller advised that a male had just dropped pants and "used the restroom" in the parking lot. We will just say a "number 2." I caught up with him at I-76 and SR43. Officer Diehl joined me. The subject was arrested for his sixth OVI offense, driving under suspension and public indecency. We may never be the same.

Child abuse and neglect

Cops and kids . . . It is a time-honored relationship. Even if police officers do not have their own children, they still cringe when responding to ANY call involving a child being hurt. Traffic crashes, a fall off of a bike or skateboard—it doesn't matter. We just drive with a little more urgency.

When we deal with abuse and neglect cases, we become very frustrated.

I spent some time working in an undercover capacity. I have seen some living conditions that animals would be uncomfortable calling home. Kids who had not seen a bath in some time, wearing the same clothes for weeks. Yes, some of it has been caused by drugs. The crack houses, meth labs and heroin dens are not kid-friendly by any stretch. We have removed children from all of these locations.

I am not jabbing at my friends from any children's services organization; however, in the opinion of an insignificant chief in one small location of the world, we have to get out of the mindset of constantly thinking of reuniting abused and neglected children with their birth parents. "Reunification" is not always the best ending.

I'm going to say something that many might find offensive, so here is your "chief being chief" warning. Some people do not have the capability of being good parents. They may love their children and have the DESIRE to be a good mother or father, but they just cannot get out of their own way. They place boyfriends or girlfriends, drugs or money in the front of the line. In the end, we arrive at children who are not being fed and being taken care of, perhaps being abused by the boyfriend/girlfriend or sleeping in an upstairs bedroom while meth is being cooked in the basement. If you read this post and look at your child(ren) and see these indicators, do something or we will. Count on it. As long as I am chief here we will not sit on our thumbs and ignore those in need.

Somewhere along the path of our society, "self" has become the most important thing. As a society, we as adults need to start leading these kids. At the minimum, we need to start helping them. If you know a drug dealer or user who sells or uses when his/her kids are around, it is YOUR business . . . and mine. If you know someone who is abusing a child, it is YOUR business . . . and mine. If you suspect "Uncle Creepy" is being inappropriate with a child, it is your business . . . and mine.

If there is a child you suspect of being neglected or abused, call us without hesitating. You can also email, visit or send up a smoke signal. Just do something.

If you suspect something . . . do something.

IN THE SCHOOLS . . . We are aware of the school shooting in Chardon. Our thoughts and prayers are with the victims, parents and school staff members. Our officers are in the schools right now and we will continue to have extra staffing at the buildings.

If you are a regular follower of BPD, you know we drill and drill and drill for these things. It is an unfortunate aspect of our society today—there are those who will prey on the defenseless. I love standing at the school every morning. I love the interaction with the kids—and I love the kids. I also am sending a strong message that our officers are in the schools and we will not allow our kids to be victims without going through us.

Officer Russ Diehl with kindergarten students.

Drunk driving

Drunk drivers are morons. There is no other way to put that, from my chair. Still, as bad as that may sound, one arrest for drunk driving does not put you on the outs with me. People make mistakes. During that mistake, we pray no one gets injured or killed. That statement is not to absolve the one-time OVI driver from the responsibility to pay his or her debt to society for that infraction—do the crime, pay the time. We will gladly oblige you with handcuffs and a tow truck.

A second or higher OVI offense, though . . . If I were king of the world (someone would have to be really crazy for that to happen), a second-offense (or greater) OVI driver would go directly to jail if convicted. No pleading the case down, no high-paid attorney making a mockery out of the system . . . none of that hogwash.

See you later. One-year minimum, bye.

Society as a whole does not take drunk driving seriously. If you are drunk and possess a firearm in a vehicle, it is a felony. OVI is a misdemeanor, unless you fall into the matrix of the complex OVI law that gives you so many strikes in 20 years. I can make it simple . . . second offense, jail. Third offense, more jail. I can go to prison for a being drunk with a gun, yet I get "community sanctions" (probation and more probation) if I am drunk and operate a machine that can reach speeds of 100+ MPH and weighs thousands of pounds. Who wasn't thinking when they were discussing that law?

Criminals in general piss me off. Sorry for the language, however there is not a nice way to express that. "Frustrate me" would be a disservice to my piss-off-ed-ness. Thieves, burglars, drug dealers, rapists, robbers . . . I have zero use and tolerance for their chosen way of life. I love to catch them and love to direct my officers to do the same. OVI drivers make that list also. If you have never been on the scene of a crash caused by a drunk driver, thank God, the moon or Charlie Sheen—whomever you thank, thank them. The sounds and smells never leave you. Notifying parents, husbands, children and other relatives of the death of a love one . . . the wailing sound never gets fainter. There is no hyperbole there. That is the truth. Ask an officer anywhere and he or she will confirm it.

Potential drunk drivers . . . you are not superhuman. You cannot make it home without killing someone. Your overconfidence comes from alcohol and stupidity. Get a ride. Call me—I will come and get you, no questions asked. If you have to think about if you are sober enough to drive, don't risk it, because you are not.

What YOU believe to be sober and what we believe to be sober are not even close.

Let's stop this nonsense.

DID THIS REALLY JUST HAPPEN . . . ? Okay, after a few years of doing this job, I pretty much thought I had seen it all. Well, I guess I have not. About 15 minutes ago I was sitting at my desk typing an email. I looked out the window, as I often do, and I saw a man standing in the back parking lot. I thought perhaps he was a contractor looking at the building for the bidding process. I walked outside to speak with him. The camera I thought he was holding was not a camera . . . it was a can of Old Milwaukee beer, and he was likely one of the most intoxicated people I have ever seen. Now I'm standing there in uniform, next to a police car . . . the conversation was something close to this . . .

Chief: "Good morning, can I help you?"

Drunk guy: "Yeah . . . um, I'm here to meet a girl."

Chief: "You're here to meet a girl?"

Drunk guy: "Yes. She's a prostitute, but don't tell anyone."

Chief: {{{DUMB LOOK}}} "Okay . . ."

Drunk guy "I have my twenty dollars!"

Chief: "Sir, do you know you are at a police department?"

Drunk guy: "I am?"

Chief: "See the uniform? The gun belt? The police car?"

Drunk guy: "&*!# . . . now I do. Am I under arrest?"

I am convinced there is some type of magnet around here somewhere . . . we just keep drawing them in.

Dear Drunken Idiot,

This will be a short request.

If you cannot hold your liquor, please at least know your limit. That limit is somewhere BEFORE you get arrested for drunk driving and then feel the need to mess yourself while in our holding cell.

It's unacceptable and illegal to put innocent people at risk by driving like an idiot when you are drunk.

Messing yourself is just plain ignorant.

Jackass.

With my nose taped shut,

Chief

MIDNIGHTS . . . An OVI driver left the roadway and met with a culvert on Howe Road. The score from that one was: Culvert 1, Truck 0. The driver was removed and placed in the penalty box . . . he tested nearly a .20 BAC. Luckily, it was only his truck that was "injured."

NEW AT THE BPD . . . Today we will be opening bids for the addition and remodel of the police department. Although you cannot see me right now, trust the fact that I am dancing. I have "cabbage patched," done the "sprinkler" and I'm trying to remember the break dance I learned in the '80s; however, I am concerned about hurting something and walking with a limp.

The building we are in is an old auto-body shop. When I became chief we did some minor remodels, replacing urine-stained carpet and other chores. We did most of the work ourselves. In the current conditions, we use the same restroom as our arrestees, each lunch on the same (and only) table used to process evidence and just suffer through it. The new building is well under budget and as I stated from the beginning, we will not seek any money from taxpayers to build it. We have budgeted for it, which is one of the reasons everyone in the building agreed to wage freezes three years ago.

I'm getting ready to play a little MC Hammer and work on a moonwalk.

My responsibilities

Some of the sentiments expressed by a few of the detractors to my rants and opinions on our Facebook page are "it's not professional" and "they shouldn't have a page." Hogwash. I believe we have a very professional police department here. Speaking personally, I am not a hill-jack with a badge. I have a Master's degree in business and a Bachelor's in Criminal Justice. I am also an avid reader and have been since elementary school. I say what is on my mind because of my convictions and bubbly personality, not because I was raised by wolves.

I know lots of police chiefs. I am friends with many of those same chiefs. Not a single one of us operates our department in exactly the same fashion. Many are bootstrapped by their elected bosses. Some are fearful of lawsuits. Some are just quiet people. None of those are me. My elected bosses, for the most part, believe in me as a chief and the department as a whole. I was an opinionated guy when they hired me. It wasn't like I was sworn in as a chief and then started having a big mouth ... I have had that wonderful curse since I learned to talk. I could not care less about getting sued. I don't try to get people to sue me; however, hot coffee is supposed to be hot and restaurants have been sued for not warning us of that fact. I would imagine leading a police department into skirmishes with criminal types will result in someone trying to get paid, and we will fight that, too.

I believe in being a leader. Not a community leader, but a leader of this department. The inherent responsibility of a police department is public safety. When I give an opinion on the police page, it is the opinion of the person in charge of the department. It is for my residents and for my officers. It is also for the lawbreakers who visit our page ... and they do. It's not posted on my "personal page" because that is reserved for family, fishing and sports. When I write that a three-time convicted child molester cannot be cured and if executions for this crime were legal I would pull the lever myself—it is my opinion, as one police chief. If you believe it to be unprofessional, ignorant or just crazy ... I do not care. All the indignant foot-stomping you can muster is not going to change that. You can call the media, you can send up smoke signals and you can hate me all you want. Call or email me and

I will give you the contact information for my elected bosses. If you convince two out of three of them I am no good . . . Yahtzee.

I will not bow to being "politically correct." I have no idea how to act that way. I do not like criminals. I do not like thieves, drugs, rapists, robbers and the rest. They are dishonest and make others victims. We are a police department, not a social agency. If you need a public official who is sensitive to the needs of criminals and wants to rehabilitate the world . . . wrong guy, wrong page.

I will not change a thing.

OVERHEARD AT THE BPD . . .

Conversations with a meth cook:

Suspect: "I didn't mean to make meth."

Chief: "You didn't mean to make it?"

Suspect: "No. I was just trying to make smoke."

Chief: {Dumb look}

Suspect: "I was trying to scare the Mexicans. They're superstitious."

Chief: "Okay . . . You were trying to scare someone by making smoke?"

Suspect: "Yes, sir. I was trying to scare the Mexicans."

Chief: "But you ended up with meth."

Suspect: "Yes, I guess I did."

Chief: "You do realize this may be the dumbest thing I have ever heard. You could not come up with a better excuse for making meth than that?"

Suspect: "I thought about it and no . . . I couldn't . . . I don't want to tell on myself."

This job is amazing.

"Politics is the art of looking for trouble, finding it everywhere, diagnosing it incorrectly, and applying the wrong remedies."

—Groucho Marx

IN THE SCHOOLS . . . Conversation this morning at the elementary school, between Officer Diehl and a first-grade girl:

Officer Diehl: "Good morning, sweetie, how are you?"

Student: "I'm good. Guess what, Officer Diehl?"

Officer Diehl: "What?"

Student: "My mom has a crush on you . . . but she has a HUSBAND."

Officer Diehl's face went to RED and I fell over laughing . . . I love these children.

WEEKEND TOTALS . . . We arrested 11 people over the weekend, for various reasons . . . OVI, being intoxicated and underage, warrants, theft, the usual. We have arrested nearly 200 people in the first three months of the year; if we were the stock exchange, you would all be rich—the numbers are up. It is a very good thing that we reuse our handcuffs.

ANIMALS . . . You may have noticed us posting found dogs (and one special pig) on our FB page. A year or so back, we secured kennels from the dog warden to house found dogs on a temporary basis. We believe it is stressful for some people to discover a missing pet—and even worse when you discover the pet is at the "dog pound." We like the dog warden; he is a friend of ours. We just don't want HIS bed and breakfast full of OUR residents. If your neighbors aren't familiar with our page, get them here if only for this reason. This page has most certainly become a useful tool.

"The respect that leadership must have requires that one's ethics be without question. A leader not only stays above the line between right and wrong, he stays well clear of the gray areas."

—G. Alan Bernard

Active shooters

The recent events in Colorado caused everyone to start thinking about how safe they really are. Although you should always think about safety, active threats and shooters are not a recent thing. As early as April 9, 1891 in Newburgh, New York, a 70 year-old man wounded five students at St. Mary's Parochial School. Recent incidents at Virginia Tech and Colorado bring active threats to the forefront once again. But those incidents are always up front for me and my officers. We experienced a rampage shooter in 2005, so unfortunately we have some first-hand knowledge. Here is a fact that will likely aggravate most of you: If someone plans and then makes the decision to walk into a mall, store, school or workplace and start shooting, someone may get killed before we can get there. We have a response time that makes me proud. We get to a "hot" call, most of the time, in under three minutes. Three minutes is a long time to be under gunfire. The shootings at Columbine changed the way law enforcement officers respond to these calls. When I started in law enforcement, we were trained to "hold the perimeter" until tactical officers arrived. I always thought that idea to be odd; after all, I have guns and people need help. But still, we waited, because that is what we are trained and told to do. Now, we go towards the threat and neutralize it (that is soft language for shooting a bad guy). That is an idea I can wrap my head around . . . not the killing part, but the going to where the bad guy is hurting people portion.

The chance that you will be on the scene of an active shooter is slim, they tell me. I'm sure the children inside the Amish school in Pennsylvania believed the same; actually, they probably never thought a about it. We do.

We are going to begin developing a public presentation for residents and friends who may want to attend. This program will cover and define active threats and give reactions and suggested behaviors if you find yourself in this hell of an incident. In my opinion (yes, I am still giving opinions here), an educated public is the best weapon we have against these cowards . . . and they are supreme cowards. Anyone who can kill a woman or child can never be anything else but a weakling and an ass. I hope to have the program ready in the fall.

I understand you gun owners and CCW advocates will post about being ready. We know that. As a police department and chief, I am speaking to and advocating for those who need us, as is my custom.

Have a great day and call us if you need us; we are here and open 24/7.

DAYSHIFT . . . A man, woman and their two-year-old child leave Akron and arrive at our Walmart. The couple enter the store and begin filling a diaper bag (which had been empty) and purse with DVDs and other electronics—nearly $1,000 worth. Under the ever watchful eye of Walmart loss prevention (they work really hard to catch people, and we love it) the couple has filled their bags and are ready to leave. A Walmart loss-prevention guy approaches the two (and the innocent child), and before the employee can introduce himself he is promptly punched in the face. A struggle ensues between the men, and the child gets to watch mom jump into the fray. Mom begins assaulting the loss-prevention person, too! During the melee, the employee is punched and also bitten.

We arrive and arrest both subjects for robbery and assault. They are processed and will go to the His and Hers wings at the Gray Bar Hotel. The baby is picked up by family; the car, which was "borrowed," is towed. Child Services is on board now and they will investigate.

Folks, taking a small child with you to appear "family-like" while you commit crimes is just an ignorant thing to do. Great job today to Sgt. Knarr and Officers Atha and Sonagere.

AFTERNOON SHIFT . . . Sgt. McCarty's shift was at it again. They made a felony domestic arrest. The subject had prior arrests for hitting females. A one-year-old child was slightly injured during the ruckus. The suspect fled the scene, as cowards who hit women often do. He failed at hide-and-seek and was arrested. He is now dressed in orange and wearing anti-skid slippers at the county bed and breakfast.

McCarty and his crew were not done. They believe in earning their wages. They were called to Walmart for an intoxicated female. They met with her, and she insisted she was dropped off by a taxi. So officers called a taxi, and she and her child left to go home. Sgt. McCarty and Officer Dumont had some doubts, so they went all stealthy, sorta like ninjas, and waited to see if she returned. She did. The taxi dropped her off at her car. She barely got it into drive before the navy-blue ninjas swooped in and stopped her. She was arrested and charged with OVI and endangering children. The child is safe now.

Our children

When I was talking about our Safety School recently, someone commented that the subject matter was something parents should be teaching. We agree. Most parents do a great job teaching their children. Some parents don't. The idea behind our Safety School doesn't involve a strict curriculum of marching kids through traffic teaching them to cross the street, with push-ups as punishment for those who don't do it properly. The main idea is to allow children to meet their local safety forces and realize we are human beings and care about them.

Our police department has a very strong presence in our schools. We have a full-time officer assigned to the schools when school is in session, and officers often visit the buildings throughout the day. A high percentage of the students know at least one officer by name, even if that name is just "Chief." We believe Safety School is the opening of the door to our long-term investment in "our" children. I cannot count how many kindergarteners who have asked me if I remember them from Safety School. We are invested in our children, as officers, for another reason . . . safety. I believe in having an officer at the schools all of the time. I also believe in showing up at the buildings at all times of the day, and all days of the week. Why? Because I want any outsider who intends to commit a crime on school property to understand that the schools are not "soft targets." I want them to know there are well-trained officers who will protect our children with our lives if needed. I want our kids to know us and not only feel safe, but also believe they are safe, so they can learn without disruptions and stress. The children expect to see us in the hallway and it usually results in a lot of "group hugs."

Our world is sometimes messy. Shootings at movie theatres, malls and other public venues have left everyone on edge. The young ones know some of what is going on and need to know we are here and we have their backs, too. Safety School is the introduction to that idea . . . and we love it; and we love "our" children.

Drunk driver behavior

A drunk driver this past weekend really acted out. He had tons of statements and questions that my officers chose to ignore. They are professional like that. Me . . . not so much. I take offense when people insult the officers or the department. I thought I would clear up some of the driver's misconceptions . . .

1) Yes, we know people make mistakes. People have gotten out of the habit of atonement, though.

2) No, they couldn't have just "driven" you "home"; we are the police, not your designated drivers.

3) Yes, you were too drunk to drive—a .155% BAC level is almost twice the legal limit. Liquid intelligence always trumps common sense for those who believe they are "okay to drive."

4) No, it is not our fault you may lose your job . . . it is yours. It also would have been your fault if you had killed another motorist. Maybe it is our "fault" you didn't kill anyone. We will take THAT blame all day long.

5) Yes, it is true we would not like you to "show up at our house if you are found guilty." In the scope of things, that would be a bigger mistake than you driving drunk.

6) Yes, it is true my officers would have been disciplined if they "just drove" you "home." They likely would have been fired. Drunk drivers kill people. That practice has not existed while I have been the chief here and never will—regardless of who you are, where you work or whose salary you pay.

7) Yes, I would have found out if officers had just driven you home. I have spidey senses . . . and I hire honest officers with character.

8) Yes, giving us the double middle finger is considered a right. It is also your right to remain silent, and we sure wish you would have.

I think that answers all of the questions.

FACEBOOK . . . We have just passed 3,000 likes; I am thinking someone should get a toaster or something. I cannot or will not try to explain how we arrived at over 3,000. We are very happy you all are here and we thank you for caring.

Dear Mope Mom,

Your children saw you get arrested yesterday. I absolutely hate that. It makes me extremely bitter toward you. I don't mind that we arrested you—you needed to be arrested because you committed a theft offense. Having your two children with you when you stole those items was a horrible decision. Now the cops look like bad guys, Moron.

When you spoke with the arresting officers you told them you were "out of work" and you stole clothing items for your children to go back to school in. Although I am sensitive to economic conditions as of late, I am not sensitive to stealing while using "out of work" and being a "single mother" as excuses. There are other options; however, there is no excuse for being a thief, no justification.

I know lots of single mothers. It is a shame that many men have shirked their responsibilities and do not pay child support or spend time with their children. Absent fathers are one of the biggest causes of juvenile delinquency in our country. Taking your children with you to steal items from a store can't help the kids learn right and wrong, either. You kind of doubled down on the negative learning yesterday.

Anyway, most single mothers do not steal. We know single moms who have put themselves through college while raising children. We know single mothers who work at fast food restaurants and attend local community colleges. What do they have that you lack? Character and pride.

When speaking with my officers after they dealt with you, they described you as able-bodied and healthy. They also said you could carry on an intelligent conversation and knew right from wrong. So I have to believe that you are of the mind to short-cut life however you can. Instead of working for what you need, you steal it. You justify that behavior by reciting all of the bad turns life has given you. That's too bad. It's too bad for your kids, who will watch your personal train

MORE…

wreck and learn lessons from it, both good and bad. It's also too bad for the single mothers who choose to work non-stop and get ahead BECAUSE of the bad turns ...

It's not too late to stop being "out of work" and start being "out FOR work."

We are compassionate people here; however, excuses get old after a while.

—Chief

DAYSHIFT . . . Kudos to the Kohl's loss-prevention crew for their "detention" of a serial thief today. This person has a pending meth case, was in possession of Vicodin and Percocet AND brought her four-year-old child with her on a theft field trip today. Alert staff at Kohl's recognized her as having sticky fingers at Kohl's in other locations.

While sorting through missing UPC tags and shoe boxes, we had to request that mom take the STOLEN shoes off of not only her own feet, but also off of her four-year-old's feet. The not-so-old old shoes had replaced the stolen ones, in the shoe box, on the shelf. Officers and loss-prevention people also recovered numerous other stolen items. This led to the speech of the day, from Officer John Pettit—who, in-spite of his Godfather-like personality, is really a teddy bear.

Officer Pettit to suspect:

"I don't care what you do. Steal all you want. I'll arrest you and do all the paper work involved. That's my job. Do NOT bring your kid with you to steal. What kind of example are you setting when you bring your four-year-old with you to steal?"

I'm not sure any of our officers would have changed a word, had he or she been in the same situation. We usually do not give advice; however, when there is a child involved, we become infomercial-like motivational speakers.

The child is with family, and the suspect is going to the Gray Bar Motel . . . room for one.

"The impersonal hand of government can never replace the helping hand of a neighbor."

—Hubert H. Humphrey

What we see

Over the last couple of days there has been conversation around the department about phone calls and visits some of the officers have received. The United States Department of Agriculture (USDA) Rural Development is funding the police department renovation and addition. As part of that process, they make calls and personal visits and ask officers if they are aware of any "discrimination" that takes place in our department. Officer Dumont called me on Tuesday to let me know he had received a call asking about discrimination and if any took place under my command. We had a chuckle over it and moved on. Officer Sonagere also had a conversation with a representative of the USDA. Yesterday, Officer Allen told me he received a call inquiring if HE was aware of any discrimination in the workplace. It was kind of a funny conversation. Officer Allen: "I got a call today asking if there was discrimination in the workplace."

Chief: "They called you, too? How many people are they going to ask? Why did they call you?"

Officer Allen: "I'm a minority, Chief . . . I'm black."

Chief: "Oh yeah. That makes sense, I guess . . . Now I get it . . . Dumont is of Chinese descent and Sonagere is a female . . . I guess I forgot."

Here is the humorous thing. I was the first chief here to hire a full-time "minority" officer . We have three different races and two female officers. I don't hire people because of race or sex. I hire based on character and desire. I also only discriminate against laziness. It seems the only people who keep bringing up race are the ones who want to keep count.

Officers Allen, Dumont and Sonagere are not "minorities" to me. They are MY officers. The only way I would ever treat them differently is if they suddenly turned into lazy vacuums of tax dollars. I understand the requirements of securing federal funding for projects like ours. The only issue I have is a simple one: If everyone keeps focusing on our differences in a negative way, if they all keep looking back, how do we ever move forward? Thanks for reading.

Chief's . . . Rant?

Well . . . another news story yesterday. I think that covers all of the Cleveland TV stations, all of the local newspapers, radio and Internet sources for news, and here we still are, having a conversation with all of you. Holy SMOKES!

The news stories have been mostly positive, with a few people who have questioned why we post on FB, whether I post "on the clock" (yes, and off the clock too) and commenters on those news pieces complaining about me offering an "opinion" on those we arrest and also issues that impact this community. After all, police chiefs are supposed to be "professional" and the chief of "blank" city police department is not posting on FB and otherwise interacting with people in this fashion . . .

Blah, blah, blah . . . that's all I hear. I am oblivious to all of you whiners and criers.

Real police work is not like it is portrayed on television. In real life, human beings (police officers) are tasked with cleaning up the mental and physical messes of their fellow citizens. Men hit women . . . we go. Shots fired in the dark . . . yep, that's our call too. A drunk driver kills a 90 year-old grandmother and puts three other family members in the hospital? We are there. A mother cooks meth with her son sleeping 10 feet from her . . . ditto. We console weeping family members, deliver death notices and take verbal abuse from at least 75% of the people we deal with. When my officers and I experience these things and I want to tell you about it, guess what? You get told. You should know what is going on.

As far as my opinion, you are stuck with it. I owe it to my officers to be very public about the things they deal with. If we can shame some criminals into not acting like mopes, good. At the minimum, criminals may hear about this department and this community and perhaps not want to tangle with us, and go anywhere but here. I also do it because police departments need community support. I know we do.

If you are among the 3% of people who disagree with this page, or dislike me greatly, call the Brimfield Township Trustees—they hire and fire the police chief in Brimfield. They know me. They know I say what I think and they also know the overwhelming passion I have for the concept of "protect and serve." They tolerate my shenanigans because my officers get results and the people who live here believe in us. Whatever you decide to do, stop telling me about how unprofessional I am (or whatever other descriptors you choose to use). It's been over two years, folks, and I'm not backing down. There are people out there who commit crimes and otherwise act like idiots, and you all should know about it . . . and I should have some fun telling you.

DAYSHIFT . . . Pettit and Sonagere with two arrests from the same vehicle. The operative thing to remember: If your license is suspended, it is far better to have a valid driver drive you around. Knowingly letting a suspended driver operate your car is not a great idea. I would also choose one minus the extensive criminal history with cautions, alerts and parole status . . . but that's just me; I'm a little PERSNICKETY.

IN THE SCHOOLS . . . Well, it's official. This morning, to a very loud chorus of "EWWwwwwwww," it was announced at a school assembly that if the students reach the goal of $1,500 in box tops, I would indeed kiss a cow. There is no backing out now. There is a push to sell tickets to the event for a small donation to the program. I'm on record saying I'm opposed to that many witnesses . . . and I'm confident that everyone would have FAR more important things to do on that day. Anything for the kids . . . anything for the kids . . . anything for the kids.

NEW AT THE BPD . . . Congratulations are in order for one of our officers; he has just became a father . . . sort of. Congrats to Officer Jerry Dumont; we were informed that his new K-9 partner was born yesterday! The new four-legged officer will spend some time with his mother before coming to join his new family. Rumor has it that Officer Dumont will take leave under FMLA to stay home to feed and potty-train the new German Shepherd. The new puppy, when trained, will be a utility police K-9, trained in explosives and bomb detection. We are all excited for you, Officer Dumont.

"Always go to other people's funerals, otherwise they won't come to yours."

—Yogi Berra

AFTERNOON SHIFT . . . We were called to the Super 8 for an intox subject and greeted by . . . 11 "undocumented workers." Someone, somewhere must be working on a HUGE building project. Officers Atha and Sonagere dealt with the illegals, and once again we called the feds . . . and once again we were told it was not a priority. We were told if we could arrest them and hold them for a few days, maybe something could be done. However, they are not violating local or state laws; immigration is federal jurisdiction. So, give us a fake name and DOB and move on, please. It is not the ICE agents making this policy; the bosses make the decisions. Someone in the chain is weak and not making decisions based on the law.

NEW AT THE BPD . . . Just to clear up a "communication" issue . . . Officer Dumont is NOT on family medical leave to "train his dog." He is at work, and the dog is still with the doggie mother. That was chief humor, just like calling Officer Dumont a "new father."

When the puppy is ready to work, he will join us here. For the talk radio caller, who phoned a local show today to inform the host that we were using "family leave" to train a dog . . . either my humor was misunderstood, or you are a moron. We do not operate like that here. We are not dishonest. We do not abuse the system or misuse tax dollars; however, I think you already know that.

PHOTO: Some professions are really fun. Police work is one of them. Although there is some stress and also sadness, frustration and other emotions . . . some things are just funny—like this picture of Sgt. McCarty being attacked by a ferret.

We were called to Edson Road park for a loose and aggressive ferret. It wasn't going smoothly. Sgt. McCarty attempted to negotiate . . . and was unsuccessful, as you all can see if you look at his left foot. Officer Dumont was on scene but could not aid his sergeant with this resisting lawbreaker. Officer Dumont was to busy snapping a picture to send to the chief . . . and we love him for it.

On keeping children safe

Mrs. Chief and I have "that house." It's the house where all of the kids congregate. I try to interact with the children in this community the same way as I do in my own house. Children need to know the police are the good guys. They need to see us joke and laugh. Mrs. Chief tells me I am "funny dad" . . . the dad who tries to crack down on his children, but the children can't stop laughing at dad being the enforcer, and then dad starts laughing. She's right.

We are at the schools constantly here. You count on your children being safe when they are away from you. That is a motivator for me. Children, by nature, are usually defenseless. The police are defenders and protectors by choice, so it is a natural fit. I am motivated by the fact that there are people out there who will intentionally hurt a child. I have met them and put more than my share in prison. I have spoken to some of the worst and most deliberate offenders you can imagine. I see things a little differently than some.

People who are inappropriate with children cannot and will not change. You can medicate, motivate, counsel and analyze . . . it's all a waste of time. For them, in their own twisted world, their attraction to children is no different from mine to Mrs. Chief or yours to your spouse/mate/BF/GF, and therein is the problem for me. I am not tolerant of anyone who abuses a child, period. There are no excuses. There is no hugging of trees or speaking of "curing" a "sickness." There is prison for life and the loss of the key to the cell. No parole, no probation—first offense, mandatory life in prison, see ya.

As parents, you need to know we are there. When we stand outside the school slapping high fives, when we walk the halls, or when we get out of the car and play basketball in a neighborhood, I want people to see it. I want the person who may have those inclinations to see us and know he has to come through us to get to them . . . and he will not make it. I want the kids to know it too. In a time of being pummeled with news stories about child abuse, murders, kidnappings and the like, I want the kids to see us and know they are safe and have the feeling we have their backs. If they need a hug, that's okay too. I may even kiss a cow for them. Have a great day.

On being a media hound

A reporter friend posted on our page yesterday a conversation she had with an elected official, not from Brimfield. It was pretty consistent with what I hear from many elected people and other public officials in our region. Well, I don't hear it from them . . . I hear it from others who attribute it to the officials. They say I am a media hound.

Malcontents, all of them.

In 2012 I have submitted three press releases to the media, all after getting a request for information. What I have done differently from most is show up here on our page every day, sometimes at odd hours ("Do you ever sleep, Chief?") and let you all know what is going on. I also talk to reporters. When they call, I answer the phone. Most of them have my cell number. I refuse to be listed in the article as the guy who "can't be reached for comment" or "did not return our calls." That will not happen. See, the news will go on. The stories will be written, aired or talked about. If I do not submit the police side of the story, the story still goes on. I will be damned if I will let a mope and his attorney smack us around without answering with a swift kick to the . . . shin.

So, for you elected people and other public officials . . . quit whining. If you have a message you want heard, get it out. My bosses here are great at it. There is this great thing called the Internet. On this Internet is a web of social media similar to this page. I think computers and the Internet will be around for a while, so do your thing. Come in to your office at the crack of dawn and say good morning to all of your constituents. Interact with them. They will ask you questions, so be ready. Some of them will insult you, too. It's kind of fun. One more piece of Oliver wisdom, if I may: Trust a person in the media unless he or she gives you a reason not to. Being done wrong by one reporter and putting the whole profession in time out is like people hating all police officers because of one bad cop. We good cops hate that feeling, and so do the good reporters.

As the chief here, I have a message to get out. The message involves our day-to-day activity. It includes what to look for, what we see and hear (and sometimes smell) and a long line of mopes and aggravated mopery. The people who live here have a right to know what goes on. I have a duty to keep them informed.

Dear College Students,

Welcome back—or just welcome, if it is your first semester at one of our area colleges. We are happy you have taken the step to get a higher education. We hope you act like you have been away from home at least once before in your life.

I would like to offer some suggestions to help you have the best possible experience off-campus. I believe it is my duty to do so, since we have so many college apartments in our fine community. Please observe the following advice:

• You are a visitor here. That means you should behave. You are out among strangers, in their community. Regardless of what your parents did or did not teach you, you do NOT act as though you were raised by a band of moonshiners when you visit others.

• If you have a party at the residence you are renting, expect at least 300 people to show up. Word spreads quickly—the whole social media thing has caught on.

• If 300 people show up for your party, we will likely be among them. Although I have been known to dance quite a bit, my officers are not ones to "robot," "cabbage patch," or "sprinkler" when they attend college parties. They are the ultimate buzz-kills. Sorry.

• If you are under 21 years old, it is illegal to drink alcoholic beverages in Ohio. I know, you can vote, fight in a war and do many other things. I have heard it all. We don't make the rules; complaining to us doesn't help. We will listen, though, because we are good listeners.

• If we come out to your party, we will likely issue a disorderly conduct warning. That means you should be quiet and bring the party to an end. If we come back a second time, we give you a free ride to our department. The ride comes complete with handcuffs, a souvenir picture of you and a personal autograph from one of our officers. You also have to appear in court and pay some fines, but every silver lining has some dark cloud in it ...

• We know you have taken some criminal justice courses. I have

MORE...

taken history courses, but that does not make me George Washington. We are aware of your rights. Your reciting them to us when you are drunk makes you look silly.

• If you throw up in our car or department, we will have you clean it up—fair warning.

I hope this advice helps you during the coming school year. If you have any questions, ask them before the test.

—Chief

MIDNIGHTS . . . Officers responded to the Days Inn overnight for a large fight involving drunk people. The large crew returned from Kent on a party bus. A fight started on the bus and spilled out into the lot of the hotel. It resulted in several people with cuts and lacerations and shots being fired. Of course, when we arrived on scene no one could give us a description of the shooter(s) and everyone ran away.

Drunk stupid people: In case you missed science classes, let me take you back to school for a minute. Bullets don't magically disappear when fired into the air . . . it has something to do with gravity. When you fire a gun, the bullet always lands somewhere. Next time it could land in a person . . . and you will land in prison and be the soul-mate of someone who has been lifting weights for the last 20 years.

MIDNIGHTS . . . Officer Gyoker, Diehl and Dumont were called to the area of SR43 and Brimfield Drive for two pedestrians; the call came in as the male pointing a gun at the female. Officers met with them and, as officers put it, "The male didn't have a gun, but he did have a warrant." He was wanted for drug offenses. While officers were arresting him, the girlfriend began to fight with officers. She was warned she would be arrested, and told officers to "go ahead and arrest" her, and continued to be a trouble, so . . . she was arrested. Because our number-one goal is to please people. Bed and breakfast for two, please.

"The line separating good and evil passes not through states, nor between classes nor between parties either—but right through the human heart."

—Alexandr Solzhenitzyn

Meth

I have had it with meth. This morning I had two girls in our holding cell . . . 15 and 17 years old. Both used meth last night and you could really see the drug at work. I wanted to scream. Actually I did, but then regained my calm demeanor and went back to work, trying to figure out who the jackass is who would supply these girls with meth. As a society, a people, a community, we should be outraged at the epidemic of meth we are facing. If this epidemic was an H1N1 virus, the bird flu or West Nile Virus, the federal and state politicians would be going berserk. Federal dollars would be pouring into communities like rainfall. We would be handing out masks, getting everyone vaccinated and all we would see and hear on the nightly news would be ways to NOT get the latest strain of whatever exotic disease is floating around.

This epidemic is not related to mosquitoes, cattle, birds or pigs. It is related to bad choices and the need to escape whatever reality is facing those who want to ignore that reality.

In the meantime, meth is a blight on our way of life.

Meth manufacture and use is reducing people and neighborhoods to the appearance of Third World countries. Meth addicts are wandering around in a daze, snorting toxic chemicals up their nose on a daily basis, sometimes several times a day. Meth cooks are concocting their poison in hotel rooms, apartments, houses, garages, sheds and cars . . . anywhere they can.

To get an accurate picture of a meth operation, think of a beehive. There is a queen bee who is the meth cook. The worker bees are the meth users who forage all day for the pollen of the meth lab . . . the ingredients to make meth. They go to any store that sells pseudoephedrine, muriatic acid, lye, red phosphorus and the other makings of the "honey," also known as meth. They fly in and out of the hive, bringing back the needed mix. In the end, they get meth for the risks they take, and life goes on.

We have all heard about the "war on drugs." On a federal level, that fight is a joke. It doesn't exist. Some 30 years ago the feds declared a war on drugs and sometime during the last few years they left local law enforcement on the front lines, while they all went home and had a cold beer. Drink up, legislators. I also hope the state politicians thought of us when they passed the recent senate bill allowing felons out of jail, making some felonies punishable only with probation and reinstating shock and judicial release. Our state's elected folks are not innocent in this issue. Somewhere along the lines of trying to keep getting elected, our elected people have failed us.

Together the whole group of elected representatives could not organize a trip to the bathroom.

If we do not direct some energy to these problems as a society, we will pay the consequences. We will lose sleep while waiting for things to disappear out of our cars, garages and homes. We will suffer identity and credit card thefts at an increasing rate. Neighborhoods will decline and become more unsafe. Lives will be forever altered.

We are on our own here. I don't believe we are getting any money or reinforcements anytime soon. After all, most in Washington are too busy fussing with each other to accomplish much of anything.

So, here is what everyone has my word on. If you make or sell meth here—or any other illegal drug—we are going to arrest you. We will arrest you 100 times if needed. We are going to seize your house and sell it. Your car, too. If you sell it out of your house we are going to get a warrant and I will kick the door myself. A 15 and 17 year-old with meth? You degenerates can't keep it amongst yourselves? If you are the one who sold meth to these girls, we will find you.

I don't care if the local officers are the last ones fighting this battle, it's the right thing to do. If you saw these girls this morning—if you saw what we saw—you would understand. It is reprehensible and should shock the conscience.

If you see any drug activity, report it.

This has got to end.

IN THE COMMUNITY . . . Police officers often wonder if they are making a difference. Most days we REALLY wonder. And then sometimes . . .

Tonight at around 9 p.m., I had just fueled up and was inside Speedway to sign for the fuel. The door flung open, and in ran one of our elementary school students. She grabbed me and hugged me . . . then she told me that she and her mother were driving by and she saw my police truck, and she "made" her mother stop so she could come in and give me a hug.

THAT, I believe, is a difference.

Drunk driving (Part II)

You cannot get far without reading, hearing or seeing a public service announcement on drunk driving. We are exposed to so many warnings in today's society. These announcements show officers pulling vehicles over and the driver's door being opened and beer flooding out; officers appearing to be like shadows and following drunk drivers; cars hitting cars with airbags deploying all over every channel of the television. All of this saturation leaves me asking . . . What is wrong with people? How does anyone STILL make the decision to get behind the wheel of a 2,000-pound unguided missile and mosey down the road, putting other motorists and themselves at risk?

People who drive drunk are not only intoxicated, they are selfish and lack vision. By lacking vision I simply mean they do not have the ability (or block it) to see past the immediate moment. So, they walk or stagger to their vehicle, fire up the engine and off they go, oblivious to their terrible driving and most other things in their periphery. They can make it home . . . they are okay . . . they will be fine . . . Me, me, me.

I cannot count how many times I have heard the phrase "I've only had two beers." The other common answer is "I am not too drunk to drive." If you have ever been behind a drunk driver (and I have been behind a few) the driving is unmistakable. There is usually weaving back and forth between the center and edge lines, then a constant drift to the left, over the yellow line, and then the near death of at least 17 mailboxes on the right side of the road. The driving is a mess, and so is the aftermath of an alcohol related crash.

If you drive drunk or even drive "buzzed," this message is for you. The word is out, all over earth. Drunk driving causes irreparable harm. You are going to kill someone. You are going to crash into a mother, father, grandmother or best friend. You will likely walk away without injuries while we work frantically to save the life of the innocent recipient of your stupidity. The world does not revolve around you, contrary to your alcohol-fueled view of the universe. I do not care about how bad your childhood was; your relationship status; your overdue bills . . . all of that pales in comparison to the walk from my police car to the front door of a residence to deliver the news to a family that their loved one is dead. The water I have to give to them to carry for the rest of their lives is a burden no one should have. In 2011, in Ohio, there were 12,639 alcohol related crashes with 369 deaths and 7,574 injuries.

There should have been ZERO.

DAYSHIFT . . . Among other calls, we engaged in some parenting for adults. We were called for some "adults" throwing and smashing beer bottles against the back of a commercial building. Their apartment is close to the property, so Officers Pettit and Sonagere made the knuckleheads get a broom, clean up the mess and apologize to the business. A little police-supervised instant community service.

MIDNIGHTS . . . Officers Diehl and Putnam continue to pursue and arrest drunk drivers. The line of the night came from Officer Diehl, who was "checked out" by a very drunk female passenger of one of the drunk drivers. Officer Diehl reported, "The female passenger that tagged along kept calling me 'Officer Fancy Pants' and wouldn't stop looking at me . . . I was uncomfortable." There is not a CHANCE we won't be calling him that for the next 20 years.

FACEBOOK . . . Well . . . we just arrived at 3,500 "likes." I saw the number this morning and I am still shaking my head. As I have said before, when we started the page I was hoping to have a couple hundred people to get some information and messages to.

I am humbled that you all check in with us from time to time and also that many of you post and share your opinion and experiences. We have something very special going on between us . . . and without you, there is no "us."

We will continue to keep you updated and from time to time rant about crime-related issues, the human element and perhaps even people who just don't get it. Thanks for being here and we love you all.

"The gap in our economy is between what we have and what we think we ought to have—and that is a moral problem, not an economic one."

—Paul Heyne

The Presidential visit

Now that the President of the United States has come and gone, we can chat about some of the logistics involved in a visit.

The last time the President drove through our community, I talked about the traffic jam. The haters came out of the bushes and from every rock in the ground. It was not a political statement. I think most federal politicians are less then genuine and say only what the particular group they are talking to wants to hear. I'm not a big fan of any candidate. I spoke on behalf of the people who could not get to work, the doctor's appointment, the babysitter, school or other appointments, because traffic was backed up all the way to Philadelphia. I usually don't speak about something unless it impacts this community. I won't even mention the overtime associated with these visits . . . not that I would send anyone a bill. I don't do or say things, like send a bill to a candidate, for public posturing or to make someone look bad. Most candidates do that on their own.

Back to this visit . . .

We got advanced notice of a visit about a week or so prior to the visit date. The Secret Service contacted us and gave us the potential route and requested we all come to a central location for a big meeting. We love meetings (not). Sgt. Adkins was our representative there. I put him in charge of the Brimfield portion of the motorcade as it moved through. I can't attend those types of meetings, because I end up staring out the window and thinking about flying kites. Sgt. Knarr had operational command of the stationary units and perimeter while Sgt. McCarty handled our actual police responsibilities . . . like calls and traffic. Sgt. Adkins may have had the best assignment. He rode in the lead car in the motorcade with the Secret Service while the rest of us stood in the rain. He was also on the tarmac when Air Force One arrived and departed. I like jets.

The motorcade came through town and we closed SR43 from I-76 into Kent. The President made his speech in Kent and then we did the whole thing all over again. It was more akin to a 60 mile an hour parade than a motorcade. It moved fast and there were more cars than in our Brimfest parade, I think. Traffic was generally backed up in every direction between Kent and I-76. Fun times.

Some more of my thoughts and observations while working the motorcade:

- 60 degrees isn't cold . . . unless it's raining.
- The Presidential limo is one NICE car (actually there were two of them). Too bad it's not available for weddings and proms.
- That military helicopter flying in circles overhead is awesome. How do I get one?
- Who drives through town, with 50 police cars in sight, stoned out of his mind on weed? Officer Allen made an arrest as the motorcade was moving north on SR43. The arrest was at Old Forge and SR43 . . . and was the guy's seventh offense for OVI. He fell asleep at the traffic light. YIKES.
- The mix of Tea Party people and an Obama supporter at Howe and SR43 was an interesting conversation. Tense, but interesting. I wish we could all be a little nicer to each other. Both sides.
- It was an honor to have a Brimfield sergeant in the motorcade and another leading the multi-agency briefing before the motorcade arrived. I had a little tear in my eye.
- If any politician ever shows up on time, I will fall over dead.
- I actually saw guys in dark suits wearing sunglasses . . . in the rain.
- I bet there were more weapons on SR43 yesterday than in some countries.
- I wish I was blocking the roads for Elvis. Elvis before 1976. Without the cape.
- I am so happy I am a police chief and not elected, and two-thirds of my bosses must like me. I can say what I think, without being politically correct. If I get fired, I can go fishing while I look for another job.

And lastly . . . love my officers. They hustle all of the time without complaints, no matter what I throw at them.

"I have found that if you love life, life will love you back."

—Arthur Rubinstein

DAYSHIFT . . . Officers were out at the Days Inn with a stolen vehicle. They worked hard on identifying anyone involved, and ended up finding the suspect in a room there—and that's not all. When the dust settled, officers had LOTS of drugs: about an ounce of heroin, packaged for sale; about an ounce of cocaine, lots of prescription pills, cash, scales and two safes. The two suspects had all of these drugs alongside their two children. The female was arrested; the male is on the run; the kids are taken care of and JFS will be on board with us to remove these children.

Drug dealers: We know it's all about money to you. Selling in Brimfield is a losing proposition. We will catch you and take your money, drugs, car and anything else we can, legally. We are relentless. We have a nationally certified drug K-9 on every shift and human officers who will come at you even faster.

The female is being processed. The male will soon have warrants for his arrest and we will pull out all stops and favors to bring him in.

Anywhere but here . . .

Great job, officers Atha and Sonagere (and Dumont with the assist). A GREAT piece of police work, as we have come to expect.

DAYSHIFT UPDATE . . . For a drug dealer who has a warrant for his arrest . . .

We are not too far behind you. As a matter of fact, I believe K-9 Havoc JUST missed you early this morning. You must be exhausted. We aren't tired at all. We are used to having very little sleep . . . coffee is awesome.

Here's the deal . . . I don't believe you have had a great life. I also believe you have made some mistakes along the way. Neither of those can be an excuse this time. This incident was not a mistake. You brought a whole BUNCH of drugs into our community and set up shop here (allegedly?). We take that personally.

Now you have warrants, and that sucks for you. It is not a good thing to be a fugitive. You probably don't know who to trust, and it may be hard for you to make money at this point. After all, your next customer may be the one who gives you up. You know how you can't trust anyone in "the game."

I strongly encourage you to call me and surrender. I can be trusted. We will take you to jail, and you can have your day in court. After all, you will be entering a Not Guilty plea, right? You will likely place all of the blame on your girl, which is cool, I guess, or at least expected. Give me a call; I will come get you myself. Until you do, you are just going to be jumpy, and I don't like jumpy alleged drug dealers; they put my officers at risk and I love police officers.

Give me a call.

DAYSHIFT UPDATE . . . A fugitive is in custody. He was caught . . . IN BRIM-FIELD.

The story goes like this . . .

We have been receiving tips for the last three days. Our phones and FB messaging have been going crazy. One anonymous tip we received put the suspect in an apartment in Brimfield, which to us seemed like it would be a little crazy. We understand the hiding-in-plain-sight logic; however that usually only applies to car keys.

Sgt. Knarr ran the lead down and we took a drive over to an apartment on Sandy Lake Road. Sgt. Knarr, K-9 Havoc and Officer Sonagere watched the back of the residence while Officer Pettit and I knocked on the door. After a few minutes we were met by the renter and . . . the fugitive's girlfriend, who is out on bond from our arrest on Sunday. An initial search of the residence turned up nothing; however, an attic access made Sgt. Knarr and Officer Pettit curious.

The attic was full of loose insulation and no one appeared to be in there, and no one responded to our commands to come out. Sgt. Knarr thought perhaps K-9 Havoc would tell us if anyone was hiding in there. Havoc was lifted up into the attic . . . and immediately began going bonkers . . . and out popped a head from under two feet of insulation. Drug dealer captured, thank you Havoc (and Sgt. Knarr and Officer Pettit).

The girlfriend was arrested AGAIN, and so was the renter. Both will be charged with obstructing justice, for concealing and harboring a fugitive.

Thank you to our FB and media friends; your help was invaluable.

MIDNIGHTS . . . The question of the night: We publicized the checkpoint . . . there are flashing lights and signs. Who would drive through an OVI checkpoint with an open container of beer? One cited for open container in a motor vehicle.

"Policies are many, Principles are few, Policies will change, Principles never do."

—John C. Maxwell

Memorial Day

Monday is Memorial Day. There will be barbeques, games, swimming and other fun all weekend. Summer is arriving in the Northern Hemisphere . . . let's celebrate.

Let's also celebrate and honor those who inspired the holiday: Our military who have died while serving our country; police officers who have died while keeping us safe on our own streets; firefighters who have died while trying to save others; and friends and family who have passed. We miss them all and are a little less than whole without them.

If you are a veteran of the military of any era and/or any branch, thanks for your service. We at the BPD love all of you and are eternally grateful for what you have provided and sustained for us.

I would like to say a special "Welcome Home" to all of our veterans of the war in Vietnam. Many of you were not treated very well when you arrived at airports on your return home. The people who called you names, spit on you and otherwise acted like they had no upbringing should hang their heads in shame. Thank you for your sacrifices. Thank you for being 18 years old and going to a foreign country to fight an unidentifiable enemy—while our politicians refused to give you the tools and strategy to succeed. We respect and honor you all.

To all of our armed forces . . . we love you.

My father, Frank Oliver, was in Europe in World War II. He was with the 645th Tank Destroyer Battalion. Their sacrifice and valor during 605 days in combat, 515 of them on the line, distinguish the men of the 645th Tank Destroyer Battalion. They fought from North Africa to Germany, ending in Munich and Dachau.

What's your story?

Thanks again to our veterans . . . you are MY heroes.

DAYSHIFT . . . We are in the soup again. After a short investigation, officers obtained a search warrant for a residence in the 3000 block of Sunnybrook Road. We recovered components for a meth lab (tubing, chemicals, filters) and some finished meth. The subject attempted to burn some evidence, too.

The parade of police vehicles at town hall was the Ohio State Highway Patrol SWAT team, who we called for entry to the residence after the subject on the inside refused to answer the door. Before the team deployed, he phoned dispatch and I spoke with him. He asked why officers were surrounding his house and I told him it was likely because he was cooking meth, and we frown on that, with big frowns. He stated that he had "just woke up" and didn't know what I was talking about. I instructed him to come out. He said he would come out but wouldn't answer questions, because he had called his attorney before calling us . . . which I guess would be MY first choice if the police knocked on MY door.

He's with us now and will be charged with several felonies.

IN THE SCHOOLS . . . Well . . . the deed is done; the cow has been smooched. Thank you to all of the parent volunteers who assisted with the box top program. Thanks to all of you, the school collected more than 20,000 box tops, resulting in an extra $2,000+ for the school. Anything for the kids.

MIDNIGHTS . . . While you were sleeping, Officer Putnam arrested a subject for OVI. The intoxicated driver tested a .221% BAC . . . and happens to be an attorney. He requested that officers lower the charge for him. That will never happen. He then stated it was "probably best" if he didn't "drink in Brimfield anymore." That's a YAHTZEE!

ANIMALS . . . We rounded up a loose horse early this morning. Each of our vehicles is equipped with leads and other horse-catching tools; we are well-rounded. Sgt. Knarr advised that Officer Putnam kept asking to "ride the horsey." We think that may be a true story.

NEW AT THE BPD . . . Congratulations to Joker, Havoc and Drogen and handlers, Sergeants Knarr and Adkins and Officer Allen: All three K-9s earned national certifications in narcotics finds today. Bad news for the drug dealers. Great job, all.

Dear Car Thieves,

You got caught. We are sorry you chose to take up a life of crime. We are also sorry you creep around houses at night time, breaking into garages and stealing cars. Last, we are sorry you suck at your chosen profession, which is being a mope.

In order to help you understand a little about why you got caught, please observe the following:

• When breaking in somewhere, you should wear some type of self-contained suit. Make sure no skin cells, hair or other parts of your body are left behind.

• When stealing a vehicle, tell your partner to NOT smoke marijuana and leave the leftover joint in the ashtray. It's called DNA, and we nailed him on it; it was a perfect match—not that the hair and skin cells wouldn't have been just as good.

• You should not "hock" out of a window. First of all it is seriously GROSS. Next, you are horrible at "hocking"—you got it all over the truck. Don't worry, Detective Atha cleaned it up ... and then submitted it to the lab. YAHTZEE! ... another match!

I can't think of anything else. Did I already call you a mope?

Congratulations to Det. Atha for two more DNA matches received today involving the theft of a truck and a bunch of other items, including a couple of four-wheelers. I would also like to thank him profusely for having the stomach to collect the evidence ... it would have made me a little queasy.

Great job Det. Atha.

—Chief

OVERHEARD AT THE BPD . . .

Officers were called to Walmart for a theft today. The subject also had a warrant for his arrest, from our department, for a prior assault offense. He was placed under arrest and the following conversation took place.

Chief: "Do you have anything on you illegal to possess?"

Subject: "These aren't my pants."

Officer Rafferty: "Huh?"

Subject: "These aren't my pants."

Chief: "Do you have anything illegal in the pants you are wearing that do not belong to you?"

Subject: "Yes. But these aren't my pants."

Chief: "Yeah, we got that part. What do you have in the pants that aren't yours?"

Subject: "A pill to help me pass a drug test. I'm getting a new job. And another pill that is illegal."

Chief: "In the off chance I put on pants that weren't mine and THEN found drugs in them . . . "

Subject: "That's what happened."

Officer Rafferty: "Are you wearing your own underwear?"

Subject: "Yep. The underwear is definitely mine."

Chief: "I'm losing IQ points here."

The subject was arrested and charged with theft, and will be charged with possession of drugs. A reminder to all: If you mistakenly grab the wrong pants . . . never mind . . .

AFTERNOON SHIFT AND MIDNIGHTS . . . We would like to thank the neighbors on Powdermill Road for inviting us to the party being held by some college students. We love attending social functions and meeting others. We took eight of the attendees with us when we left the party, all for underage drinking and possession of various drugs and paraphernalia. Great teamwork, both shifts.

Handicapped parking

Handicapped parking was designed for people who have trouble moving around. Some are in wheelchairs; some use canes; some just have trouble walking great distances. Some have incurable diseases; some have heart or lung issues. Some have the affliction which will get us all someday, "TMB" . . . Too Many Birthdays.

Handicapped parking is a basic common-sense thing. It is yes or no; black or white. Either YOU need the space or YOU do not. Either the handicapped placards or plates belong to YOU or not. In simple terms, it means if you drive your 99 year-old grandmother around and have a placard, God bless and thanks for caring. When she is not in the car, YOU DO NOT NEED THE SPACE. Save it for someone who does.

Some other tips from us, because we care . . . and slackers make us want to bang our heads on car hoods.

- If you use a handicapped space and you jump out of the vehicle, all healthy-like, as if someone is dangling free cheeseburgers on a stick, expect people to stare at you and get angry. You are milking the system and it aggravates those of us who play by the rules. Ignoring us does not make you invisible. We see you, loser.

- If your 99 year-old grandmother or other qualifying relative is not with you, park in a regular spot, like the rest of us. We do not care if you are going in the store to "get her medicine." Don't be a mope.

- It is highly disrespectful to use a dead person's handicapped pass. If you do this, I hope lightning strikes you as you are walking towards the store. I will bring the marshmallows.

- I am not a skinny guy. I know . . . you are all shocked . . . I rant and post like a skinny guy. It's a nice quality. If you use a handicapped permit because you are "husky," "big-boned," "short for your weight" or any other term used for being overweight, you are missing the boat. You should walk. This also applies to the little electric carts in the store. Walk. You are not handicapped. You are overweight. That is not a handicap. It's a choice. Movement is the cure.

- If you are not supposed to park in a handicapped space and

do so, we will ticket you. We may even tow your car. No pleading, no excuses . . . no love. There are people who have the
need for those spaces. We will make sure they have access.
It's a right or wrong proposition. We all should know the difference.

UPDATE (2 DAYS LATER) . . .

To clear up an issue on the handicapped parking post: A new
"poster" to our page, Katie, is very upset with me. I do find some faults
in my posting. So I will share them . . .

There are people out there with disabilities you may not see—MS,
heart issues and other diseases. These are invisible to the eye. It is
not the right thing for us to judge them or make assumptions based
on only what we see. Katie, I am sorry for offending you and others if
that was the case.

I want to make a point with this. The post was not directed to
people who should be parking in a handicapped space, and are legally allowed to do that. The post WAS 100% about people who have
no honor and use these spaces meant for those among us who truly
need them. Period. Any other inferences should not be used.

Now, for my "short for my weight people" . . . relax. I have been
short for my weight since the eighth grade. The Beacon Journal refers
to me as "portly" . . . nice, guys, and thanks. If there is a medical reason
for you to have a permit, God bless. If there is not, that's on you and
your character.

I love social media. It has been great for the police department and
our communication. Please, please read the posts and understand
one thing . . . If how you act is according to law, I am NOT directing
anything your way.

UPDATE (3 DAYS LATER) . . .

Who would have thought a rant on parking spaces would have created such drama? Not me, for sure. One news outlet wrote that I told
"overweight people to walk." YIKES. If that appeared to be the main
idea of the rant, I need to learn a new primary language, because English is not working for me. I like my friends in the media; however,
that story was a mess.

Letters from the elementary school

Gather around, gang. It's time to open the mailbag and read some of the letters we have received from some of our 2,000 children . . .

Dear Brimfield Police,

Thank you for everything you have done around Brimfield. You save banks and people.

Megan

Dear Chief Oliver,

Thank You for saving people s lives. We are grateful to have such a great chief. I am lucky to know there will be a policeman at the door whenever I am in trouble.

Your Friend. Micah

Dear Brimfield Police Department,

Thank-you for arresting bad guys. You work too hard.

Sincerely, Gavin

Dear Police Officers,

Thank-you so much for protecting us. You guys make me laugh.

God Bless, Julia

I have to thank you for all the good things you helped us with. You are the best. You guys showed up at my 4-H Club with your dogs.

Sincerely, Shelby

Thank-you for stopping traffic so we could cross 43. We are grateful to have the best police department in Portage County.

Sincerely, Dylan

Dear Police,

Thank-you a lot for keeping us safe. If you weren't here, my PS3 probably wouldn't be in my house. All of the criminals are gone because you have great police skills. You are all very nice and friendly.

PS . . . Chief Oliver . . . Pittsburgh rocks and so does anyone who beats the Browns.

Your Friend, Colin

Thank you for letting us take a tour of the department. Petting Havoc was a great part of the trip. The jail cells do not look very comfortable, but bad people deserve to be uncomfortable.

Sincerely, Ava

I had so much fun at the police department. Thanks for letting the whole 4th grade come there and thanks for protecting Ohio. Thanks for letting us pet Havoc. He is so soft.

From: Taryn

Thank-you for giving us a tour of the police department. My favorite part was going in the jail cells. The bed was hard, but prisoners have to deal with it.

From: Kalei

IN THE SCHOOLS . . . I think by now you all understand how important the children in this community are to us. We spend a lot of time at our schools interacting with "our kids." This morning, we were given quite the surprise when we were asked to attend an assembly at Brimfield Elementary. For the school's "Act of Random Kindness" week, the students donated nearly 400 stuffed animals to the police department. We give these stuffed animals away to kids during calls for traffic crashes and other incidents during which we may find a child who needs some uplifting. We are honored and humbled by "our kids" and we love them all. We will continue to serve and protect them with the fiercest efforts.

Work time

One of the most irritating things I hear about our FB page, from a small amount of dimwits, is the canned response of "I hope he's not posting on work time." Well, of course I am. I'm not sure I have "personal time." I'm usually working, even at home. This is a work page. The heading is "Brimfield Police Department" and I am the Chief of Police. We engage in social media. Social media in law enforcement is a relatively new thing for many departments. Not us. We are a "real time" agency.

I get lots of messages on our page, both in the form of public posts and private messages. To me, these are no different from an email or phone call. When I post crashes, delays or information about our arrests, I am keeping the public informed. The FB page is actually quite demanding. I usually get 15-20 messages a day, most from residents and most needing a response. Some just tell us we are swell . . . which we also read and love. I have been nominated for President at least 12 times on our page. I have declined them all, because I do not like lying to people.

So how is this any different than an email, phone call or visit from someone with a question? I believe it's a little better. It is kind of like a 9,000 person conference call or an email with 9,000 "CC" entries.

There are those among us who cannot grasp the concept of a chief of police using social media. There are those who just hate police officers and take a swing at us every chance they get. There are those who swing at anyone they can, because they themselves are miserable. There are trolls who stir the pot.

What do I think about all of this? I don't care. Say what you want. Talk to my bosses. They can be reached at 330-678-0739; ask to speak to a Township Trustee. Call them and whine. I'm not changing. I'm doing my thing here. I am leading a department that makes lots of great arrests, stands in the cold at "Fill-a-Cruiser" events to help the needy, checks on our senior residents and loves the children in our school district. We are crime fighters and community advocates. One of my responsibilities is to have a relationship with the community. You know . . . networking with our residents. They should know us and should know what we do, what we see and anything else they want to know. As the leader of the department I will ALWAYS speak out on things impacting this community . . . whether it is handicapped parking, drug dealers or mopery in general. It's just who I am.

End of babble.

FACEBOOK . . . As we approach 4,000 likes, I want to thank all of you for your steady presence in our virtual community. I am sure at one point or another during your visits here you will laugh, cry, reflect . . . or even want to punch me in the face. I understand.

If we make you "LOL," great . . . we love laughter. The main purpose of this page is to keep you informed on a local government function. We do not expect to make all of you happy all of the time. In fact, we are likely to make some of you upset some of the time. I am not a "people pleaser," saying different things to different audiences . . . and my officers are not either. For those of you who are residents, you will know everything we do, as quickly as we can get it to you. For those who don't live here . . . we are wondering when you will be moving in.

Again, thanks for the support—but mainly, thanks for caring about what goes on in your community. If you would have told me two years ago we would be close to 4,000 "likes," we would have requested sobriety tests.

MIDNIGHTS . . . Advice to criminals who have warrants for their arrest: When you have a warrant, you should lay low. When you fail to appear for court, assume the police are looking for you, and, in the spirit of real-life "hide and seek," give us a chance to seek you . . . before walking down a five-lane state highway (in the center turning lane), drunk and waiving your arms at 3 in the morning. Timing in life is everything. Officer Putnam was stopped by a female who was wildly waving her arms in the center turn lane on SR43 at Howe. Turns out she was tired of walking and wanted a ride. She got one . . . and a weekend at the county spa for women.

FACEBOOK . . . In our most recent Facebook stats, we have over 2,000 people "talking about this page" on a daily basis (which means they share or post something about the BPD page). And there are over 35,000 "unique" visitors each month—each visitor counted one time . . . amazing to me still. Lastly, the page is "hit" over 140,000 times per month . . . YIKES! That much hitting is bound to leave some marks. Thanks for your support and for being here.

Dear Meth Mopes,

Because you continue to come here and get arrested for possession of meth, manufacturing meth and possession of the chemicals to make meth, I feel the need to give you some advice. Please observe the following:

Do not come here and commit drug-related crimes. You are not from here. Stay in your own yard and commit crimes. It could have ended it there, but then we wouldn't have had any fun.

Regardless of what you believe, you are known by the company you keep. Hanging out with other mopes, including ones who have warrants for meth-related crimes, is not wise.

Have a valid driver. It sounds simple; however, it appears there seems to be a shortage of valid drivers in the world of methamphetamine users. We arrest and tow for driving under suspension, which means we can then find out what's in the vehicle.

Attempting to buy 3,293 packs (poetic license used) of pseudoephedrine and having warrants for that offense already out on you—we call that a "clue" in police work. What do you have, a herd of elephants with flu-like symptoms?

We are lied to on a regular basis. You are not slick enough to get away with it. For example, having "stove fluid" because you are going camping is like you buying rubber gloves because you are going to do dishes. We've seen the inside of your car. You do not do dishes. The point is, we have been riding in this rodeo for a while now. The clowns come and go; we are the constant. Save the excuses; they have been used. Particularly the one called, "I'm buying this stuff for a friend."

We have a drug-certified K-9 on every shift. Please, roll the dice.
—Chief

AFTERNOON SHIFT. . . A traffic stop resulted in the driver being arrested for driving under suspension and OVI. Then a passenger mope dropped some drugs out of his pant leg. The subject then grabbed the drugs and put them in his mouth. We told him not to, but he would not listen . . . and he started fighting with us. Sgt. McCarty said, "We rolled around the side of I-76 for a while." The subject had to be subdued by use of a TASER while fighting with officers. THEN, another subject came to the scene to pick up a third passenger from the vehicle . . . and he was arrested on a warrant. The guy who swallowed the drugs was transported to the hospital; we went with him, just to hang out. He was checked out, given a Band-Aid for his boo-boo and then taken to the bed and breakfast. He was charged with tampering with evidence, two counts of assault on an officer and resisting arrest.

WHILE YOU WERE SLEEPING . . . Brimfield was invaded by the Vans Warped Tour overnight. That's a tour of young'ns, playing that rock and roll music. They had just finished up a big show at Blossom Music Center and were pretty hungry, so 20 tour buses exited the interstate and landed in the Brimfield Triangle . . . at Walmart. The tour includes such names as "Pierce the Veil", "Lostprophets", "All Time Low" and LOTS of others.

Inside the store, items began to be thrown. Employees hit the panic button, and the cavalry, consisting of Sgt. Knarr, K-9 Havoc and Officer Putnam, responded. The good guys convinced the posse of rockers that the plush tour buses were far more comfortable than the county bed and breakfast. Officers talked the crew back onto their buses and waved good-bye as the group drove on to Pittsburgh to pluck their magic twangers for Steelers fans. Go Browns!

MIDNIGHT . . . Four arrests, including two very lucky 19-year-old young men who flipped their vehicle on Edson near Sherman. The driver was arrested for OVI and underage drinking, the passenger for underage drinking. It could have been much worse. Learn something from this, boys, and hug your family today.

MIDNIGHTS . . . Officers were called to a hotel at I-76 and SR43 for a fist fight over one person failing to provide the other person with the agreed upon amount of crack cocaine. They were both arrested; one went to the hospital, the other to jail. Neither are welcome back until they stop smoking crack and hitting people.

Hannah

I met Hannah in 1999. I was a mopey looking bearded fellow, with an eyebrow ring, some other piercings and long hair. I was working as an undercover narcotics investigator. Hannah had been hanging with her (then) boyfriend and some others in one of our Brimfield hotels. I was watching the room, because I knew some of the visitors. We ended up getting some cocaine out of the room, and Hannah was "left holding the bag." She had rented the room, had an argument with her boyfriend and she left. A drug party ensued. We hit the room, found drugs, and I called her to come in and speak with me. She and her parents came to see me at the Brimfield Police Department.

I was impressed with Hannah. I found her to be an articulate, well-groomed and a pretty young lady. She could have been any-one's 18-year-old daughter. It worried me she was hanging out with the crowd I knew was at that hotel. To say that crowd had the knack for finding trouble would underestimate their talents greatly. At the time, they were card-carrying mopes, and she looked like she would not touch a drug if you made her. I spoke with her and her parents for several hours. They asked me to reassure Hannah that she was indeed headed for trouble hanging with this crew. I had a heart-to-heart talk with her in front of her parents. I explained the street drug culture to her and the likelihood of bullets flying or otherwise being an innocent bystander while hanging with dopers. During my "make her see the light" talk, I said these words to her: "If you keep hanging with this crew, you will be dead in six months." I have said that once in my career . . . on that day. I just truly believed she was way out of her element. There was some type of innocence there. Hannah cried, her mom cried, we hugged and off she went. I spoke with her mother a few days after and heard that all was well. I called Hannah's boyfriend and he admitted the cocaine was his and drove to the department and fessed up. Besides Hannah and everyone else telling me it was NOT hers, I had that strong feeling it truly was not. This was a bad case of a really good girl hanging with the really wrong crowd.

Not too long after that her mother called for me. She desperately wanted me to check my sources to see if I could locate Hannah. Her mother was as distraught as can be. She advised me that Hannah had not come home the night before and that Hannah always checked in. Hannah was found a few days later. She had been murdered and placed in the trunk of her vehicle which was left parked on a street in Akron. Girls like Hannah—and there are hundreds if not thousands a year—should not be murdered at age 18. It is incomprehensible. The person responsible was found guilty last week, over 10 years after the killing.

To the Akron officers and detectives who worked this case, including Lt. Hughes and others, hats off to all of you. A conviction 10+ years after the crime is monumental. You don't work with me; however, I want to thank you, from the heart.

May her family find comfort and may Hannah rest in peace.

"Moral courage is the most valuable and usually the most absent characteristic in men."

—General George S. Patton Jr.

The "war on drugs"

Most of you, if you have been around here for longer than a minute, know I have very little use for the federal government. For the most part, I believe it to be a giant collection of people who are long on talk on and short on action. Both sides and all parties. They also are short on telling the truth. I believe any politician who is caught in a lie should be forced to go home and get a real job. Enough of that . . .

Whenever we make a drug arrest here, I get a small segment (2-3%) of posters who chime in about the "failed war on drugs" and all of the money spent on that effort. We hear the "legalize" nonsense and all about how poor non-violent drug dealers are in jail. Blah, blah, blah. So, let's clear up a few of the issues on this topic. First, the federal war on drugs IS a monumental failure. Huge. Huge. Failure. If a private company put that much money into a project with these results, they would have been bankrupt years ago. Only the feds can run something so unsuccessful and sustain it for so long without results. There are just too many suits at the table, and not enough people who know how to get results on the street. Here's the catch: Local law enforcement gets results. I know, because I have worked in and with drug units my entire career. I do not know any chief of any local department who has received federal money to direct towards drug enforcement. The prime example is our department. There are grant openings on the federal level a couple of times per year. We always apply and we are always rejected. We make 1,000 arrests a year, have three drug detection certified dogs and I have officers who want to work nonstop, and we do it all on our local budget.

See, the feds direct all of the money for law enforcement to "hot button" issues, and always a year or two late. The local level saw a dramatic rise in meth labs during the last five years. Dramatic may be an understatement. Yet, the feds "ran out of money" for these very expensive lab clean-ups, and now locals have to pay for the hazmat crews to come in and remove the elements and chemicals. Meth is no longer important. Now we are focused on "human trafficking." Well, we aren't focused on it . . . THEY are focused on it. We seem to have a shortage of human trafficking cases, fortunately. We do, however, happen to be focused on the people dropping over from heroin overdoses, and the explosion of very cheap and plentiful heroin all over the place. I have never seen heroin as often as we see it now. And for God's sake, legalizing it won't change anything. An addict has trouble holding down a job, so unless you are also going to have Uncle Sam supply them with daily doses of heroin, pipe down.

The war on drugs has turned into local pockets of guerilla fighters. That's a lot of comparison to war, but I didn't start it. These local "guerilla" fighters are local officers, in uniform or undercover, who show up to work daily and try to have an impact on their specific communities. They are led by their chiefs and sheriffs and get no money or support from the feds. Why? Because the feds do not care about crime. They only care about getting re-elected. They will tell you all that your safety and security is paramount; however, after they are done running their mouths, they walk away and leave your protection to us.

So, in the future, when you see on our page we have made drug or other arrests, don't start whining about the ineffective war on drugs. We are not involved in that war. We will not be lumped in with poor planning, policies and methods in general. We are local and state law enforcement.

We get results and we work for a living.

MIDNIGHTS . . . Officer Gyoker found a suspicious-looking vehicle with occupants in the plaza near one of the "casino" establishments. When approaching the vehicle, Officer Gyoker reported the occupants were . . . umm . . . engaged in certain acts. Some things cannot be "unseen." The subjects told Officer Gyoker they were "tickling" each other. I could offer a bevy of jokes related to that excuse; however, I will let the "tickling" speak for itself. They were not real tickled when we took their heroin, needles and pills though. Two arrested for drug offenses; great job, Officers Gyoker and Diehl.

AFTERNOON SHIFT TODAY . . . An OVI arrest early in the shift. The drunk driver stopped off at one of our gas stations to ask directions to a . . . ummm . . . an adult "dancing establishment" east of here. He was intoxicated enough for the clerk to call us. He made it to the entrance ramp on I-76, where he was stopped by the officers. He was arrested for OVI and tested over a .260% BAC. We hope his attorney takes payment in all one-dollar bills.

The Page

Well, we passed another mile marker on our FB journey over the weekend . . . 7,000 "likes." Yikes! My officers and I rarely make it anywhere in public without someone mentioning our page. The comments come at just about every opportunity, including when we are making an arrest, which is sort of funny. Over the weekend I was out on one of the OVI arrests and THREE of the witnesses told us they read our page every day. We sure hope we don't start acting like divas. The recent FB stats are in and they are astounding to us. Last week we received a call from the FB people who would like to assign us an "account rep." They said we have their attention. That rep would help us market and get more people to like us. I passed on that, but told them to tell everyone I said "hello" from Brimfield, Ohio.

Last week, over 100,000 different people saw something associated with our page—a post, picture or some other item. Over 4,000 people shared or liked something on our page. Our "friends of friends" (combined people you all know) is well over one million people. (I'm throwing in another "yikes!" there.)

Our strongest base is right here in the Brimfield/Kent/Akron area; however, we have friends in 31 states and 16 countries. Our "reach"—people who read something on our page last week—consists of an unusual mix of countries . . . 436 in the United Kingdom; 305 from Canada; 222 from Hungary; 164 from Germany; 150 in Australia; 77 in Philippines; 76 in Italy; 54 in India; 48 in France; 42 in Brazil; 41 in Belgium; 38 in Thailand; 37 in Netherlands; 35 in Japan; 32 in Greece; 30 in Spain; 30 from Turkey; 30 from Mexico; and 30 in Ireland. I have no idea what all of that means, and other than to thank you all, I'm not sure what to say. We appreciate you all being here and sharing with us. We appreciate all of you being here and CARING about crime in general . . . and caring about police officers who wear bulletproof vests to work every day and hope they can get home to be with their own families after the shift. We may not always agree with all of you; however, regardless of our opinions, we still love you all . . . and care about you.

Thanks for being here and making this a special gathering place.

Trying to please everyone in police work

As a public official I used to be a people pleaser. I failed at that effort because I hate to compromise integrity and principles to make 4% of the people I deal with happy. I'm not just speaking of residents; this applies to politicians, vendors, lawyers and everyone else.

Two examples that come to mind are the new building/renovation and our police vehicles. Let's start with the new building. For the last 20 years we operated out of a remodeled auto body shop. An addition was put on during that time, which consisted of a three-bay garage constructed largely as a frame building with garage doors and a roof. Our old patrol room was originally a garage bay with our admin offices being the old shop offices. Although it was remodeled to the best of the budget and ability by the former powers to be, the place was generally laughable as a police department. When arrested people make comments like "Dude, this place is a dump," you know your home base is bad. In 2005 we identified the need for a new police department. In 2011 the ball got rolling and we decided that in lieu of buying and building, we would stay here and add on. The bids came in at $500,000 under budget and we immediately returned money to our funding source, the U.S.D.A. Rural Development program. All told, when it is done, we will have been $300,000 under the original budget and have one of the most modern departments in the area . . . with no unneeded bells, whistles or gold toilet seats. Still, when I post about the building, a very small few make comments about the "electric bill" and other nonsense. Really? Our systems are far more efficient, the lighting draws far less power and the heating and cooling systems will cost less than the drafty old building. So, that is just bitterness. Our police vehicles: When I became chief I inherited six police vehicles. All had over 100,000 miles and three were dead in the lot. So I had three police cars that worked, all having over 100,000 miles . . . nice. We implemented our impound lot program shortly after that. Before that, when we towed a vehicle because the person was arrested, drunk, driving under suspension, possessed drugs . . . whatever the reason, the cars went to the tow yards and they collected the impound fees. We built our own lot and started having the cars towed here. Every black police vehicle you see on the roadway now was bought with these criminal proceeds and NOT TAX DOLLARS. This was a way to relieve some burden from those who pay taxes. The impound fund is strong enough now to buy our cars, equip them and pay for fuel for an entire year for every vehicle. Fiscal Officer John Dalziel and I believe this is the best way to relieve pressure from the levy funds and use them solely for operations. Now we are on a program to replace vehicles every four years, so we do not have the huge expenses associated with using a vehicle with over 100,000 miles on the odometer, and those are not miles added by driving to church on Sunday. Still, a select few say things like "Why don't you buy some more cars, chief . . . gee, do you have enough?"

In simplest terms, I am not a people pleaser. I have a limited budget and stretch it until I can get no more. I spend your dollars very carefully and demand maximum return for every penny. I can line up vendors out the door who will tell you they hate negotiating with me because I am not one who just says "Hey, it's not MY money, so I don't care." They will tell you it is quite the opposite and I always tell them I am spending the public's money and I will be damned if I am not getting the most for it.

As long as I am here with this team, from the trustees and fiscal officer to my officers and admin people, we will always hustle. If that doesn't make the naysayers happy, they may have other issues . . . like suffering from bitterness.

AT THE BPD . . . With the Olympics in mind . . . Although our officers perform at a consistently high level, they do not use any performance-enhancing drugs. I believe a few do take fish oil though . . .

The Brimfield Police Department Reaches 7,000 "Likes"

And we are still shaking our heads . . .

OVERHEARD AT THE BPD . . . Conversations with a drunken guy . . . Over the weekend a drunk driver hit a couple cars and forced a few more off the road. He ended up at an apartment where he was staying. He was sitting on the couch in a stupor when Officer Allen and I shared a few moments with him.

Chief: "Were you driving a vehicle this evening?"

Drunk: "Yep. It's wrecked."

Chief: "You wrecked your car?"

Drunk: "Yep. I hit a couple cars . . . but you can't prove it!"

Chief: "Well, we will see. You're coming with us now. Can you walk?"

Drunk: "Yep." (as he stands up and falls back onto the couch)

We get him (almost carry him) outside and he sees his vehicle under lights.

Drunk: "[Expletive], my car is smashed!"

Chief: "Yeah, you hit some cars, remember?"

Drunk: "Yep. I hit at least two . . . but you can't prove it."

Chief: "Right. You told me. You got us. You are too smart for us."

Drunk: "Am I being arrested?"

Chief: "Without a doubt."

Drunk: "That's not too smart."

Chief: "Right . . . I can prove THAT."

Later, Officer Allen offered the subject a breath test, after the subject refused all of the field tests . . .

Drunk: "I'm not gonna take the breath test. The last DUI I had I took the test and you guys used it against me in court. I'm drunk and you already know it. Just write in your report that I am very intoxicated and hit some cars . . . but you will never prove it."

Chief: "Officer Allen, he has requested you note all of that in your report."

Officer Allen: "No problem. It would be my pleasure, Chief."

Drunk: "Thanks. You guys are pretty cool."

I'm not sure I have ever witnessed a more intoxicated person. I'm so thankful no one was hurt during his attempt to make it home. Folks, please, do not drive after drinking—and call us if you see someone driving drunk.

Driving while intoxicated can lead to things that can't be undone.

Dear Meth Cook,

Dude . . . I'll bet you were close to messing your pants when you saw officers on Tallmadge Road making traffic stops. They were mope hunting. I'm pretty sure you saw K-9 Havoc also. He is a big, black German Shepherd. He is the one with four legs and a badge. He looks sort of like a grizzly bear. He is really intelligent and does lots of neat tricks, one of which is finding drugs. You hide, he seeks . . . He loves that game!

I'll have to take you to the woodshed today, and I will not apologize. What kind of mope ducks the cops and then drops his meth lab in the middle of a residential street? In an act based solely on self-preservation and fear, when you saw us, you motored down a side street, came to an intersection and dropped your meth-in-a-bag project right into our laps, so to speak. My issue, other than the volatility of lab—that means it could make a loud boom—is the fact that there are CHILDREN on that street, and children are curious. That was selfish and ignorant. It kind of freaked out the people who found it, too.

We are sending your glassware and plastic to the crime lab for fingerprints. We hope to have a personal discussion with you real soon. Until then, I wish you no luck in any of your future endeavors, except they be lawful.

Great job handling this incident, Sgt. Knarr and Officers Putnam and Diehl.

—Chief

September 11th

There are moments in time you can remember exactly where you were. When President Reagan and John Lennon were shot, I remember where I was. I know where I was when the space shuttle blew up. It's the same with 9/11, but on a bigger scale because of my chosen career and the magnitude. I remember hearing on morning radio when the first jet hit the first building. I was on my way to a court appearance. I had been a sergeant for about two months and was just transferred back to uniform duties after five years working undercover. It was my first day back in uniform. I remember thinking that perhaps a small aircraft had gone astray. A judge and I began watching the news coverage in one of the conference rooms while we waited on a defendant to appear for court; we watched the second jet hit the second building. I turned to the judge and told him we were under attack and I was leaving. When he asked where I was going, I told him I did not know—but I was going to do something police-related.

I drove back to Brimfield. I came to the department, spoke with the chief for about three seconds and then started getting officers near our schools and other "soft targets." I did not know what else was going to happen, but I would be damned if was going to let it happen without giving whomever it was the fight of their life. I genuinely had no idea where it would end. I also remember our gas stations closing because they had all ran out of gas. Later, as I watched police officers and firefighters running TOWARDS what everyone else was running AWAY from, I knew the remains of the buildings contained a lot of graves of true heroes.

The events of 9/11 changed our country and changed us. They also changed police work. I think about those events regularly. I am not a paranoid guy by any stretch; however, I read everything I can about the terrorists and terrorism. I firmly believe the threat is not over.

Our lives have returned to as normal as can be (taking shoes off at the airport notwithstanding) and as a country we move forward, but we cannot forget. We cannot forget the loved ones in the buildings. We cannot forget the safety service workers who were climbing countless stairs to rescue others. We cannot forget the heroes at the Pentagon who ducked flames to pull co-workers from that inferno. We cannot forget the heroes of Flight 93 who said "Let's Roll" and rushed the cockpit to take control of a 500-mph unguided missile. In spite of the talking heads in Washington D.C. making everything, including 9/11, a hot political mess . . . we cannot forget all that has happened.

Tomorrow, on 9/11, please remember all of those who suffer because of the events on 9/11/2001. Our thoughts and prayers go to all who were left behind.

DAYSHIFT . . . Officer Pettit loves Sunday jogs . . . Officers were called to Walmart for a subject who pushed a TV and home surround sound system out the emergency exit, in a cart. Officer Pettit saw a subject pushing a cart containing those items down Tallmadge Road. In police work, that is know as a clue—or at least a "person of interest." Officer Pettit pulled up to the subject and ordered him to stop. He didn't, and the foot chase was on. Thankfully, Officer Pettit has been a faithful student of both P90X and Insanity workouts; it was a short run. The suspect was arrested and taken to the bed and breakfast, where he will work on not smoking and hopefully get some cardio work in during "yard time." Great job, Officer Pettit!

IN THE SCHOOLS . . . Parents of Field Schools students: Nice job this morning—all of the kids looked great in their "back to school" clothes. Officers were at all of the buildings. I was at the elementary school and confirmed how much I was ready for summer to be done; the high-fives were fantastic and I believe some of the students missed us as much as we missed them. We could tell from all of the hugging that was going on.

FACEBOOK UPDATE . . . Last week a total of 98,490 people visited our page—no person was counted twice—Facebook calls it "unique people." We think you are all unique. Thanks for being here and checking in from time to time. The purpose of this whole FB journey is to keep all of you informed on what we are doing . . . and what others are doing when we meet up with them. Once in a while (or more) we try to add some humor and emotion . . . and I even spout off about things. We appreciate all of you being here.

"The most important thing a father can do for his children is to love their mother."

—Theodore M. Hesburgh

Politics and crime

I hate politics. Today's politics in particular are pretty unnerving for me and likely for some of you also. In my lifetime I have never seen so much hatred and mudslinging in every political race, from top to bottom. Watching these knuckleheads and their surrogates campaign is like watching an episode of Jerry Springer: Old ladies in wheel chairs being pushed over cliffs; grainy pictures of opponents with words spliced and arranged to make voters angry . . . folks, they all think we are pretty stupid. From my perspective, as a public official, it is an embarrassment. NO ONE is telling us what they can do to be a leader; they are only telling us how bad the other guy is.

Here's the problem I have: crime and disorder. Among all of their failures, including even passing a budget for the last three years, no one gives a crap about crime and disorder. Both parties should be fired and sent packing. All of their failures contribute to the workload of police officers across the United States. The economy does have some impact on crime; however, crime and disorder is still largely an issue of character. When your leaders display no character, you are left to your environment and upbringing. Unfortunately, many do not have a solid family foundation, so the cycle begins. Drug abuse, theft, crimes of violence . . . no one is leading, because everyone has to please as many people as possible in order to get elected or move to the next highest office. We are led by people who cannot get off of the fence. When is the last time an elected person answered a "yes or no" question with a "yes" or "no"? How about all of the national and state level politicians answer one specific question for me? Here it is . . . "Is the average American citizen safer today than 10 years ago?" I don't mean safer from Al Qaeda. I mean safer from the thief, carjacker, rapist, robber, burglar, child abuser. Are we safer? Bueller? . . . Bueller? . . . Bueller? ('80s humor). Do any of you feel safer? I don't mean because of what the police do. Are you and your personal belongings safer than at any other time in your lifetime?

I love our country. If you love something or someone, you have stock in that person or thing. You have a desire to have that person or thing succeed. What I see from many elected people is a desire for personal (or party) success and not one for the country. This country needs character in our leadership. We need someone who is offended by crime and disorder and will hold people accountable for breaking laws we have established to make our lives better and more safe. We do not need elected people to reduce prison sentences because of jails being overcrowded—that is a symptom, not the problem. If the problem is crime you do not legalize crime . . . you build more jails.

If we are not going to build more jails, then we damn well better start building character.

AFTERNOON SHIFT . . . From the "I didn't get that memo" file . . . In the middle of downed trees and alarms going off, officers were called to the Walmart for a theft. After a foot pursuit to the area of the Applebee's, the suspect was arrested. After returning her to the scene, officers were parked outside of the store . . . and out runs another thief, straight into the arms of a very surprised Officer Allen. Kind of a two-fer deal on arrests, we guess.

The second arrestee was a suspended driver and swore she did not drive to the store, that she was dropped off. So, she makes bond on the misdemeanor theft and gets released. Less than 30 minutes later Officer Allen sees her . . . driving out of the Walmart parking lot. She gets stopped, because she is not a valid driver. She gets arrested and gets to wear the silver bracelets again . . . and Officer Allen and K-9 Drogen also find meth, needles and other drug related items in the car. No more bond, but a trip to the bed and breakfast. Being arrested twice in two hours elevates her to mope status.

IN THE SCHOOLS . . . Parents, we have an issue . . . I just had lunch with some kindergarten students. I'm not sure there was a full set of teeth (other than mine) at the whole table. Three students had three loose teeth each! Missing front teeth, top teeth, bottom teeth . . . it's a good thing they were serving mac and cheese! Some students are getting two dollars a tooth and NOT ONE OF THEM would pull a few of my teeth so I could get in on the profit. Mac and cheese, peas, chocolate milk and a few "you have to be a little quieter" visits from the teachers . . . and at least 973 knock knock jokes. What a blast.

"People pay for what they do, and still more, for what they have allowed themselves to become. And they pay for it simply: by the lives they lead."

—James Baldwin

Addiction vs. disease

When we post about drug arrests, we often get divided opinions on drug users. Most of what is said is the fuss about drug users making a choice or having a "disease." I am not a politically correct guy, so if you think drug addiction is a disease, stop reading now, because I am not trying to frustrate you.

My father died of cancer. He left for World War II as a kid and returned from Europe as a battle hardened First Sergeant who smoked three packs of cigarettes a day. He was addicted to nicotine. That addiction caused a disease . . . cancer.

In a "Psychology Today" magazine article, an M.D. named Lance Dodes wrote about addiction vs. disease. In part he stated: "In addiction there is no infectious agent (as in tuberculosis), no pathological biological process (as in diabetes), and no biologically degenerative condition (as in Alzheimer's disease). The only 'disease-like' aspect of addiction is that if people do not deal with it, their lives tend to get worse."

Why bring this up? Because from my view, calling addiction to heroin, meth or any other substance a disease attempts to absolve the user from any responsibility. When addicts get locked up for drug offenses or steal from people, we hear "It's a disease . . . he can't help it." It's not a disease, it is an addiction. When cancer or heart disease attack, the person does not have a choice. Every time a person plunges a needle into their arm or snorts a drug up their nose, they are making a choice to engage in that BEHAVIOR . . . which is the strong and stark difference in my mind. They create a physical dependency on the drug. That dependency will cause them to get sick if they do not use. I get a headache when I don't have my required coffee, so is my addiction to coffee a disease? Addiction involves a behavior—it is compulsive in nature. I like to eat. I may even be a food addict; however, my appetite is not a disease. The food I choose to eat may catch up with me and cause a disease, such as heart disease or diabetes. Just like the intravenous drug user may end up with Hepatitis C or HIV . . . both diseases and a product of an addiction.

I offer this is because of one main point: accountability. If you are an addict, a recovering addict or the family member of an addict, don't let labels stop you from fighting against this addiction. The word "disease" implies you are helpless and hopeless. You are not. Addictions—and this is what drug abuse is—can be beaten. It takes effort and time . . . and usually several tries. The addict has to be ready, and only the addict can and will know when he or she is ready. They will look in the mirror one day and not recognize who they are, and their heart will change and they will know it is time.

Until then, stop with the "disease" nonsense and hold that person accountable.

OVERHEARD AT THE BPD . . . Conversation, with a suspended (and arrested) driver, occurring during the booking process, as relayed by Officer Lee Allen . . .

Suspect: "Man, I can't believe this . . . and I read your Facebook page every day."

Sgt. McCarty: "That's nice."

Suspect: "This isn't going to get posted on the Facebook page, is it?"

Sgt. McCarty: "Probably not. Routine stuff usually doesn't."

[Unless Officer Allen snitches on you.]

The Brimfield Police Department Reaches 8,000 Likes!

When will the madness end . . . ?

"Good character is more to be praised than outstanding talent. Most talents are to some extent a gift. Good character, by contrast, is not given to us. We have to build it piece by piece—by thought, choice, courage and determination."

—John Luther

OVERHEARD AT THE BPD . . . Conversation with a thief, brought to your by your friends at the BPD:

Chief: "When you stole the computer, where did you take it?"

Thief: "I didn't steal the computer."

Chief (shows thief a picture of said thief stealing a computer): "Here's a picture of you stealing the computer."

Thief: "That's not me."

Sgt. Adkins: "Dude, you are wearing the same clothes right now."

Thief: "I've been moving from my house. I haven't had a chance to change clothes."

Chief: "We would like to get the computer back. When you stole the computer, where did you take it?"

Thief: "I didn't steal a computer."

Chief: "Your buddy says it's at your house."

Thief: "I didn't take it to my house! I took it to City Park and gave it to a guy."

Chief: "Did you exchange it for drugs?"

Thief: "I don't know. I gave it to a guy and he's going to call me back later and tell me what I am getting."

Chief: "So, you took the computer that you did not steal, to a guy at a park."

Thief: "Yep."

Chief: "Okay. We don't like you coming here and stealing. We do not like criminals operating here."

Thief: "I know. My wife is on your Facebook page . . . we read your page."

Chief: (blank stare) . . .

"Be more concerned with your character than your reputation, because your character is what you really are, while your reputation is merely what others think you are."

—John Wooden

Dear Thieves,

This is your official "Welcome to Brimfield" letter, along with a warning to never come back.

You two have had a rough morning. Running from the crew at Walmart while throwing items you had just stuffed down your pants makes for a slight adrenaline dump. It's kind of funny to watch on video, too.

As is our practice with most mopes, we would like to give you some pointers on your recent failures—because we are sarcastic yet helpful, in a public service kind of way:

• When three out of four of you are either on probation or have multiple warrants for theft, we take notice. Like the kids on "Blue's Clues," we all form a circle and yell, "A clue! A clue!"

• Giving a bogus name to police officers no longer works. We have computers in our vehicles and can see a picture of you. You didn't look anything like the person who you claimed to be, and we mean it wasn't even close. We understand you have six warrants for your arrest. The best advice I can give is: STOP STEALING. And try telling the truth—it works.

• Baggy pants are some kind of fashion statement, we guess. Wearing baggy pants does not help you conceal game controllers, headsets, video games and other electronics. You looked silly. You had baggy pants . . . with lots of lumps.

• Running while wearing baggy pants is just short of hysterical. The baggy pants-sprint while reaching down into your pants, removing stolen items and tossing them aside . . . priceless.

• We are not "ruining" your life. You have six warrants for your arrest. You seem to be doing okay at setting yourself up to fail. If you don't break the law, we won't show up. It's a cause-and-effect thing: You cause the crime, we effect the arrest. It's life mixed with logic.

• While we strongly encourage visitors to come here and spend

MORE...

money, we are strongly discouraging you from coming here at all. It's not personal; it's business. ("Godfather" reference.)

We hope you take our advice, particularly the hint to not come back to our fine community. We know all of you, we know your vehicle, and we know you do not believe you should pay for things that you would like to acquire. If you decide to return, I am willing to assign you a personal shopping assistant in a new program I like to call "Shop-with-a-Mope." Your shopping assistant will be one of my officers and maybe even a drug certified K-9 . . . and we will make sure you are assisted in every way possible.

Good luck at the bed and breakfast. We hear the scrambled eggs are . . . scrambled.

—Chief

Back-to-School Shop-with-a-Cop.

Don't poke the bear

This little diatribe pertains to Brimfield police officers. Some of it may be relevant to officers in other departments . . . they can decide that for themselves.

• Most police officers do not eat donuts. Long ago, on night shift, donut shops were the only businesses open. That was during a time when the gas station pumped your gas, washed your windows and checked your oil. Stores closed at 10 p.m. and were never open on Sunday. Donut shops opened at 2 a.m. to "make the donuts." Midnight cops usually love coffee, so they stopped at the donut shop for COFFEE.

• Most officers don't give a damn about skin color, sexual orientation, socioeconomic status or other hot-button discrimination topics. Ignorance comes in all shades, shapes, sizes and genders. We are not stopping you because you are white, black, straight, gay or have been pierced more than a Halloween pumpkin. It's hard to see any of that when you are approaching us at 87 mph in a 35 mph zone . . . we can barely determine you are not a Scud missile. Give all of the other stuff a break and take responsibility for driving like a moonshiner running from the revenuers.

• Stop texting and driving. Next time you may run over a jogger and not a mailbox.

• If you get arrested, my officers are not going to call me at 2 a.m. so you can talk to me, because you "know me." I know lots of people. Some of those people are good friends. They do not call me at 2 a.m. Don't poke the bear.

• We do not stop women because they are "hot." Guys either. Along those lines, flirting with us or "giving us a show" has no bearing on our enforcement of the laws. It makes us a little nervous. If you will "do anything" to not be arrested or get a ticket, anything includes making up some wild story about us. So, when you say you will "do anything," cops will appear like a David Copperfield show in Vegas. They are there as witnesses, not spectators. I happen to like my career, reputation and house. I am not giving any of them to you . . . button your shirt, please.

• Drugs are illegal. We are the police. This is a police Facebook page. Take a breath, hit the bong and surf to another page. We will give you no shelter here. Call a legislator and throw money at them . . . it seems to work.

• We know you have only had one beer. It was apparently consumed through a straw attached to a kid's swimming pool. Now, stand on the line. We have some tests for you to complete.

• Yes, you pay our salary. It's called a social compact. We put on bulletproof vests to protect us from our own population. The 95% of the population that are not mopes like having us around.

I think that covers it for today.

DAYSHIFT . . . Officers were called to the Circle K for a counterfeit $20 bill. Workers there pegged a perfect description of the mope and his vehicle. Officers Dinkelman and Pettit swooped in and stopped the vehicle on SR43. After speaking with Mr. Mope, he told us he had sold drugs to a "dude" who paid him in counterfeit cash. Later her told us what really happened. He was making the money at home, and had tried to use it at several other locations in town. Officers recovered 16 counterfeit $20 bills and a Chihuahua. Cute dog.

The bad guy was arrested. After he was fitted in nice bracelets and brought to the department, we searched his apartment. Officers recovered a scanner with more counterfeit money, heroin, 50+ used needles, marijuana and other drug-related items. We released the nice doggie to a neighbor . . . and took the bad guy to the bed and breakfast . . . where, we hear, the chipped beef is not counterfeit.

The Brimfield Police Department Reaches 9,000 "Likes"

We are beginning to believe the Mayans were correct . . .

WEEKEND HAPPENINGS . . . Nine arrests over the past weekend. The highlight for Sgt. Knarr was arresting three people for being highly intoxicated and also underage. They are from out of town and were staying at one of our local hotels and running around the area gas stations, causing problems. Usually such routine arrests are not a highlight; however, we all believe it is a keeper because one of the very drunk females, a 16-year-old, became combative and kicked Sgt. Knarr in the . . . umm . . . the . . . "nether region." He has regained his color and no longer has a queasy look. I'm not sure what has happened to parenting. I would never have thought to strike a police officer when I was 16—not many in my age group would. The female, instead of being released to parents, is now at the bed and breakfast for juveniles. The judge will be less than pleased.

FACEBOOK . . . Last week, 118,706 "unique" (each person only counted once) people visited our Facebook Page. Will the person who lives in Romania please stand up? Azerbaijan? . . . Madagascar? . . . Venezuela? . . . Cambodia? Although I am teasing, we are still amazed at the relationship we have built with all of you. This is my weekly "thank you for being here" post; I usually do that after getting the stats from Facebook . . . and staring in disbelief.

OVERHEARD AT THE BPD . . . Brimfield has heavily developed areas, yet still has farming. We have drug-testing kits in our cars . . . along with leads for stray horses. You can go from a violent domestic or meth lab to loose critters—which happened yesterday. We had a "stray" cow wander into the roadway. The radio traffic heard by those of us who were in the office brought a chuckle . . .

Officer Pettit: "I'm out with it . . . see if you can find a phone number for the owner of the cow."

Dispatch: "Can I get a better 39 [location]?"

Officer Pettit: "I'm on Sandy Lake, just south of Tallmadge Road."

Dispatch: "Copy. Can I get a description of the cow?"

Officer Pettit: "Umm . . . it looks like a COW . . . it has a tag on its ear . . . "

Unknown Officer, over the air: "Mooooooooooooooooo."

A sense of humor is priceless.

Community programs

First, a huge thank-you to all of you who stopped to see us during the Thanksgiving Fill-a-Cruiser event. We collected an amazing amount of food and also $2,724.10 in cash for the community food cupboard. The program is all-volunteer, so all of that money will be used to purchase food for those who may need a little help this year. If you are one of those, call us and we will get you in touch with the food cupboard.

A few times during the Fill-a-Cruiser, we heard about our efforts to collect food and money for those in need. We heard about the "benefits" available from the feds . . . we heard about welfare, EBT cards and big screen TVs. Great. You want to know want my answer was and continues to be?

You can't pick your parents.

See, I do not care even a smidgeon about what character a parent has. If they are able-bodied yet under- motivated, lazy, taking advantage of the system, or they are truly in need. All of that does not matter to me. What matters are the children. Some of the kids are brought into this world in bad situations. They are the result of a bad relationship, bad economics or poor choices. Teens having babies, people who are not financially ready for children having MORE children . . . we all know the story. My view is very simply this: If the children need something, we will help them out. Some parents make bad choices. They buy cigarettes instead of cereal, beer instead of milk and pay for cable or satellite television instead of school clothes. Other parents just cannot make ends meet, no matter how hard they try. It makes no difference to us.

Our willingness to help a child cannot be based on the level of parental participation the child receives or does not receive. We hold the Fill-a-Cruisers and Shop-with-a-Cop to help families . . . particularly the children. It just doesn't matter to us what other departments do or don't do, what other agencies can or can't do, or what the feds provide or don't provide. Part of our job is service and part of that service, as long as I am chief here, is centered on taking care of and helping the children who live here.

We are not ones to stand around when things need to be done.

Reality check

I get it now. Every few weeks I am going to have to type some mundane thesis on what we do here and why we do it. We have new folks joining us regularly and I am beginning to believe when you all share posts with your friends, they become somewhat confused about a police chief talking so much. In turn, they post their colorful opinions and sometimes use colorful words, and the fighting starts. So, heads up to the following . . .

We post police-related (usually) information on this page. It is relative to this community. Some may find it relative to their own situations, and some are here to see how long it will be before I am fired or done in by some type of explosion. Here is the rest . . .

• When I babble or rant, my opinions are my opinions. I am refined enough to have an opinion and not let it impact the way I do my job, which is according to law and not my opinion.

• I do not like crimes and those include drug sale and use. This is a police page and not anything more. We arrest people for lots of things, including drug offenses. We are not counselors. When we arrest someone, our playbook says nothing about it being a "disease" or "choice." It's a crime, period. Call your congressperson and have him or her change the law if you believe people who have a "disease" like drug addiction should not be arrested. Our book does not specify.

• Cop humor is weird. Ask a cop. In addition to cop humor, I am sarcastic at times. So are my kids. Oops.

• Believe it or not, a large majority of people DO NOT LIKE CRIME and are tired of living with it.

• If you advocate violence or the death of anyone, we will see you on some other page, because you won't be here. No swearing, either. If you have an opinion, offer it without being over-the-top mean.

• We do not post names or pictures. Every crime listed here is anonymous, save for a general location and offense. If you see a picture, there is a good reason—likely a warrant for an arrest or our need to identify someone.

• Don't complain about my professionalism, or lack of whatever you believe to be a professional characteristic of a chief or leader. The same people who complain about me being "unprofessional" will give passes to generals having affairs with authors, presidents having affairs in the Oval Office, or an elected politician who used to smoke crack while he was the mayor of a major city. I hold myself accountable . . . you should try it.

• There is an "X" at the top of every webpage. When your cursor hovers over it, the word "close" comes up. If you do not like it here, for heaven's sake, leave. It's been three years and I have not changed a thing . . . we will tell you the truth, add some humor when available, and move on to the next post.

MIDNIGHTS . . . It's Halloween . . . Officers are out all over tonight in the area, particularly in neighboring Kent and here in Brimfield.

Officer Putnam with the first arrest in Brimfield tonight, a traffic stop resulting in the arrest of the driver . . . he had a felony warrant from Summit County for drug offenses. He will attend any functions this weekend (lunch, exercise and phone calls) dressed as an inmate . . . bummer. I am betting they do not have Butterfingers and Smarties.

The best radio traffic of the night so far has been Kent officers chasing someone involved in a fight—he was dressed up as an Amish guy.

MIDNIGHTS . . . Brimfield Officers ended the Halloween weekend festivities with 19 arrests last night and early this morning. Out of the 19 arrests made, eight were for Operating a Vehicle while Impaired (OVI). All subjects arrested for OVI either tested over the legal limit for Ohio or refused to take a test. Everyone who tested over the legal limit for OVI swears to having only "one beer." We are figuring by the appearance of some of the arrestees, the "one beer" was served in a 55-gallon drum.

Arrested were Mother Earth (or Mother Nature . . . she could not tell us), Red Riding Hood, the devil, a cheetah, a kitty cat, a princess of unknown origin and some type of dinosaur . . . and others. The boyfriend of the kitty cat was arrested in our lobby . . . he decided to throw a hissy and break a phone in the new waiting area, while he was waiting on the kitty to be processed. I cannot believe, as a police officer, I would ever type the above paragraph . . .

Our new holding cells are not so new anymore.

Great job to all officers for the hard work last night.

Dear College Halloween-ers,

Hello from the Brimfield Police Department and your favorite—
Not!—public servant. It's that time of year again, when you all dress
up, go to Kent and drink your favorite alcoholic beverages. The Kent
Police Department will have a bevy of officers there to ensure public
safety and watch you throw up through your Iron Man mask. We
will be sending officers, as will numerous other agencies, so I am
confident with all of the officers present, things in Kent will be under
control...

Some of you choose to go to Kent and then come back to your
off-campus housing here in Brimfield to continue the party. Please
read the following advice from your friendly neighborhood police
officers. It may save you bail money and court costs:

• Please stay out of the roadway. A couple years back, while responding to a call, I nearly mowed down all of the Disney princesses.
Although I have seen all of the Disney films and don't remember the
princesses being so scantily clothed, it was certainly Belle, Snow
White, Cinderella and a few other princesses who were highly
intoxicated. They nearly went the way of a herd of groundhogs, lying
on the side of the road with tire marks across them. I could never explain to my daughters that their father was responsible for the death
of Cinderella.

• Keep the noise to a level acceptable to sober people. Noise
draws attention. Loud noises bring the police. If we show up to Hal-
lopalooza at your apartment, someone will be leaving with us. There
will be a quick costume change from "Pirates of the Caribbean" to "O
Brother, Where Art Thou?" Read: jail clothes.

• Know your limit and be able to hold your liquor. We do NOT
want to arrest you. We want you to have fun. We really DO NOT want
to see you throw up. It makes us all a little queasy.

• It is never okay to throw bottles at us. If you do, we will chase
you down and arrest you. If we cannot catch you, our dogs run like

MORE...

Olympic sprinters. They are undefeated in foot races with people and have also kept pace with cars with six cylinders and under. When bottles start flying, the dogs get very protective of us. Place all of your glass in the proper recycling containers.

• If you fail to heed these little nuggets of advice and get arrested, you will be coming to a modern department with cameras located everywhere. Although in a drunken state it may seem "cool" to moon the camera or shout obscenities, in the long haul, it can be detrimental to finding gainful employment. What we do is public record, and we are a transparent group. "Drunken Captain America Moons Police Camera" might sound funny ... until a potential employer sees it while doing a background check. Yikes! That's embarrassing.

Have fun, be safe and act responsibly.

—Chief

NEW AT THE BPD . . . We knew it wouldn't take long . . . The first adult arrestee took our new holding cells for a test drive. Officer Pettit made the arrest; the subject was wanted on a warrant for "swindling" in Minnesota. Minnesota police confirmed they will provide the ride to that fine state, so we provided one to our cells and then to the bed and breakfast. Both Officer Pettit and the arrested guy will be getting a toaster for being the first customer in the brand new digs.

FACEBOOK . . . Wow! . . . 11,000 "likes." We are amazed and humbled by all of you being here and interacting with us. It is a concept that has worked well and, we believe, brought a community closer . . . and added a few thousand new virtual residents to Brimfield, Ohio.

FACEBOOK . . . In the last seven days, the BPD Facebook page has 774 new "Likes" and 97,686 people who have visited our page. We keep chugging forward with all of you. Thanks for being here and giving a hoot about things in general.

"Too often we give children answers to remember rather than problems to solve."

—Roger Lewin

This time of year

As we get geared up for our "busy" time of the year, I want to offer some background on our holiday programs. I don't use the word holiday as a generic term, but with Thanksgiving and Christmas close together, it's easier to type "holiday" . . . although I just typed every word in the dictionary in this first paragraph, so brevity be gone. I love this time of year, not because of the commercial aspect . . . because it is a time for us to demonstrate one of our guiding principles, which is Community. Not to get on a federal government rant again, but that branch of reps should not be focused on helping people with food and clothing. That, by the very definition, should be done by a community. Neighbors helping neighbors. And as politically correct as I am (Ha!), that help and assistance should never be providing for a second or third generation. End of insensitivity . . .

Coming up in the next two months we will collect over two tons of food, eight truckloads of toys, clothing and other personal items. We will also take at least 120 kids to Shop-with-a-Cop, with each spending $100. All of this is through donations, so those of you who bust my chops all of the time can be gone—no tax dollars are used.

Last year we took our highest number of kids ever, 137, to the shopping program. We will come close to that number again. If you have ever attended that event, it is impossible to forget. That may be my most favorite day of the year.

All of the collected items from our two days of "Fill-a-Cruiser" go to the Brimfield Community Food Cupboard. If you need some help with food and other items, call them.

Police Officers sometimes do things which people do not like—arrests, tickets, answering domestics. However, many of us also are present when you need other types of help. I have had people question our spearheading of these events. My theory is and will continue to be this: If there is a void, we will try to fill it. If there is a need, it is our job to help.

We are problem solvers.

FROM OUR "YOU HAVE TO BE KIDDING" FILE . . . Officers were called to the Brimfield Plaza for two suspicious males. They were hanging around the Dollar General and had been customers at the "casino" there. When we arrived, one subject was inside the Dollar General; the other left the area in an SUV.

We met with the subject inside of the Dollar General. He was later deemed to be a mope. He was "looking for socks." After identifying him, we discovered he had three warrants for his arrest, for burglary and receiving stolen property. He was arrested inside the store.

As we were putting him in the car, his buddy came back, driving, and pulled into a spot at the "casino" and started to head in. We met with him. He was driving with a suspended license and in possession of meth and a used needle. So, thinking about things, we went back into the store to see if the first bad guy left anything behind. You know, when you see the cops, you ditch your stuff . . .

Thanks to some very alert store employees, we recovered a used needle and meth, on the shelf, with the socks. I was less than pleased that a mope would endanger innocent people by leaving drugs and a used needle hanging around. After all, there are no victims when it comes to drugs (that was extreme sarcasm).

They both are going to the county bed and breakfast, courtesy of BPD Travel . . . providing trips for mopes for over 20 years.

Great job, Officer Pettit!

MIDNIGHTS . . . Officer Atha with the arrest of a female for possession of meth and prescription pain medicine. She did not have a prescription. Shocking, we know. The arrest was a result of a traffic stop. By the way, if you are committing crimes and driving around . . . have valid license plates. The object is to NOT get caught. She is at the county spa now, no pedicures or seaweed wraps are scheduled.

"A two-year-old is kind of like having a blender, but you don't have a top for it."

—Jerry Seinfeld

Tolerance of crime

Tolerance is defined several ways. One definition is "the acceptance of the differing views of other people." Another is "the act of putting up with somebody or something irritating or otherwise unpleasant." I think there is some confusion on the word and the proper definition when it comes to crime and criminals. Preaching tolerance to people about different views is okay by me. You can be a liberal, conservative, white, black, straight, gay, god-fearing or mother earth worshiping . . . who cares? You should not have any more or any less freedom than anyone not in your group. If a football team WANTS to say a prayer before a game, mind your own business. If you are not a part of the team, community or function, get lost. Part of "tolerance" as it is emphasized is being tolerant yourself. Which brings me to my wonderful rant subject . . . When did it become "cool" to tolerate crime?

• Crime is not a different view, race, religion or any other subsection. It's crime. It's illegal. Against the law. Laws keep order in an otherwise goofy society. Order is good, disorder is chaos. What gives?

• If you have ever come home to find your stuff missing; if you have been the victim of any crime . . . assault, sexual assault, identity theft, burglary, car theft, the list goes on . . . it takes something else from you. It takes your sense of order, your sense of security.

• We have subdivided crime into delineating if there are "victims," how badly the victims were impacted and also if the perpetrator had some awful thing in his or her past that made him or her become a criminal. We also have to now be faced with the dilemma of guilt if we act on a drug addict, because they now have an AMA-recognized illness—addiction. Land sakes!

Here is where I differ from some: Tolerance of crime is hogwash. I cannot stand excuses, reasons or mitigating circumstances. The only thing that should come into play is right and wrong. Unless a person truly is insane and cannot differentiate between what is right or wrong or legal and illegal, they must pay the price agreed upon by all of us as a society. It's called the law. If you break into a house and are lucky enough not to get shot by the resident, you should go to jail. Your drug use, childhood experiences or bitterness for society is irrelevant to the crime. Right is right, wrong is wrong. DO NOT give me the dance about drugs being a victimless crime. That is bull. I can show you neighborhoods taken over by drugs and crime. I can take you to hotels in suburban America where drugs are sold and used daily. That activity brings other crime, like thefts, robberies and prostitution.

To our residents: We will pursue every person who breaks the law in the same fashion. We will turn them over to the courts for a judgment . . . and, if found guilty, a sentence. It is up to you to vote in prosecutors and judges who follow the law and sentence appropriately. At the beginning of 2013 we will be following all of our cases through to sentencing. I will be attending as many sentencing hearings as possible. If a person is found guilty I will advise you of the finding and the sentence. I will also tell you what court and judge handled the case. You all need to be educated in this process, find the weak link, if there is one, and vote accordingly. If a judge is bound by weak sentencing guidelines, that is an elected representative problem. If a judge has the tools and does not use them, then it falls on that judge.

If you intend to commit a crime here, think twice. All eyes will be on this system, this community and this process. It is time everyone in the system is held accountable. Cops all over this nation are doing their jobs. It's time for the rest of the system to carry some water, too.

DAY SHIFT . . . This morning, around shift change, we were called for a death. The couple was traveling from out of town and the husband passed away unexpectedly. The scene when I arrived was heartbreaking—yet comforting to me. Officer Atha was sitting on the floor of a hallway, back against the wall, directly beside a very distraught widow. He had never met her before today, yet they were talking like they were family. Officer Atha was a 6' 4", 290-pound teddy bear.

I have said it before . . . law enforcement is not just about tickets and arrests. Those things are important, because of safety and order. Another very important thing missed by many in the public is the large amount of consoling we do, on a day-to-day basis.

Officer Atha, you did a great thing today.

Veteran's Day

Everyday is Veterans Day for me. I am so thankful for men and women who choose to serve our country. These men and women enlist, attend basic training and then live away from their home and loved ones, by choice, for the next several years . . . some while being shot at on a daily basis. Oh, and the pay is bad.

So, from me, my officers and staff, thanks to all of our veterans who have served or continue to serve. Thank-you to the World War II vets—you are all my heroes. Every time I see one of you I am in awe and close to tears.

Korean vets, you are not forgotten. Our Vietnam vets . . . thanks and as always, welcome home. If I had been at an airport and saw people spitting at you, I would have put my foot in their backside. THAT was the beginning of mopery. Thanks to all of you who have served in the sandboxes in the last decades, and in Kosovo, Grenada and Panama. Thanks to all of you who never left the U.S.; you kept things safe here.

I have the softest spot possible for veterans. I don't care if the person served in a war, in peace time, or guarded a patch of strawberries. If you served, I love you.

Thanks from all of us at the BPD.

DAYSHIFT . . . Crash on Tallmadge Road, slight delays in the area while the cars are removed. To the nice female in the silver Toyota: Please hang up the phone when driving through a crash scene.

Love,
The guy you almost hit,
Chief

---

*"It doesn't take a hero to order men into battle.
It takes a hero to be one of those men who goes
into battle."*

—Norman Schwarzkopf

Dear Veteran,

I wanted to write a note of appreciation to convey how much I love you and everything you have done to protect my life in freedom. Some of my thoughts may ramble at times. That is because of my slightly goofy personality and also because of how emotional I get when I address someone from our military, no matter where or when he or she served. So here it goes . . .

Thank you for everything. Thanks for leaving the comforts of your house and hometown and going to another country to battle for us. Thanks for going to boot camp and listening to big guys scream at you for several months. Thanks for doing all that running while carrying packs full of whatever you put in those big packs. Thanks for sleeping outside in the rain, snow and blistering hot sun. For you younger vets, thanks for all that time you spent in the sand . . . that much sand should have an ocean and those little drinks with umbrellas nearby.

Thanks for lying in foxholes for days and days while the bad guys shot at you. Thanks for stopping Hitler. He was one of the worst. Thanks for jumping out of perfectly good airplanes with a hundred or more pounds of gear on . . . and landing behind enemy lines . . . on purpose. Thanks for riding inside of tanks and submarines. Yikes. Thanks for being on ships (not boats) for a year or more at a time. Thanks for logging thousands of hours of flight time while tracers, missiles and other nasty projectiles came flying in.

Thanks for being in heated battles and seeing things that you cannot un-see. Thanks for being next to that other guy when he died—you provided him with comfort. Although you thought you would lose your mind, you held it together for him. Thanks for being second-guessed by a bunch of people who have nothing better to do than run their mouths. Thanks to those of you who were sent to war by a government that could not make up its mind and then all but forgot about you.

MORE...

Thanks for everything you have done. Thanks for doing most of it before you turned 30. Thanks for coming home without all of the body parts or with the peace of mind you left home with. Thanks for subjecting yourselves to nightmares and flashbacks so my family and I can live our lives in freedom. We owe all of you so much that I refuse to use just one day per year to acknowledge your contribution to our way of life.

We love, respect, honor and thank all of you . . . always.

—Chief

DAYSHIFT . . . The loud "boom" heard yesterday: Aliens, or . . . ? It may have been a binary explosive, commonly known by the trademark name "Tannerite." Primarily made from ammonium nitrate/ aluminum powder, the product is shot with a firearm and explodes. Large amounts, when detonated, send small shock waves and make one HECK of a boom—100 pounds of it being set off can be heard over five miles away. It is legal, but it has caused lots of changes of shorts by unsuspecting neighbors.

WEEKEND . . . Officer Dumont returned from vacation to receive a knee in the groin from a drunk person who didn't want to be arrested. It did not work . . . and now the suspect gets an assault on a police officer charge, too.

"The world is not dangerous because of those who do harm, but because of those who look at it without doing anything."

—Albert Einstein

Internet casinos

I comment from time to time on the "Internet casinos" that have opened in Brimfield, and many of you post your disdain for the establishments. Others want to let people make their own decisions on what they do with their money. I understand both arguments.

When the storefront casinos began popping up, I had some concerns. However, the township could do very little but watch. Local townships (like Brimfield) rely on state laws to keep the peace and accomplish other police work. The state had not and still has not passed any laws regulating these establishments. Our state government is frustrating at times. I know that is news to most of you.

In Ohio gambling is illegal, apparently, unless the state is running it and making money. When these new games and locations came into the picture, owners of the big casinos and their high-priced attorneys argued that these "Internet casinos" offered games of "skill" and not games of "chance," which threw the legal system into a tizzy. Lots of attorneys made money, as did the owners, because the rooms stayed open. A court ruled them to be illegal and a bunch of games were seized and many of the locations went out of business. Another judge in a southern Ohio county ruled them to be games of skill, and thereby legal. The payout had to be in "Internet minutes" or gift cards, but you could trade those in on the spot for cash.

And here we are. If you live in a city, the city government can pass laws banning the stores. Townships do not have that authority, but do have zoning laws. All three locations currently in Brimfield opened up in direct violation of zoning laws . . . and back to court we all go. The wheels of justice are turning . . . slowly.

The Brimfield Board of Trustees has passed a resolution preventing any new casinos to be opened in Brimfield until the state removes their thumbs from their . . . ears . . . and either outlaws or regulates the ventures. I can tell you from my perspective, having worked off-duty on some nights, that there is a lot of "rent money" being parted with.

The issue for many of you appears to be the element these locations bring to a community. I have been to these locations and have worked at one of them in an off-duty capacity. One location here pays for an officer and police vehicle for a security detail. We have made arrests at all three locations for warrants, drugs and driving offenses. There are also "little old ladies" and other very nice people who go there to gamble. The question seems to be our "moral compass."

Gambling was made illegal because leaders during that time were tired of hearing about loved ones losing all of their money to schemes . . . and yes, it does become an addiction. I have personally witnessed someone say "I don't know how I am going to pay the rent now" after losing a bunch of money at one of the casinos here in Brimfield. It is unfathomable to me that a person would choose to gamble over paying rent . . . but they do.

What do we tolerate as a society? In an age when everyone is talking about personal responsibility (and very few are taking action) do we make laws to protect the families of people who won't look out for themselves or their loved ones? Not unlike a drug addict, gambling addicts commit crimes to support their habit. And one of the largest purveyors of their "drug" is the state government. Nice job, elected people . . . well played.

MIDNIGHTS . . . Hello from Walmart and our Black Friday extravaganza . . . brought to you by the BPD, because we have unshakable holiday spirit—and because we are working. The Walmart parking lot is full; cars are now parking in the lots of closed stores in the Cascades Shopping Center. The crowd is very well-behaved . . . though we have seen some grandmothers who look like a deer in headlights . . . and some who look like the car bearing down on the deer . . .

MIDNIGHTS . . . Update: Only one arrest at the Black Friday event last night/ early this morning—a male subject walked into the store VERY intoxicated. While we are a patient group for the most part, Black Friday, lots of people and a slobbering drunk guy just is not a good mix. We gave him several warnings and then changed his status to "black and white Friday" and provided him a free ride in a police car. Thank you to the shoppers who behaved and to my officers who worked on Thanksgiving.

Dear Domestic Violence Mope,

You are a BEAUTY. That was not a compliment. I refuse to get into excuses or reasons why you chose to assault your wife and two stepchildren last night. I don't want anyone to talk about anger issues, mental health or you just being "frustrated" over your life. You, sir, are a mope.

There is no excuse to "get pissed" enough at children to kick one of them across the room, batter their mother who is defending her child, then assault your stepson, who is defending his mother. Geez, Dude, were you raised by professional wrestlers? MMA fighters? Wolves?

Men do not deal with family issues by beating the tar out of the family. If your desire to have control is so overwhelming, buy a gold-fish. They stay in a bowl, eat when you want them to and aren't much on conversation—perfect for you. Men do NOT hit, kick or otherwise assault children or women.

None of us are perfect. We have raised voices and said things to loved ones we wish we had not said. Some, in our younger days, have punched walls, doors or other things in frustration. You are not in the "younger days" category, and walls and doors do not go to the hospital with broken bones . . . like last night. You displayed violence in the household to young minds. Will they now believe that is how a man acts?

Well . . . enjoy your stay at the Mope Motel. I hope that control thing works out for you in the clink. I also hope the victim sees exactly what you are and puts your stuff on the curb, in the rain.

Oh . . . and one other thing. If you come back here to that house in violation of a protection order, we will be there.

We have the children's backs.

—Chief

Ticket revenue

One of the reasons the general public has issues with police officers is the issuing of citations for traffic offenses and misdemeanors. A constant theme on our pages is the outcry over local government making money by giving you all tickets. A week seldom goes by without someone posting about us "making money" by writing tickets. Here is the truth, without any sugar . . .

Many departments make money by writing citations. These departments are usually located in cities and villages and write citations under local ordinances (laws) which mirror the state laws. So, for example, the state law lists speeding as an offense in the Ohio Revised Code. The city or village makes it a local law also, the police write a ticket under the local offense . . . and the municipality keeps the money. The state and feds have cut so much local government funding in the past years, and the money from citations helps make up some of those costs. The subject usually isn't talked about, because it fires people up. Many believe they pay taxes and should not support the government further by sending them $200 for speeding.

More truth: Citations can be avoided by driving the speed limit, being a valid driver, not driving drunk or causing a crash. Citations are a monetary penalty for breaking the laws established to make us safe and keep order. Although some of you would LOVE to not have a speed limit and may be able to handle the driving at 100 MPH, some are just not mature or aware enough to drive at high speeds and still have time to react if the need arises.

At the BPD, we issue very few citations. That is my decision and I own it.

We make very little money on citations here. We do not make enough to pay for our fuel for a year or for half of the salary of one officer.

I truly do not believe in padding my budget with the hard-earned money of construction workers, teachers, office workers and others. Everyone pays enough taxes already. Before daylight we all get up and come to work. There may be a morning when you are a little heavy on the gas pedal. When we stop you the first time, it is our educational obligation to tell you the dangers of driving too fast. If you are lucky enough to get me, I will tell you some nasty stories about deaths related to driving too fast. In my opinion and my opinion ONLY . . . how does handing you a $185 citation HELP you? After all, isn't that what we want to do? I understand the punishment aspect of a citation; however, I also believe in sending a clear warning and providing some education.

Now, if we see you speeding again, things will be different. If you have 163 prior speeding tickets, you will leave with your 164th. If you cause a crash . . . ticket. If you speed through a school zone . . . sign here. If you are driving and commit an arrestable offense . . . you get arrested. That is our line in the sand. There are some among us who cannot grasp gentleness, so we provide a change of pace.

I do not like giving people tickets. I prefer to catch criminals. Our way is to stop a lot of vehicles looking for the worst who operate among us. Our officers get special training on criminal patrol and interdiction. We look for knuckleheads who make you a victim. We do write citations for minor traffic offenses at times, but you have to be trying to get that particular autograph from the officer.

That's just who we are.

IN THE COMMUNITY . . . To show that the crew is not all enforcement oriented, the Fill-a-Cruiser was held Saturday. The cars were filled with toys and food approximately 20 times, and we collected over $5,000 in cash, which is the highest total ever. There is no way we help people at Thanksgiving and Christmas without all of you. I am overwhelmed most of the time by all of the support and encouragement you give us. We have a great partnership and we all are honored and humbled by all of you. Thanks for everything.

FACEBOOK . . . We picked up lots of new "likes" yesterday. Welcome to all of you and we hope you enjoy being here . . . if not, sorry. We can be kind of mouthy at times—don't take it personal, unless you are a criminal. Then, take it to heart.

"Everybody needs a hug.
It changes your metabolism."

—Leo Buscaglia

SHOP-WITH-A-COP . . . I am thrilled to tell all of you that we will be taking at LEAST 125 children shopping this Saturday for our Shop-with-a-Cop day out. The morning starts with all of us meeting for breakfast, held at and donated by Applebee's in the Cascades Shopping Center; then it is off to Walmart for shopping, where each child will be spending $100 on whatever they want . . . as long as a parent (and maybe the chief) approves. If you have not guessed, this is one of my favorite events (along with the Christmas breakfasts for our senior residents, which are being held next week). If you have never seen 125+ kids going shopping with us . . . it is a life-changing event. Thank you to all of our donors and volunteers for making this day possible.

Four more days until the police department and 125+ young'ins invade Walmart. I'm worse than the kids anticipating this event. Hurry up, Saturday . . .

Three more days to go before I experience the short-circuit effect . . . Shop-with-a-Cop is Saturday . . . 127 kids, with police officers and volunteers . . . I cannot wait. My head may explode. There is something about the expression on faces during that event; it is a one-of-a-kind feeling.

Tomorrow is Shop-with-a-Cop. 128 children will be attending a breakfast with officers and volunteers (thank you, Applebee's) and then off we go . . . each child gets to spend $100 on whatever they REALLY want for Christmas. A HUGE, HUGE thanks to all of the people and businesses for the donations to make this happen. We will get some pictures and let all of you know how the day went. One of my favorite days of the year!

The Brimfield Police Department Reaches 17,000 "Likes"

We are humbled by all of you being here, with us.

On the school shooting

I have been thinking about kindergarten students all day. Five and six year-old kids with no cares and with eyes on Santa coming soon. I see kindergarteners every day at our elementary school; you can always spot them, because of their book bags. They are small, innocent and love the world . . . and they give the BEST high fives, ever. They high five with love and eagerness, unaware of this nasty world we live in and the fact that monsters really do exist, in the form of killers, like the one who showed up at a school in Connecticut today.

When disasters like this happen, we as a society tend to go way off, one direction or another. Moving to either extreme is not the answer, in my very humble opinion. We should not ban guns. We should not arm teachers.

I am a gun enthusiast. I am an NRA member. I am not a right-wing extremist. I have been around guns since birth and have always had one in the house. For those who want to make guns illegal, I have a comparison . . . cocaine and heroin are illegal. Making something illegal just means that those with a moral compass will not possess or use it. Criminals still will. I do not know about the rest of you, but when I am backed into a corner, and have to protect my family from harm or death, I do not want to take a baseball bat to a gunfight.

On the other hand, my gun enthusiast friends need to simmer a little. The talk of "criminal" or "gun free zones" is also a little dramatic. The world is not collapsing. There are not bands of roving killers who prey on people because they enter stores or buildings where guns are not permitted. Teachers should not be armed in a school. I do not want teachers having the responsibility of being in a shoot/don't shoot scenario or worrying about proper backdrop. We constantly work those scenarios and they are unnerving at best. Mrs. Crabtree should not have to worry about breaking out her Glock while also trying to give directions to 25 screaming first-graders.

Additionally, a small fraction of the gun people who "talk the talk" about what they would do in a life or death situation would most certainly not "walk the walk." It's very easy to say or type "If I was there with my concealed carry, I would have killed him" . . . it's not so easy to put that play in motion. Many would shoot themselves in the leg, and then urinate. Again, that's a fraction of the gun people, so don't come unglued.

So we had another mass killing at a school. Innocent children . . . angels . . . gone. I have said it for years, to anyone who will listen: It is time to direct tax money to every school in this nation. It is time to make our schools secure. The time for talk is done. It was done YEARS ago. There should be NO one in the building during the school day except for staff, students and police. Dedicate a secure room/vestibule near the entrance for conferences or meetings with parents. Set a perimeter of cameras and locked doors, so these kids can be safe, the teachers can be safe, and the building can function as a school and not a murder scene.

Fed and State elected people, nationwide, listen up . . . You have taxed beyond belief. You have attempted education reform numerous times and failed. You are failing children and teachers in a way that is reprehensible, and they are dying. Stop lining the pockets of your lobbyists and start securing these schools. If you can fund the study of methane gas released by cattle, you can damn sure make these schools safer. And yes, it is on you. You have taxed at a federal and state level so much that you have caused the locals giant issues with passing ANY taxes.

These children leave the safety of home every day. It is our job to return them home, safely. Let's start making schools a "safe zone" and not just show up for photo ops when kids die. Lead, or get out of the way.

Thoughts and prayers to all involved. I just cannot grasp your agony.

Update (3 days later) . . .

My resolve has not wavered since my post on Friday.

National and state lawmakers, politicians, elected reps . . . If someone intends to do you harm where you all congregate, they cannot get to you. You are all protected by armed security and multiple physical barriers.

All of you are no more important than the children of this country.

This is not a new song and dance for me. I've been singing it for years. I care about children and senior citizens. It's time for you to start funneling money away from pet projects and other nations and towards the children and teachers of the United States, who meet every day, at the same time and location, without the benefits of armed police, bulletproof windows and other security measures.

Until you do this, I will call your offices and send you emails and letters . . . regularly. Because I am a swell guy.

SHOP-WITH-A-COP . . . I want to thank my officers, their families, the elected officials, civilian volunteers and all of the donors who made our 2012 Shop-with-a-Cop a huge success. I was overwhelmed by the smiles and laughter of 127 children, all shopping for Christmas presents.

Many of these children are aware of what happened yesterday in Connecticut. I know this, because many of them told me. We owe something to these kids and kids all over our great country . . . we owe them a little civility. We owe them answers to their fears; however, so far, all I am hearing is bickering about guns, mental illness and schools being turned into prisons . . . adults, being kids.

Let's all of us stop placing blame and start solving problems.

I lost count of the crying grandmothers, mothers, aunts and others who hugged me while crying over lost kids several states away. A few told me they came to the event today just to look at some happiness. I cannot imagine what those close to the scene are feeling.

To all of you who assisted in this project . . . thank you for all you did today.

Christmas Shop-with-a-Cop.

For you new folks . . .

We have had lots of new friends join us over the past few days. We had 1,544,000 visits this weekend. Facebook thought we were giving away LCD televisions.

Some of you new people messaged me LOTS of questions. I figured a quick post would answer many of them.

• Yes, this is REALLY a police FB page.

• No. I have no interest in running for any office. In my younger days I would have, because I would say anything to anyone. Times have changed. I also figure that together, politicians get very little done. My crew here is one of the best, and they get results.

• Brimfield is in northeastern Ohio. It's a great place to live, work and visit.

• A "mope" is someone who leeches off of society and is involved in criminal activity.

• I am tired of politics and everything associated with it. So make your stand for or against guns, abortions, mental health, global warming and all of the other hip social issues somewhere else. If you believe in God, believe He will deal with people who do wrong. If you believe in karma, the same applies. If you believe in nothing, I have no advice for you.

• Yes, I am not "politically correct." I also do not use that as a license to insult people. If you commit a crime here, we will take you to the woodshed . . . other than that, your life is not my business.

• Color, money, looks or any other "labels" do not matter. Heart and character do.

• I ABHOR people who prey on kids and our senior citizens. If you want a long term stay at the bed and breakfast, try that nonsense here.

• Your local police officers probably do lots of great things. You just do not hear about them.

• If you do not like what we do here, see you down the road. Until my bosses replace me . . . it's me. Whining only makes you tired and my eyes burn.

• I'm not sure on the definition of "Alpha" male. If it's bad, then yes . . . I probably am. Sorry.

Have a great evening.

MIDNIGHTS . . . A traffic stop at Mogadore and Howe resulted in the arrest of two mopes on felony drug charges. Mopes, remember: If you are going to hang around each other, make sure at least one of you has a valid driver's license. And it also helps if you are not wanted on an outstanding warrant.

The stop results in the seizure of three baggies of crack; three baggies of powder cocaine; and three containing heroin. The officers also found a digital scale and some other drug items.

Off to the county bed and breakfast, drug dealers. Enjoy the oatmeal . . . it's . . . tasty. And you are now on Santa's Mope List.

Great job, Sgt. McCarty and Officer Dumont; thanks for guarding the gate while we sleep.

FACEBOOK . . . We haven't changed a bit since becoming Internet sensations, with the exception of the bedazzled jump suit, cape and the hiring of back-up singers. The rumor I am requiring the playing of the theme from "2001: A Space Odyssey" every time I enter a room is just not true. I miss Elvis.

IN THE COMMUNITY . . . Today, we will be delivering gift bags to the 180+ seniors who could not attend our breakfasts. There will be more hugging, and the more emotional ladies cry a little . . . which is okay with us.

The Brimfield Police Department Reaches 19,000 "Likes"

Okay . . . now, it's a little odd . . .

"Above all else: go out with a sense of humor. It is needed armor. Joy in one's heart and some laughter on one's lips is a sign that the person down deep has a pretty good grasp of life."

—Hugh Sidey

FACEBOOK . . . In the last seven days, 2,025,664 people visited the BPD Facebook page . . . land sakes! We are very grateful for all of you being here; particularly, we are thrilled you all care. We may not all always agree, but the conversation is never boring.

MIDNIGHTS . . . From the "Man, I wish I had Facebook" files . . . A few weeks back we posted pictures of two female mope-types who stole the March of Dimes donation bottle from the Circle K store. Last night, one of the female mope-types returned to the scene of the crime. She had a male with her; his job was to distract the clerk while Mrs. Mope stole some lottery tickets. As they made their getaway, the clerk phoned us. Officers Atha and Putnam caught up with the love birds at one of the Internet casinos, near SR43. The lottery tickets were recovered and both subjects were arrested. Officers also recovered used needles and a crack pipe.

So, Merry Christmas and Happy New Year to both of you. We hope you enjoy your stay at the bed and breakfast . . . where you will find no confetti, nice party hats or live reports from Times Square . . . but you may get a surprise bed check. And don't come back to Brimfield; anyone who steals from sick children is a mope and is never welcome.

FACEBOOK . . . Well, the world did not end in 2012. All of the hype was . . . hype. So, here we are again, in a new year, all of us together, solving the world's problems; or at least talking about some important issues from time to time.

As we start the new year, I must once again say thanks to all of you for being here. I know I say thanks a lot; however, I believe those who are grateful should give thanks. When we started the FB page a couple years back, I believed if we could get 500 people to pay attention to what was going on in our community, we would be successful. I have no idea how to measure 22,800 "likes" on a success meter. The continued notice by various media outlets and the continued growth of the page indicates we (you all and us) have gotten a recipe right . . . now, does anyone know what exactly we are cooking?

The Brimfield Police Department Reaches 20,000 "Likes"

We are so happy it happened before the end of the world

. . .

IN THE SCHOOLS . . . I had to miss a morning at the elementary school this week because of needing to give testimony in court for a mope. I hate missing my morning high-fives. That and my large black coffee are the perfect start to the day.

The next day a kindergarten girl walked up to me, threw her arms around me (which is no easy task) and said:

"My name is Ella and I missed you yesterday. Where were you?"

Mopes, we may need to move court back an hour, so sleep in.

FACEBOOK . . . We passed 27,000 likes last evening. We aren't sure who the toaster and autographed picture are supposed to go to . . . it all happened so fast. We appreciate all of you being here and checking in from time-to-time. We are having a blast.

WEATHER REPORT . . . The roads are pretty sloppy today. Most are either snow covered or slushy. Side roads have a coating of snow. The main thing to remember is this: It does not matter how fast you can go . . . it matters how fast you can stop. The stopping part seems to be confusing at times. Slow down as you approach intersections, lest you be the one who white-knuckles with an open mouth, bouncing off of curbs and cars.

The Brimfield Police Department Reaches 27,000 "Likes"

Is everyone sure they understand this is a POLICE department Facebook page?

"There's a hole in the moral ozone and it's getting bigger."

—Michael Josephson, American ethicist

Dealing with gun violence . . .

I have received lots of emails and messages about the plan announced this week on gun violence and safety. Every one of those has asked for an opinion. I am so shy and introverted, I hesitate to give an opinion. But I did take my Vitamin B Complex this morning, so I feel pretty confident and clear headed.

The "Gun Violence Reduction Executive Actions," as released by the White House, list 24 objectives for the reduction of gun violence. Only four deal with mental health issues. The others are related to acquiring guns, registering guns, reviewing gun locks and safes, launching a responsible gun ownership campaign and many other objectives. As honestly as I can say this . . . this is what happens when politicians of ANY party form committees and start studying problems.

If you do independent study—independent as in not affiliated to anyone or any organization which makes a profit from the argument—firearms used in most active-shooter or mass-killing incidents were not bought by the shooter. The weapons were acquired from family members, friends or others who acquired them legally. These shooters have some mental illness issues, folks . . . plain and simple.

Decades ago we began closing mental health facilities and shoving the mentally ill out the doors. They were left in the hands of relatives, friends or homeless shelters. The mentally ill, born or diagnosed since that time, are among us, with very little input on a diagnoses or anyone to make sure they have the correct medication and are taking it. So they continue to suffer and often act out.

I have no issue with people owning firearms who can lawfully do so. I have some issues with 30 round magazines, simply because an experienced shooter does not need them. The experienced shooter (recreational) can switch out an empty mag for a loaded one without missing a beat. It's the inexperienced, angry shooters I have a problem with having these mags, period. That said, guns and magazines should not turn into a money-infused fight between the two political parties.

Until our elected people . . . ALL of them . . . stop engaging in party politics and taking money from lobbyists who push an agenda using a bulldozer covered in money, nothing meaningful will get done.

There are far too many voices in the room.

Dear Dispatchers (ours and all others) . . .

This week is your recognition week. It's called Telecommunicators' Week. (I apologize for the humor in advance, but are the police now Mope Neutralization Engineers? Okay, I'm done.)

We are very thankful for all of you for various reasons. First and foremost, thanks for putting up with the firefighters you have to deal with. They are so much more high maintenance than we police officers.

Now, to the real thanks:

• Thanks for dealing with people who dial 911 because their french fries are cold.

• Thanks for your calm demeanor when the assault victim calls, screaming, and all we really need is an address so we can get there to help.

• Thanks for taking calls from dying people and giving them reassurance.

• Thanks for dealing with us police officers. That is not an easy task, particularly when we are on the radio asking you to do everything EXCEPT answer your phone—like finding people, addresses or contact numbers for an alarm drop on a person whose last known address is from 17 years ago.

• Thanks for doing 29 things at once, including talking on the radio, talking on the phone, entering info to get to us on the in-car computers . . . all while working in a room that is far too small and never the correct temperature.

On behalf of police officers everywhere, most of whom I am not licensed to speak for (although I'm sure they won't mind) . . .

A great big thank you with our love to all of our "telecommunications" people, our dispatchers.

—Chief

The murders

I don't talk about the triple homicide much. It gets to me, still. I often thought about having a community meeting when the case was over, just to fill everyone in on the details. Frankly, I'm not sure I could make it through a question-and-answer in a public forum. It is an emotional thing.

On January 21, 2005, I got the call at about 8:30 p.m. I was at home with my family, watching a movie. Sgt. Knarr and another officer, who has since left, were on duty. They got the call from dispatch advising a man had just shot and killed his girlfriend and her seven-year-old son. The suspect had reportedly left the residence in his truck. The officers were on their way there when Sgt. Knarr was called off, to go to another location for a man dressed in "camo" who had held two people hostage at gunpoint and then let them go . . . so, two officers, two different calls. Both mutual-aided other agencies for help. We were assisted on the original call by the Sheriff's Office; Sgt. Knarr was aided by Tallmadge and KSU police.

Our officer on the first scene arrived and noticed the truck was still there. When back-up arrived, the two officers searched the area. Through the back bedroom window they saw an unimaginable sight. The mother and son were both dead from multiple gunshot wounds. On the other scene, Sgt. Knarr and the other officers were taking direct gunfire from the suspect . . . the same guy who had just killed a mother and her child. He had left the house on foot, well-armed. I had arrived at the first scene and heard my sergeant and officers, one an old friend from Tallmadge PD, getting shot at by this mope. I had called the SWAT team on the way in and told our dispatchers (who were awesome during this entire incident) to find me more cops from anywhere they could. We secured the first scene and set perimeters on the gunman. When radios were used near the gunman, I could hear the shots being fired over the open microphones. He fired hundreds of rounds at us that night.

The gunman eventually entered the apartment of a 22 year-old college student. He took her hostage and forced her to call 911. We negotiated with him and he told us he needed two hours to make some calls and settle some things. He said after that, he would let her go and kill himself. That was fine with me. After we made the agreement, he hung up the phone and shot her. When I interviewed him later, he stated he did that to "find a way out of the house and escape, if there was one."

I made the decision to have the SWAT team enter the house just before daylight. The suspect had been shooting at officers all night and we could not subject surrounding houses to gunfire. The SWAT team arrested him in an upstairs bathroom. Both guns were found with him. He had been subjected to a few hours of tear gas. During the trial, his attorney lacked honor. My opinion, only. There were stories made up about me, the police and also the victims. The subject and his attorney said he was abused by officers after his arrest, which was an outright lie. They said I authorized a "sniper" to enter the residence, which was also an outright lie. Believe me, if one sniper advised me that he had a clear shot, I would have green-lighted that without thinking twice. It never happened.

So, in spite of stories in the papers or those spun by attorneys and murderers, you have a glimpse of what happened those two days. It was horrific for all of those involved. I cannot fathom the loss felt by the families . . . and won't even speculate. Two of the victims are in the cemetery behind the police department. We chat regularly.

And my heart hurts for them every single day.

"The hottest places in Hell are reserved for those who remain neutral in time of great moral crisis."

—Dante Alighieri

January 21st

January 21st. There are a select group of people who will always look back and reflect on the happenings in Brimfield on that particular date in 2005. I will until my last day on earth. I know many, many family members who will also. Along with other police officers, dispatchers, residents, potential victims, doctors, nurses, attorneys . . . the list goes on.

Since starting the Facebook page, we have taken January 21 as a breather from being funny, sarcastic and generally displaying the wittiness that endears us to the ladies. Will we do so again today, for the rest of the day, in honor of Renee, Dakota and Sarah, who were all the victims of an ignorant control freak on January 21, 2005. This man, whose name is not worthy of ever being mentioned in the same breath as the victims, is on death row now. He was found guilty of shooting all three, in addition to other crimes. I will attend his execution, if the appeals process ever finishes, and I will pray every day that my face is the last he sees before meeting his maker. This morning, I would like to offer some thanks . . .

- To our dispatchers that night, Kat and Nikki . . . you two did the best job imaginable under these conditions. You had a lot to handle for a long period of time. You both are class acts. We love you.
- To our negotiators from SWAT and OHSP . . . Mike and Rick. Both of you were absolutely wonderful. You consoled a hostage and dealt with a jackass who counted on having the upper hand. We know now what a coward he was—one who shoots women and children. You both are fantastic human beings.
- To members of SWAT in all of the jurisdictions who responded . . . Thanks for being here that night. Thanks for lying in a foot of snow, in 8 degree weather, for hours on end.
- To Sgt. Knarr, Mike, Jeff and Bernie . . . Thanks for walking face first towards gunfire. You faced a well-trained gunman and never flinched. He could fire indiscriminately in any direction. You four could not, because of homes and people. Sports players are not heroes; officers like you are.

Heroin

Folks . . . we have a problem.

I'm not an alarmist by any stretch. Swine flu, West Nile, pandemic this, pandemic that; I keep moving and working and sometimes spray "OFF" when I am outside. You can't stop living to avoid dying.

But for the first time since I have been a police officer, I am concerned about what is or could be an epidemic: Heroin. It's bad, and I am nowhere near exaggeration in that statement.

Ten years ago, if a K-9 alerted on a vehicle, indicating there were drugs present, I would have guessed there was an 80% chance the drugs in the vehicle were marijuana or cocaine. Today, if a dog hits, I will give you 50/50 odds on the drug being heroin. We have seen more heroin in the last two years than in my prior 18 years in police work, including five years working undercover and buying drugs.

So far this year my officers have seized more dirty needles, burned spoons, cotton balls and heroin than in any prior year. We had two heroin-related arrests yesterday, and nine this month already. We have had seven overdose calls in the last 18 months. Yesterday we found 50+ used (dirty) needles in one user's bedroom.

This drug gets a grip on people and refuses to let go. When it has someone hooked, that someone turns into a person his or her loved ones do not recognize. The person will steal, use someone's identity, hurt loved ones and engage in prostitution to feed the habit. If the habit is not fed, the person becomes physically ill . . . and I mean SICK. When the addiction reaches that point, users are only using in order to not be sick. They have to use heroin in order to live a "normal" life.

I'm a hard core anti-crime guy. I am not giving the users a pass on this by justifying their behavior. They and they alone are responsible for making the decision to jab a needle in their arms and escape the world we live in. It is their choice. The biggest issue I have with the entire mess is the collateral damage they leave. Regular heroin, crack and meth users cannot maintain employment, so they resort to burglary, theft, forgery and other crimes, making all of us potential victims. They steal from our houses, our cars, our stores and businesses. They solicit for sex and bring that risk into our neighborhoods. I know

... another "victimless crime" ... until your neighbor has a parade of customers stopping by. Then it's an issue.

I know what we will do on our end, in our little corner of the world. We will continue to take the fight to the dealers ... and the addicts. Although they are different in nature, they both bring risk to the community.

We need your help, too. We need you to talk to your children and loved ones. They need to know the risk associated and present with this drug. They need to understand that when heroin gets a hold of them they will be in a very real fight which could cost them their lives or freedom. You all are our eyes and ears. Use our smartphone app, email, telephone or tie a note to a rock and throw it through my office window. Get us any information you have. If you see something that looks suspicious, looks like drug activity, drug use or the byproduct of one of these (thefts, etc.) get us any info you have.

The "cure" is education, enforcement and discussion. Heads out of sand, please. We need the "anywhere but here" attitude in every community in the world.

Let's get moving on this.

"One problem with gazing too frequently into the past is that we may turn around to find the future has run out on us."

—Michael Cibenko

AFTERNOON SHIFT . . . An intoxicated driver pulled into a business on SR43 . . . and just kept driving. He drove through the lot, beside the building, out of the lot and into the swamp. Unlike military-type vehicles, his Cadillac was not meant to . . . float.

Sgt. Knarr and his frogman, Officer Putnam, waded in and retrieved the driver from the vehicle. During field sobriety tests, the driver page homage to E.T. by following Sgt. Knarr's finger with his own finger instead of using his eyes. Land sakes!

Oh, and the driver also was chowing down on some tasty fried chicken when he drove into the swamp.

He was arrested for OVI (DUI, DWI for you old-school folks) and transported to headquarters. He tested a .206% BAC. He went to the bed and breakfast, where they only give one aspirin per headache.

By the way, Sergeant Knarr may have uttered a combination of words never before said by a police officer. When approaching the vehicle—and standing in knee-deep water in 10-degree temperatures—Sgt. Knarr could be heard several times saying:

"Sir, put down the chicken . . . and get out of the vehicle . . . Sir . . . put down the chicken and get out of the car . . . "

AFTERNOON SHIFT . . . Sgt. Knarr (K-9 Havoc) and Officer Putnam (K-9 Nitro), proving to all of us that they just cannot mind their own business . . . Officers saw a vehicle at one of our hotels. The vehicle is associated with a person who has a couple warrants, including one for felony robbery from the Tallmadge PD. Knarr and Putnam went to the room, which was registered to the person who has the warrants. The dynamic duo heard voices inside the room—in addition to the television. After they knocked and said "police department," the conversation inside the room stopped . . . and the TV volume became really low. In police work, that is called a clue.

After several tense minutes of negotiation, the mope's girlfriend opened the door. The subject was arrested, as was his girlfriend . . . who also had warrants.

Mopes . . . although we love visitors, we are not a "weekend getaway" or place to hide because you have warrants for your arrest. If you stay here, we will visit.

NO MOPES ALLOWED

Fame

Just about every day, someone posts, sends an email or tells me in person . . . "You are famous." I have some ideas on that concept.

• I do not care about fame. Not one bit. I may not operate as most chiefs do, but I am not most chiefs. I am going to make as much noise as possible about criminal behavior. I am going to publicly commend my sergeants and officers every chance I get. They deserve it.

• Elvis was/is famous. I have yet to sell one CD. I do sing a nice rendition of "Suspicious Minds," though . . . usually while I'm driving.

• I do not call the press, unless I need to tease them about something. Most of them have my cell number and are not shy about using it. I am very, very public about what we do. Our residents should know what we see, hear and experience. Even if it involves women's unmentionables. When we post stories, I get calls. I like most of the media I have met, so I share.

• I wake up in the morning, get dressed and come to work like most everyone else. When I get home, my kids are not impressed with the "Internet sensation." Actually, they tease me and I become humble. Quickly.

• No amount of TV or radio interviews, newspaper articles or T-shirts can change who I am. I believe people have the right to move about freely without being the victim of mopery, and own stuff without having to worry about that stuff ending up at a pawnshop. I also like John Wayne movies, bluegrass music and dogs. I do not like boring meetings, because I get restless.

In a nutshell, I have certain beliefs about how we should treat each other. If I have a nice TV because I work hard and like to watch westerns, a mope should not steal my TV. A mope should work hard and buy his own TV, so he can watch "Moonshiners," "Honey Boo Boo" or whatever else he would like to watch.

I don't want the three dollars in change I have in my truck stolen while I sleep. That is my coffee money. If you want coffee money, work for it. I also do not want my children or the children in this community to worry about their safety. I don't want parents to worry either. So, as a department, we take the fight to the bad guys.

With all of these things said, if people want to talk about them, write about them or interview me about them . . . good. Maybe the idea will catch on.

It's not about fame. It's about doing what is right.

STORY TIME . . . Once upon a time there was a truck driver. He stopped at one of our businesses that allow parking for big trucks. He also had a little vehicle (carriage) at his disposal and decided to wander off in search of his princess.

His search led him to a place where potential princesses gather. These princesses dance and gyrate for princes while wearing very little . . . or no . . . clothing. The princes pay the princesses-in-training, usually in one-dollar increments. The prince met a female, who he desired to take back to his castle on wheels. The two left the enchanted exotic dance castle on a journey to . . . the truck lot. Oh, and the princess had been drinking NUMEROUS spirited beverages. She was tipsy.

The prince and princess spent some time together in the castle on wheels. It was at this time the prince realized he may not have his soul mate. Alas, when the prince was without pants, the princess fled the area in his little carriage . . . Yep, she stole his car. YIKES!

Never fear, dear readers . . . the local peace-keepers were in the area. The Sergeant of the shift, Sir Sergeant Matthew McCarty of Brimfield, saw the princess and vehicle and caused her to stop.

The stripper was arrested for stealing the car and driving while drunk . . . and we aren't sure if any of them, except for us, are living happily ever after.

Nice job Sgt. McCarty, Officer Atha and Officer Allen.

"The respect that leadership must have requires that one's ethics be without question. A leader not only stays above the line between right and wrong, he stays well clear of the gray areas."

—G. Alan Bernard

Gun control

I get lots of emails and messages every day asking me if I will support the federal government taking away guns. The questions are pretty point blank (pun intended) and usually ask "Will you defy the constitution and enforce unconstitutional laws and confiscate guns if told to do so by the federal government?" Yikes. Both sides sure are worked up over guns. I have found if you are too hot for anything, you can be blinded by passion, anger and hyperbole.

I've been around for a minute or two in law enforcement. I have seen these battles and heard these words lots of times. The old "pry my gun from my cold dead hands" surfaced first in 1976 and again in 2000. Both sides like getting everyone whipped into a frenzy. There is a LOT of money being spent right now, all to get the attention of one side or another. We have the "they are going to take our guns" side versus the "guns are evil and kill people" side. Both sides are pretty susceptible to being sucked into a battle that isn't as bad as it seems. I don't get involved. I watch and feel kind of sad over friends and countrymen (and women) fussing.

Here's the skinny, from one small town police chief, in one little corner of a huge planet. People are the problem. I can rattle off scores of serial killers who never killed any of their victims with a gun. So, let's ban serial killers . . . oops, never mind . . . we have done that already. Yes, there are people who commit rampage or revenge killings with guns. What do these people have in common with serial killers who never used a gun, yet killed lots of other people? Mental illness.

Guns are not evil. Guns are inanimate objects. So are knives, meth labs and rockets. People are the problem. Mentally ill people with guns . . . problem. Until we start caring, and I stress TRULY caring for people who have a thought process that isn't "firing right," we will suffer as a society.

To my friends on both sides of the debate . . . relax. Don't get duped into believing everything your side offers without proper research. There are dollars being thrown at this every second of the day. No one is going to "take your guns." There are also not thousands of "crazy" gun owners the "other side" should be fearful of. If you want to correct some of the problem, concentrate on mental illness . . . oh yeah . . . and all of the CRIMINALS, felons and drug dealers who buy black-market guns and are killing each other at a record rate.

No matter how stringent the rules, someone is always ready to break them.

MIDNIGHTS . . . Mopes, I have a word of advice from Sgt. Adkins. He says if you are going to steal something from a business and then run out of that business in an attempt to flee . . . DO NOT HIDE NEXT TO THE MARKED POLICE CAR. Particularly the one that is marked "Caution, Police K-9."

Sgt. Adkins happened to be in one of the "casino" lots last night, when a female came running out the door and hid behind the police vehicle containing Sgt. Adkins and K-9 Joker. Joker barks at strangers. Loudly. The female had just stolen a cell phone from inside the store. She was arrested and taken to the Brimfield Police "Home for Wayward Mopes."

Parents, please encourage your children to play outside more. The concept of "Hide and Seek" may need some review.

The Brimfield Police Department Reaches 30,000 "Likes"

We may need a bigger place for our summer picnic . . .

School safety

Today it is one year since the killings at Chardon High School. Our thoughts and prayers go out to the families who lost loved ones.

Sometimes when the police talk about school safety or just safety in general, some who don't think things through accuse us of being "fear mongers" and hyping up what they perceive to be rare occurrences or anomalies in law enforcement. That is particularly true with school shootings. "It won't happen here." Here is my advice to those people . . . take a hike. A long one.

In 2004 when I became chief of police, if you had told me we were going to have a rampage shooter within the next 10 months and he would kill three people, I would have doubted it. Who expects a shooting at THEIR schools? Did Chardon, Sandy Hook, Columbine, Nickel Mines, Virginia Tech or any other school expect it? Probably not. Expectations and preparations are very different. The police and school staff in Chardon were most definitely prepared and their training and preparation showed that day. They are all class acts.

Being prepared is not being a "fear monger." I am the chief law enforcement officer in this jurisdiction. It is my duty and obligation to prepare for the worst, and to PREVENT it, of possible. Putting policies and procedures in place, training officers and school staff and students is not instilling fear in them. It is encouraging them to not be a victim and displaying that this police department is always training, studying and preparing.

If suspicious people are observed around the schools, we will ask them questions. If threats are received, we will act on them. We are constantly on the lookout for danger from the outside and from within. We still need parents to be involved. As I have said before, check Facebook and Twitter accounts. Read texts and emails. Your children should NOT have important secrets or "hidden" events they keep from you—at least not ones concerning violence, firearms, bombs and other weapons. Don't be THAT parent. Don't be the parent who lets life pass while their child is posting rants and threats on social media sites or snapping pictures holding guns. All of this is not to make people fearful; it is to empower them. Ignoring the dangers in our society does not make those dangers go away. As with everything we do here, there will be open conversation about the risks to our residents, schools and our 2,000+ students, all of whom we love.

We owe each victim ever killed during school violence one thing, and that is to learn from those incidents.

AFTERNOON SHIFT . . . Officers Putnam, Gramlich and Sergeant Knarr were called to an area "watering hole" for a subject who was highly intoxicated and disorderly. He may have made comments about "killing people." After spending a few short quality minutes with the subject, it was determined he needed to be arrested. His ability to reason was not available.

After his arrest and transport to the BPD mope holding area, he made the decision to launch a saliva projectile at Officer Putnam. He also made the decision to assault Sgt. Knarr. I stopped by long enough to lend a hand and have him mistakenly call me by a first name beginning with the letter "F", along with some other slurred names.

His alcohol-induced disorderly charge became assault on an officer . . . times 2.

He is at the county bed and breakfast, looking forward to scrambled eggs and toast for that morning hangover. We hope the cell doors "going clank" sound during the night does not make that headache any worse. Nice job to all officers . . . way to keep your composure.

The Brimfield Police Department Reaches 34,000 "Likes"

We hope you ALL don't bring baked beans to the picnic . . .

"If you want children to keep their feet on the ground, put some responsibility on their shoulders."

—Abigail Van Buren

MIDNIGHTS . . . From the "Am I really seeing this?" files . . . Officer Atha was checking our businesses, as usual. He observed a van with a male inside, parked in a closed business. Officer Atha made contact with the male driver to determine why he was parked in a closed business.

After the normal routine of "Why are you harassing me?" and "I have rights," Officer Atha kindly explained to the subject that the business was closed. The subject told the officer he was having some relationship problems and was using available wifi to pass the time. Officer Atha explained we have thefts at nighttime and told the person to move along and away from a closed business. Easy enough; he moved on.

A short while later, while on patrol, Officer Atha observed the vehicle and same subject leaving another closed business at which we have had lots of metal thefts. Officer Atha traffic-stopped the vehicle, exited his vehicle and approached . . . and probably wished he had not.

When Officer Atha made contact with the driver he immediately noticed the driver was without pants. He also immediately noticed that the undergarments worn by the subject were not designed for or intended to be worn by males. Yes, he was in ladies' underwear. No pants.

After a lengthy conversation and consent search of the vehicle (which contained . . . adult . . . um . . . paraphernalia), the subject was warned to leave the area and not return, unless businesses were open for business—not for free WIFI access during really dark hours. We have his info, as do most of our surrounding departments now.

Officer Atha is still walking around the department, mumbling.

OVERHEARD AT THE BPD . . . Nice job to Sgt. McCarty on handling the very intoxicated female yesterday morning at a hotel. She ended up in adult time out. They had this exchange . . .

Sgt. McCarty: "Ma'am, you have to go to your room or we are going to arrest you." (She was knocking on room doors.)

Woman: "Okay . . . Bring me a jar of peanut butter, a large coffee and turn on my television."

Sgt. McCarty: "Ma'am . . . I'm not the bell boy."

Woman: "You're not?"

Sounding off on the bronze statue

Our local paper here is the Record-Courier. It is the epitome of the hometown paper concept. The people who work there are nice. I enjoy working with all of them. The only thing I dislike about the paper is the "Sound Off" section. People can call or email their opinions and the paper publishes those opinions. Oh . . . and you can remain anonymous.

It's the journalistic equivalent of a drive-by shooting.

In today's Sound Off, as on many days, a coward offered an opinion about good ol' me. This miscreant isn't too pleased with the T-shirt and coffee mug sales, particularly because my face is on them, I suppose. He or she says my job is supposed to be "about protect and serve, not self serve" and offered that the next thing I would want is a bronze statue of me.

I think that is a great idea.

I would like a bronze statue of me, for one purpose. When it is erected in front of the police department, I will invite the person with "keyboard courage" to come on over to my statue and kiss my bronze butt. Pucker up, buttercup. Knucklehead, in case you missed every newscast in northern Ohio for the last two months, the money from sales of merchandise from the BPD goes towards school security. So far we have installed panic buttons in all five buildings. Next up are the cameras and intercoms. The Oliver paycheck doesn't change. I get no money from any of this, nor would I take it. I am a public servant. I serve the public. It is not my chosen profession, it is my way of life. I would much rather NOT see T-shirts and coffee mugs with my face on them; it's kind of . . . weird. However, those who do this for a living believed it would fit nicely because my face is funny, I guess. Just like our page.

So I will await that bronze statue. The coward should bring some ChapStick.

Dear Meth Cooks,

I know you both only just got arrested. However, I have to strike while the iron is hot.

You made some errors while driving through town today. I would like to assist you by doing a little debriefing of your mopery.

First, you broke one of the cardinal rules of criminality: Don't speed or commit other driving infractions when you are "driving dirty." You want to be inconspicuous. The object is to NOT be arrested.

Second, use your turn signals. See rule #1 about driving dirty.

Third, we know most of the people who live in our community. If we don't know them by name, we know their houses and vehicles. We drive around on patrol every day and learn which vehicle belongs at which house. This plays into your mistake. It's like the old "Sesame Street" song: "One of these things just doesn't belong." When you try to duck us by pulling into a driveway where you do not live and do not belong, that's a clue in police work. Hiding in plain sight only works for car keys and the cable remote; never for mopes. Try wearing camo pants and dressing like a bush next time.

Last, I would like to thank Officers Gramlich and Putnam for their traffic stop and for arresting you. It sounds harsh to thank them, but sooner or later you meth "Iron Chefs" have to realize that you are driving around with explosives. You are endangering more than just yourselves when you pull stunts like the "ol' mobile meth lab" trick.

Well . . . that's about it. Enjoy your stay at the bed and breakfast. You will be there over Memorial Day, while the rest of us honor our fallen military heroes. I'm sure when they were storming beaches and taking incoming fire, the last thing they were thinking was, "I hope they enjoy their meth back home."

Thanks for contributing nothing to society. Enjoy the orange jumpsuits, anti-skid slippers . . . and the oatmeal.

—Chief

IN THE SCHOOLS . . . We have sold enough "No Mopes" merchandise to cover the installation of the "panic buttons" in all five school buildings. All of these have been installed and are operational. If there is a threat, staff can alert us without picking up a phone. And the alarms ring straight to dispatch . . . there is no middle company fielding the alert.

IN THE SCHOOLS . . . Well . . . The panic buttons at the elementary school are in fine working order. We are sure of it—and so is one of the adult office work-ers, who thought the button was to open the door leading into the office from the lobby. She was embarrassed to find cops falling out of the sky, all over the building. No worries; as with all new systems, there is some trial and . . . "What's this button for?" errors. We will call it a high-speed training and preparedness exercise. We have to keep the machine oiled and working . . . and at least one officer may need to change his shorts.

IN THE SCHOOLS . . . This morning, outside of one of our schools, a nice little lady approached me. If this is your daughter . . . you are doing a great thing as a parent.

Girl: "Chief, I have a question for you."

Chief: "I have an answer, sweetie."

Girl: "Could you please put (name not used) on your list and take him to Shop-with-a-Cop . . . he really needs it."

Chief: (again rendered speechless by a child)

Girl: "He is really nice to everyone but could use some help."

Chief: "He is now on the list. Thank you for looking out for him."

Girl hugs chief . . . chief hugs back.

She is younger than 10, I believe . . . with a great heart.

IN THE SCHOOLS . . . A very nice anonymous lady just left the department. She read here on our page and in the paper about our new program for back-to-school shopping for our school-aged kids. She brought us a $1,000 check to kick off the program. The check was written in honor of her husband, who passed away in December. I'm not going to be shy about this; she received a HUGE, HUGE chief hug . . . HUGE hug. We all thank her.

Our first 10 kids are paid for. This will be our first year doing this program. We are attempting to take at least 50 kids who may need some help buying some school clothes, shoes, socks, book bags, supplies . . . you get the idea.

Weed

Today I posted about a little over a half-pound of weed recovered by officers last night. The driver was driving under suspension, was stopped for a moving violation and subsequently arrested . . . and the weed aficionados came out of the woodwork like a swarm of locusts.

Here's the deal, weed smokers: It's illegal. Whether it is legal in Colorado, Oregon or the planet Mars, it's illegal in Ohio. At this agency, we do not and cannot operate on "should be legal," "will be legal" or "arrest someone who is committing a real crime." In Ohio, trafficking in marijuana is a real crime. It's in the 2925 section of the Ohio Revised Code.

Police work isn't fishing. We don't troll around catching people and throwing the ones who "aren't committing real crimes" back in the lake. This guy had 14 ounces of weed—at an ELEMENTARY SCHOOL! So, while some of you weed proponents may be in favor of legalizing it, do you let your fourth grader smoke with you? Why not? It's "safe" and from "mother earth," right?

I realize some of this may seem like a direct attack on weed smokers. I am a fairly easygoing dude. What gets to me is your willingness to attack good law enforcement with arguments about legalization and "wasting tax dollars" by enforcing laws. My oath of office didn't read that I would enforce all laws except for ones that you don't like. So, although the law may change . . . it hasn't.

Lastly, PLEASE do not start the "non-violent drug offenders in prison" nonsense with me. While I will give points to weed smokers for usually not being violent, the traffickers are, and I have witnessed it personally. Drug dealers are usually armed and willing to, at the minimum, let you know they are. There are drug-related shootings all over the U.S. on a daily basis.

And most weed dealers never see the inside of a prison. Most are on probation and spend a year or two trying to figure out how to beat a urine test. If they had studied for the math or science test as hard as the urine test, we could have cured cancer by now.

Marijuana is illegal, at least for now. It is a drug. We are the police. You expect quarter here . . . for real?

OVERHEARD AT THE BPD . . . Conversation with lost travelers from New York state this morning, after pulling up to the vehicle . . . at 4:30 a.m. . . .

Female: "We're lost."

Chief: "I can tell. Where are you trying to go?"

Female: "To southern Ohio."

Chief: "You missed . . . but you did get to northern Ohio. You're in Brimfield, Ohio."

Female: "How do we get to southern Ohio from here?"

Chief (jokingly): "You head south . . . "

Female: "You're the chief? In Brimfield?"

Chief: "Yes. But only until someone discovers they made a mistake. It's taking longer than I thought."

Female: "We follow you on Facebook!"

Chief: "Yikes."

So, two girls, a mom and dad received a hug this morning, on the side of the road . . . at 4:40 a.m. The girls may have received some stuffed animals. Driving with a furry friend is always more fun.

We all thought it was humorous that they landed in Brimfield by accident. It makes me wonder why I woke up at 3 a.m. and decided to just come to work . . .

Go figure.

The Brimfield Police Department Reaches 36,000 "Likes"

Can we have the taller people move to the back, please? . . . We weren't expecting such a big crowd . . .

On kids driving

It's been a rough week in northeast Ohio. Field schools lost a recent graduate to a traffic crash last week. We had another roll-over crash Saturday evening, involving young drivers. In Warren, six young people were killed when the vehicle they were riding in lost control, flipped and ended up in a pond, under water. There were eight in that vehicle; two survived.

To the families of all of the victims and to all of the police, fire, medics and dispatchers who dealt with those events . . . our thoughts and prayers are for you.

The hand of fate is exactly that. There are things we cannot avoid, no matter how hard we try. There are events we fear as parents. Losing a child is at the top of that list, and an unimaginable circumstance.

Parents . . . take some time to review safe driving with your children. The 16-21 years of age group is very vulnerable to distracted driving, speeding and "over correcting" when driving off of the side of the road. Explain the dangers of being distracted while behind the wheel. Distractions come in many forms . . . cell phones, passengers, jamming to Vanilla Ice or Poison . . . and all should be avoided. Speed has long been a factor in many fatal crashes. Over-correcting was a factor in at least one of these crashes. This occurs when the driver suddenly realizes the car is going off the right side of the roadway, and "yanks" the wheel too fast and too far the other direction, causing the vehicle to flip. It happens a lot with young drivers.

Most importantly, explain to them how precious life is and how, during one brief moment, it all changes. Keep the passengers in their vehicles to a minimum, and keep on them constantly . . . and we will, too.

Oh . . . and regardless of how frustrated they make us; tell them you love them every time they leave.

"Few men think, yet all will have opinions."

—George Berkele

Death notifications

MADD just sent me an email. I love my ladies (and gentlemen) from our local MADD chapter. They are great huggers. The email they sent was for some training the organization is offering for police personnel. The title of the course . . . "Death Notifications."

When I started in law enforcement, we didn't have a death notification course. We sent the guy with the rank or the gift of gab. I usually had one or both, so I have done my share of giving bad news . . . at least 15 of those talks, to the best of my recollection. I also think I went because of my propensity to give hugs. I always felt as if I needed to be the one to tell the family.

Guess why I am babbling about MADD and death notifications? Yep . . . St. Patrick's Day. One of the biggest drinking and driving days of the year. It's ironic that officers all over will be reading about available training on Death Notifications, sponsored by an organization whose membership is comprised of family members who have been the recipients of that very same "death talk." It gives me chills.

This weekend, please do NOT drink and drive. There is no reason for it. Being very blunt . . . you are absolutely ignorant if you get behind the wheel while "buzzed" or intoxicated. When (not if) you are stopped, you will be field tested and arrested if you are impaired. Your vehicle will be towed and you will be taken in handcuffs to the BPD or another fine agency. You will be asked to submit to a breath test, booked . . . complete with photo . . . and have to post bond. By the time it is all done, including court and attorney fees, you will be well over $5,000.

Me, my officers and officers all over the United States and the planet Earth are just TIRED of delivering bad news. We are just tired of hearing the screams and seeing the tears. We do not want to attempt to console the inconsolable. We do not want to tell mothers and fathers their sons or daughters are dead.

Please, drive sober or find a ride. Today, this weekend and every day.

Dear Drunk Driver,

Thanks for the call today, but it's not my problem. You should have thought about all of this before you made the CHOICE to drive drunk. You drove in from out of town, went a campus bar in the area, got hammered like a piece of wood on a home makeover and made a choice to drive drunk.

Luckily, my officers caught you before you killed someone . . . or yourself. So your litany of grievances and complaints are not my problem. Some advice:

• I'm sorry you live 50 miles away. You should hang out at home more. Home is good. You can put on some scrubby clothes, watch some TV . . .

• It is not my worry that we impounded your car. I could not care less if you have to WALK here to retrieve it; just be sober and bring a valid driver because you have a suspended license.

• You are kind of whiny. I'm not sure if anyone has ever told you that. It is NOT on us that you might lose your job, your wife is mad and you cannot find anyone to bring you to court or drive you here to get your car. Leave your car here, for all I care. I will auction it and send the money to MADD.

• You need to accept some personal responsibility for your actions. You drank, you drove, we arrested. Your actions caused a reaction. Change your actions.

• No, you did not "pass the field tests," as evidenced by your damn near causing the BAC machine to die from alcohol poisoning. Your driving sucked, your field tests looked like me attempting to break dance . . . By the way, what did you think of our new holding cells? We love them; they're just so roomy . . .

• Sorry you made us arrest you. I am also sorry for the financial hit you will be taking over this incident. I am not sorry we took you off of the street before you hit a high school kid coming from a game or date . . . I have had to take the long walk to the front porch to give par-

MORE...

ents THAT bad news, which is why we are so vigilant in our efforts to catch drunk drivers. We may have avoided a family having a real-life nightmare and we may have helped you avoid committing an act you would have had to relive for the rest of your life.

Think of it as an intervention, with a smile . . .

—Chief

CHANGES AT THE BPD . . . Effective March 17th, Sgt. Chris Adkins will be known as . . . Captain Chris Adkins. Chris, who was just promoted, will assume the duties of second-command of the department. His partner, K-9 Joker, who is now seven years old, will be retiring sometime in the next couple of months. Joker will continue to live with Chris during retirement . . . and likely still chew on things when Chris is not home. We can't confirm, but we also think Joker makes is own lunch. Congratulations to Chris!

WEATHER REPORT . . . I detailed the police vehicle yesterday. Today, it will rain. Life is a continuous cycle of being the windshield, being the bug . . . We set the clocks ahead one hour over the weekend. I gained the hour back trying to figure out how to set the clock in the truck. We are now flush. I am going to set it once a week now, just to prepare for the real thing twice a year. My own little event in the Olympics of life.

MIDNIGHTS . . . Officers were called to a residence on Old Forge via 911. When Sgt. McCarty and Officer Dumont arrived on scene, they were greeted by a person holding a shotgun. The "ouchy end" was pointed towards officers, who in turn pointed the business ends of their weapons towards him. After a few tense seconds, the tie ended. No one in the house knew who or why 911 was dialed. It may be a mystery akin to the Bermuda Triangle. The man with the shotgun said he "thought" we were "burglars." Nice.

"The reason women don't play football is because eleven of them would never wear the same outfit in public."

—Phyllis Diller

"Low-level" and "non-violent" drug offenders

Often people post on our page about "low-level" and/or non-violent drug offenders. Their offering is usually about the overcrowding of our jails due to the incarceration of "low-level or non-violent drug offenders" . . . and it's not true. It was true in 1994, but not in 2013.

The Bureau of Justice Statistics' most recent study tells us that less then 23% of the prison population, both federal and state, is comprised of drug offenders. Those are drug dealers and those who possessed large amounts of drugs and could not sell the jury on "personal use." Some may fall under the "three strike" rules of some states. Mostly, people just are not going to jail or prison for users' amounts of drugs. Heck, most "low-level" drug dealers get probation unless the judge sees them one time too many.

Here's the opinion that may rub some of you the wrong way . . . so, heads up.

Drugs are illegal. If you violate a law or laws multiple times, you SHOULD be in jail or prison. First-time drug offenders usually do NOT go to jail. Read: first-time offenders. That being offered, if you get arrested a second time, see you in 1-3 years. I do not care to hear "non-violent" or "low-level" attached to a crime. Who here wants drug dealers living next to them? Embezzlers and other monetary offenders are non-violent too. However, no one is tripping over themselves complaining about Bernie Madoff being in jail, and he was a non-violent, first-time offender.

My opinion is simply this . . . we have to stop being desensitized by the constant barrage of information about drugs not being serious. Drugs are serious. Drug sales and abuse leads to burglaries, thefts, rapes, human trafficking and a bevy of other societal woes. Legalizing drugs is not the answer either, unless you are also providing a government sponsored debit card for those who are addicted to buy the drugs. Their addiction keeps them from keeping gainful employment.

My opinion is that we have become too soft on drugs, because many believe the offenses are not serious. How is that working out for us?

"Asking for it"

I know. I always have something to say.

A recent case in Steubenville made national news. Athletes, alcohol, parties . . . yikes. I am going to offer one thing on this and only one perspective. I'm not narrow minded, old school (okay, maybe a little old school) or anything else you want to label me. I just have a very defined belief matrix. One firm belief is this: No one "deserves" to be raped. I do not care to hear bad things about any victim—if they had been drinking, if they had a "past." I do not care nor do I want any justification for sexual assault.

I have been asked at least two dozen times to offer my opinion on what happened in Steubenville. The easy answer . . . I don't know. I do know that in ANY sexual assault situation, people do not get a pass for playing sports (or being politicians, cops or famous). I also know that a 16 year-old who has been drinking cannot make decisions regarding what she "wants to do."

I've been around victims my whole life. I will grant you one thing; at times people are responsible for being where they are. But they are never responsible for being attacked by another. Never. Anyone here who did not make a bad decision in their teen years, raise your hand.

Both of my hands are pocketed.

There is nothing a victim can do, no situation a female can "put herself in," which should result in rape. None. A woman can be engaged in prostitution and still reserve the right to say no.

We are a social bunch of citizens. People go out. They go to parties. They dance, they drink. That is not an invitation for unwanted and/or forceful assault . . . it's drinking and dancing. It is not an open door for violence. No is no in a whole bunch of languages. If you are too drunk to say it, it darn well should be understood.

I don't care how a person acts, dresses, talks, walks or dances . . . Sex is always consensual. Rape is not about the act, it is about control and dominance.

There is NEVER and excuse or a situation that results in blame being assigned to the victim.

That is that.

Personal responsibility

We hear a lot about rights nowadays. The right to own guns, speak freely, assemble in protest . . . everyone wants to embrace and exercise these rights. I do, too. I like owning guns and running my mouth. I don't protest much. I kind of shy away from boisterous crowds when I am not working, unless I am at a Browns game.

However, there is a duty or obligation that comes with these rights (and others) that some people seem to not want to acknowledge. It's the theory that dictates we must also observe the rights of others. Our individual rights are no more important than the rights of others. When we exercise our rights and our behavior infringes on the rights of others, it turns into a mess. We have free speech, but we cannot scream "fire!" in a crowded movie theatre. It is that concept.

Last week a drunken driver killed a pregnant mother and two of her children when he crashed into them at an intersection. Recently, a four year-old got a hold of a gun belonging to an adult and shot and killed himself. These are both tragedies, caused by people who failed to adhere to duty and obligation while exercising rights. Now, we know that most drivers and most gun owners are responsible, so don't start hammering away at me about politics. I could not care less about politics and politicians. Most are driven by whoever is providing them with the most campaign dollars. What I care about are victims, and victims usually are victims because someone is not acting in an honorable way.

Here's the boiled down version of this rant . . . If the NRA, Libertarians, Liberals, Conservatives, Independents or any other group do not want rights "whittled away," then we all need to concentrate on personal responsibility. There is NO REASON a person should drive drunk. There is NO REASON a gun should be accessible to a child. As human beings, we should not go through life screaming about rights when we don't care about anyone but ourselves.

Some adults need to act like adults.

Our senior program

There are many things we do here that could make my list of favorites; however, one of the most fun and successful is our "senior check" program.

We started the program about 10 years ago and the reception was sort of . . . slow. Now, as I type this babble, we have enrolled over 600 of our senior residents in our program. The nuts and bolts of the program are fairly simple. We call or check on members of the program monthly . . . some more and some less, depending on their individual situation. If they have family close by, are still married and still getting around okay, they may see us less. If their family is spread out and perhaps they live alone, they have 15 constant BFF's in navy blue.

On April 25th and 26th, we will be hosting another of our senior breakfasts. This one will be at Applebee's. The restaurant donates all of the food and supplies some of their staff. Officers and other volunteers serve the food, pour the coffee and I may give a hug or two . . . or 100. No one hugs like a grandmother. We usually have packed crowds on both days, raffle off some gifts and just have a great time. Did I mention we hug, too?

In addition to checking on our seniors regularly, we host four breakfasts a year and also deliver Christmas bags to all of them. If you have been on this page longer than seven seconds, you know my vision and philosophy on seniors, women and children. Our seniors have paid lots of dues in life. Some of them have paved the way for my generation. Many have been in the military, fought in wars or otherwise contributed to making us better. So, we have an obligation and duty to look out for them.

If you are a senior or know one in Brimfield, call us to get enrolled. We would love to sit and discuss things with you, from your perspective. It's how we learn and become better at what we do. Besides, we love stories. We will also likely have some laughs. Thanks to all of my officers, civilian staff and other volunteers for making this program so successful.

Dear Guys with Drugs and Warrants,

Hey, it's Chief Oliver again. I'm the guy who yelled at you in the parking lot today. I usually don't yell at people, but land sakes, you hit a nerve. Your decision to leave drugs and a used needle on the shelf of a store when you saw me was a horrible decision. Had we not gone back to check the area, a child (or adult) could have had a very bad day.

Drugs are illegal. If you are going to dance, you have to pay the band. Don't ditch your drugs in a location where they can hurt others.

As is my usual custom, here are some other great pointers:

• You two hanging out together is bad. In police work, we call it a "clue." One has multiple warrants for his arrest for burglary, drugs and a used needle; the other just used a false credit card, has meth and a used needle. You dudes need some new friends.

• Mope #2, you were GONE. I watched you drive out of the lot. I had your partner, the other officers were all tied up, and—wham—back into the lot you drove. You are not a valid driver, had meth and needles on you, and had just given a tow truck driver a false credit card number after locking your keys in your ride . . . Yikes. I think of a moth and a light bulb.

• "Am I going to jail?" was a great question. Yes, you are. You had meth and warrants, and you are a mope. Mopery is not illegal, but it IS an indicator of your potential. Welcome to Brimfield.

• Police officers in general are not dumb. We will check the area you were standing in and around. If you drop it, we will find it. You are not smart, we are not stupid . . . It's basic cops and robbers. We learned it at, like, age five.

• "It isn't mine" usually does not work if you are HOLDING it in your hands.

• We are not afraid of your lawyer. We hope he gets paid in advance and doesn't accept a credit card from you; however, he does not scare us.

MORE...

• Last, do us all a favor and stay out of our community.
With no affection and extreme intolerance,
Chief

IN THE SCHOOLS . . . From the BPD "letters we receive" file . . . When the book fair comes to the elementary school, I always pop in and buy some books for kids. Sometimes kids "forget" to bring money. Whatever the case may be, if they want a book, we make sure they get one (or three). On a personal note, I grew up kind of poor and relied on books . . . a lot. So, reading and books are important for me to pass along.

During the most recent book fair, I got some names from the staff and snatched up some kids to take them to get some books. I received a note signed by a couple of my young friends and thought I would share it . . . because it made me laugh.

"Dear Chief Oliver,

Thank you for buying us some books. We also thank you for teaching others not to jump to conclusions (everyone thought we were in trouble!).

Sincerely,
[Names removed]"

An important lesson, indeed. When you see us, it doesn't mean someone is "in trouble."

Maybe we are just doing our thing.

"The real source of almost all our crimes, if the trouble is taken to trace them to a common origin, will be found to be in idleness."

—Walter Gaston Shotwell

Morals

Something has to give. When that something finally gives, I hope the good guys win out.

You may not like this rant. It is not a "holier than thou" soapbox talk. It may shock some of you . . . but I am not an angel. Yep. I said it. Until the last several years of my life I was a mess. I didn't do drugs, drink (I have never had a drink in my life) or break the law; however, I was a tool. Let's just summarize it by saying I lacked character. People change.

Our society is filled with "tools" right now. We have segments of the population who want to legalize drugs. Much of that segment may have missed the field trips to crack houses. I have been in them, when I worked undercover, and it is not a pretty sight. Actually, you question humankind when you witness some of the things that go on there, and in heroin dens and meth labs. We have friends here who believe marijuana is "harmless," yet won't subject their kids to it, so I question "harmless." Go ahead and jump on that one, marijuana friends. I have thick skin.

We are losing our grip on right and wrong in our great country.

People drive drunk and kill others; theft, robberies and burglaries happen too frequently. A teenager is raped by football players, and coaches know about it and do not act. Somehow, we blame the victim. A coach at a major college observes a young boy in what could be a very bad situation, and does not act.

We need Elvis . . . "A little less conversation and a little more action."

Recently in northeast Ohio, a road rage incident resulted in a 50-ish years-old man punching an 80-ish years-old man in the chest. The older gentleman had recently undergone open-heart surgery and died two days later. Who would punch an 80 year-old? That is unacceptable on so many levels my head may explode. Popular culture is losing its way, due to a faulty moral compass. There . . . I said it. Morals.

I am not chirping about religion or politics. I am writing about individuals grasping the concept of being decent. It's a basic concept; however we are slowly drifting away and "tolerating" more and more, because it has become normal.

I do not care to be normal. I sure hope I am succeeding.

Quality of life

I have many friends who offer opinions on quality of life, but it usually applies to when they are going to die. I'm sure you have friends like this too. They give us the old "pull the plug" speech. If they can't have a life of quality, they do not want be resuscitated or on life support. I have no particular opinion on that. I'm too busy living.

There IS a quality of life issue I worry about daily. So do most cops, if they are approaching the job through a service mindset. It's the quality of life of day-to-day living. For me, it's the quality of life of Brimfield residents. These residents live in their homes, raise (or have raised) their children here and deserve to enjoy a good quality of life. That quality of life goal equates to some sleepless nights for me and my officers . . . but that is what we DID sign up for. We signed up to serve and protect. We signed up to chase and catch bad people.

Here is what I believe. I cannot reduce it to one sentence, because it is too complex. I believe you have the expectation of living without being robbed, raped, assaulted or threatened. I believe your TV is yours, not the mope's who breaks into your house while you are WORKING. I believe your house is your castle. I believe no one is allowed in your castle unless you (the King or Queen) allows them in . . . unless you are a criminal and we have a warrant. I believe your car is yours. So is the change in your ashtray, the sunglasses in your cup holder and the CDs in your disorganized catalogue of music. The tools in your garage? Yours. If your wife asks, the bathing suit calendar in your garage is NOT yours . . . it belongs to a friend. It still should not be stolen.

Your children and you expect to have the ability to play in your yard, or a neighbor's yard, without a panel van containing a creeper rolling up and asking them to get in. You should be able to barbeque at your house without being victims. In a better world, doors would be unlocked and mopes would be locked up. People who live here deserve a quality of life . . . a life of quality, not ducking criminals and living in fear.

As long as I am here and have my crew, our mission is to provide the best, most crime-free life of quality for you that we can. If you are the criminal type (and we KNOW the criminal types read our page) your best interest is to ply your trade elsewhere. If you come here and act like a fool, we will arrest you. If you commit a crime here and run, we will pursue you and then arrest you. We have cars and a gas card. We travel.

Spread the word . . . it's about a quality life here.

A PERSONAL NOTE . . . It is an anniversary of sorts . . . nine years ago today I was sworn in as Chief of Police for the Brimfield Police Department. Had you told me when I was sworn in as chief I would make it at least nine years, you would have heard raucous laughter. Thanks to Mike Kostensky and Sue Fields, who were on the Board of Trustees when I was appointed chief . . . and still are. Mike is the liaison to the department and is nuttier than me, which is a lot of fun. I would also like to thank Wyatt Earp, Starsky and Hutch, the cast from "S.W.A.T.," Andy Griffith and the Town of Mayberry, John Wayne, Matt Dillon from "Gunsmoke" . . . and my wife and kids, who have had some long days and nights over the last several years. Lastly, thanks to Chuck Norris, for letting me be chief . . . and allowing me to live.

With Elec Simon and friends at Brimfield Elementary.

On Facebook

Last week, 566,000+ people read at least one post on the BPD page. That post could have been on this page on in your news feed, from sharing a post on your wall.

In 2010, when we started the page, there were some peers and others who asked . . . "Why?" Why does or should a police department need a Facebook page? Once a week or so some misinformed person will post a "Why are you spending time on Facebook?" post and then proceed to tell me what my job is. I love those exchanges.

When I started in the profession, we had one computer in the department. We had no cell phones (nor did most people) and pagers were just coming into vision. During that time, if a chief had been emailing people, it would have likely been considered "playing on the computer." It's 2013 now, and I can post information, real-time, and have it reach anyone and everyone on here in a matter of seconds. Besides, I have a lot to say and a limited number of years on Earth.

When we were approaching 5,000 "likes," some of my officers and I were talking about it being the top end of our reach. That was not even close.

So, on a rainy Sunday in one small corner of a great big world, my officers and I thank you for letting us share our profession with you. Good and bad, we try to let you see what we see and experience some of the heartaches and laughs. We appreciate you being here with us, more than we can express.

It is also nice to have people now wave using all of their fingers instead of just one. Have a great evening . . . Chief Oliver

"Politicians are people who, when they see light at the end of the tunnel, go out and buy some more tunnel."

—John Quinton

Dear Heroin User,

He could have died. If it were not for the great work by the BFD medics, he would have. So let's replay this entire event and learn from your mistakes. It's kind of like we are the coaches and we are reviewing your contributions to the big game of life.

I'm not sure how many times you have bought heroin from this particular dealer. I would kick him to the curb and get the word out on the street that his stuff is bad. If you give us his name, we will handle that for you. You may not need to give us his name because we are reviewing the recordings from the 200+ cameras on the property.

While we are talking about this, stop arranging your drug deals for a crowded store parking lot in Brimfield. You are not from here; the dealer is from Akron. Stay the hell out of this community. We have three drug-certified K-9 units and highly motivated officers. Spread the word.

When you decide to use again, and you probably will, you two geniuses should not shoot up while driving down the road. Absolutely nothing good can happen from two mopes driving down the road attempting to use drugs intravenously. The car is moving . . . other traffic is moving . . . I SHOULD NOT EVEN HAVE TO EXPLAIN THIS!

Humans are not blue. We come in lots of colors, but I do not think blue is an option. Smurfs, yes. Humans, no. When a person turns blue, it is usually a sign something is wrong. Do not keep driving, do not head for a fast food restaurant, do not take the time to get rid of your fully loaded needle in a public trash can. DIAL 911 . . . Immediately!

Speaking of your decision-making ability while under stress, on what planet is it acceptable to throw a used needle loaded with heroin into a public trash can at a fast-food establishment? I happen to know the kid who is responsible for cleaning the lot and emptying the trash every day. You suck for exposing him to that mess. I am

MORE . . .

thankful my officers hate drugs and work really hard. Officer Gramlich showed great initiative by checking the trash near where you parked. This was not our first rodeo. It is SO UNLIKE a doper to put self-preservation over the safety of others (That is sarcasm). "The cops are coming! Quick, throw the dirty needle loaded with heroin into the trash! They will NEVER look there!"

Now you are in jail on two felony charges. You should consider this trip to the bed and breakfast as our gift to you: a little BPD rehab without all of the hugging and excuses. Tough love still exists; embrace it and get clean. Both of you escaped with your lives this time. The next time, your ticket may get punched.

Thanks to Officers Pettit and Gramlich and Det. Lance for her arrest of a female for possession of heroin and tampering with evidence after being called for a male who overdosed on heroin while the mopes were driving down the road after and while shooting the drug. One is now in the county spa, the other in the hospital with a ride waiting for non-stop service to the county bed and breakfast. Great job, Officers . . . I love that you all look beyond what is right in front of you.

—Chief

WEATHER REPORT . . . We have a Winter Weather Advisory in effect until noon for our area. Snow, rain, freezing rain and who knows what else may be falling from the sky . . . I haven't heard of the chance for hot lava and Cheez Whiz, but at this point I would say it's possible. We have no delays or incidents to report so far this morning.

The Brimfield Police Department Reaches 37,000 "Likes."

We are just very thankful there is not a "dislike" option . . .

Criminals

I'm not sure what happened to our society. Some of those who live among us have gone off of the rails.

We had two fine examples last night . . . a couple of knuckleheads who are too lazy to work, creeping around at nighttime, attempting to steal things that do not belong to them. They had a bag of tools and were on a mission. A witness saw them and did the right thing. He called us. My officers snuck up on them and found they were attempting to steal a truck from a dealership lot. They had "peeled" the steering column and were well on their way. Now, they are sitting in the county jail, wearing matching orange jumpsuits and very fashionable slippers.

At what point in our great country did committing crimes become a "job"? There are lots of people who do this for a living. Check area pawnshops and Internet sites like Craigslist and you can find hundreds of items that used to belong to someone else. Some of our friends will say "it's the economy." That is a load of . . . hogwash. I have relatives who lived during the Great Depression and they didn't steal a thing. I'm sure many of you have the same story. You and I may have had some rough times, yet did not CHOOSE to steal. It's not the economy, it's not the "hand they are dealt." It is one thing plain and simple. It is CHARACTER.

People who steal and commit other crimes lack character. The have no moral compass. They creep around at night when we are sleeping and take the things we have worked to buy; they sell drugs for the money and laugh at the addicted; they rob the defenseless. They are weakening the fiber of our great quilt of a country.

Legislators and other elected people should be outraged. Instead, last year, Ohio legislators made it LESS of a crime to steal, by increasing the amount triggering a felony from $500 to $1,000. So . . . for you criminals . . . you can steal MORE now, without it being a felony! We were told it was due to the budget. So, justice does have a price. If prison overcrowding is a problem, build more prisons. Stop sending billions to other countries while our own country collapses. Of course, politicians, with their private cars, security details and secure, guarded houses do not have these worries.

Maybe, since there is no place to put criminals, we should shuttle them all to the legislators' neighborhoods.

After all, they are just petty thieves and non-violent offenders, right?

WEEKEND . . . The officers did a nice job of removing drunks from the roadway and a few hotel rooms over the weekend. I believe we had 8 arrests or so . . . I'm still sorting it out. We love out-of-town visitors, with the exception of the ones who live less than 10 miles from here and rent hotel rooms just to get drunk and act like . . . drunk people. So, we attended a party or two over the weekend—because we like fun as much as the next person. A word of advice: When we attend a party and tell you to find a ride home or go to jail, we are giving you an opportunity to NOT BE ARRESTED. Changing your mind later, when the sally port doors open at the county bed and breakfast, is not an option.

AFTERNOON SHIFT YESTERDAY . . . Our afternoon shift are some nosy officers. A "chief's hug" to Officer Paul Gramlich. Paul is one of those who comes into work and gets right on it.

Yesterday Officer Gramlich received information that some subjects were at a local store buying ingredients to make meth. Being the busy-body he is, he decided to act on it immediately. When one of the suspects exited the store, she walked into the waiting arms of Officer Gramlich. It was not a romantic meeting.

After some on-scene investigation, Officers Gramlich, Gyoker and Sgt. McCarty arrested two adults and a juvenile for assembly of the chemicals for the manufacture of meth. They were taken to the county bed and breakfast for a tasty powdered-egg-and-cold-toast breakfast.

Great job to all officers involved. I am thrilled you are proactive.

The Brimfield Police Department Reaches 38,000 "Likes"

Suffering from the pressure of reaching 38,000 likes . . . the chief immediately requested a week of vacation . . .

IN THE SCHOOLS . . . First, thanks to my little buddy Carter, from Brimfield Elementary, for this excellent artwork. I believe it looks just like me. Thank-you, Carter . . . I love it.

Ellah, a student at Brimfield Elementary gives me a hug (and high-five) every morning. Today she added a little heart-melting phrase . . .

"Chief Oliver, you make my days SO HAPPY."

Enough said.

Illustration by Carter Wood of Brimfield Elementary.

MIDNIGHTS . . . Officer Dumont made a traffic stop on a subject coming out of the Beechcrest area. After a little roadside chat and some field tests, the subject was arrested for OVI (drunken driving) . . . Oh, and the nice man also had a couple grams of meth and some chemicals and ingredients to make MORE meth. That's a YAHTZEE!

The mope is on his way to the bed and breakfast; alas, he is late for the first meal of the day. He may have his orange jumpsuit and anti-skid slippers before lunch. We hope he gets the toasted cheese-food sandwich, with a side of "guess the meat" soup . . .

Don't drive drunk here. Don't make meth here. Don't use drugs here. We think it's pretty simple.

K-9S . . . Nice job to K-9's Havoc and Drogen, who both have become kill-joys in the game of "hide the drugs." A heartfelt "bummer" to the dopers who try really hard. Sorry about your luck. There are no prizes for second place.

IN THE COMMUNITY . . . The last Thursday and Friday in April we are hosting our twice-per-year Senior Breakfast at Applebee's. We have taken reservations for almost 200 seniors so far and we expect both days to be at capacity. Officer and volunteers serve breakfast to our senior residents during those two days. We love our seniors. Call for your reservation.

The stats for March have arrived. Brimfield officers handled 1,171 calls for service in March. Officers traffic-stopped 454 vehicles and gave 391 warnings. The citations involved driving under suspension, drunken driving and some other moving violations. Officers arrested 95 people last month.

Officer Gramlich wins the prize for most arrests—22 (gasp!). The prize this month is the Boxcar Willie CD collection, along with the 16-song greatest hits CD from Slim Whitman. Enjoy, Officer Gramlich. That's some classic music. "Mule Train!," by ol' Boxcar, is a foot-stomper.

Other notable stats for March: Officer Pettit made 15 arrests and Officer Dumont made 12. Better luck next month, boys . . . we are sure the prizes for April will be just as special.

Once again, we demonstrate we are not just about "writing tickets" or "revenue." Our aim is to keep everyone safe and to keep the mope-types from hurting you, your loved ones or your property.

Questions and statements from chief-haters . . .

It's Q&A time . . . brought to you by people who have nothing better to do.

• "I wish I had a job that allowed me to play on Facebook all day" . . . Yeah, that's what I do all day. You can have this job if you work hard. Get your bachelor's and master's degrees, go the police academy, pay your dues, work hard, move up in rank, have some luck, and POOF, you have it. I will caution you on one thing, though. You cannot be anonymous in this job. Everything you say is forever preserved and you always own it. It's a far cry from posting as "I h8 police" and being ignorant. Oh, and don't count on a lot of time off. My phone is always on and rings often.

• "It's not professional for a police chief to post on Facebook" . . . I get that, if we were in the year 1956. I will use whatever method I can to communicate our message and information to the public. If that requires me to wear a sandwich board and walk along SR43, sign me up. In case you haven't noticed, computers may stay around for another minute or two and can be used for things other than Internet sniping and porn.

• "Chief Oliver insults criminals and is rude" . . . I call criminals mopes. I do not comment on them being ugly, smelly or otherwise beauty impaired, even though some are. I do not comment on their education, social status, color, sex, origin or whom they marry. I care about crime and character. If you come to Brimfield and commit a crime we are all going to talk about it. The easiest way to not be called a criminal is to not be one. It is not calculus.

• "One of these days a defense attorney is going to win a case because you talked about his client on Facebook" . . . Find a name of an arrested person on this page, posted by us. We don't list names. We don't post pictures of mopes. I have said it often: If a jury can be seated for O.J. Simpson, the Manson Family, Ted Bundy, Jeffrey Dahmer and other well-known cases, I think we will be just fine with the meth cook and the shoplifter, and Chief Oliver talking with a few friends.

We hope you all enjoyed this.

ON NOTICE . . . We are coming up on the end of the semester for area colleges. We have lots of students living here . . . and sometimes lots of parties . . . so we sometimes are the uninvited guests to parties, due to neighbors calling about naked drunk people and loud music. College people: The object tonight and over the next few weekends is to NOT get arrested. NOT get arrested. NOT.

FACEBOOK UPDATE . . . In the last seven days, 854,537 people visited the Brimfield Police Department Facebook page. Will the 316 people in New Zealand please raise your hands? Land sakes!

IN THE COMMUNITY . . . Day one of the senior breakfasts went fantastic. Applebee's did a great job with the food . . . and officers and volunteers did awesome with the serving of breakfast to some of our favorite people—our senior citizens. We had another great raffle of gifts . . . and I hugged LOTS of ladies . . . I'm not sure the morning could have gone better. Thanks to all of you who attended and all of the officers and volunteers.

AFTERNOONS . . . Great job to Officer Gramlich for a traffic stop on SR43 resulting in the seizure of meth and the chemicals to make more meth. The occupants were apparently on the way to a circus . . . because they had enough pseudo-ephedrine to cure the stuffy noses of an entire herd of elephants. They also had other ingredients for meth . . . and a blowtorch. It's sort of a caveman-type heat source for a good ol' batch of meth.

As usual, the arrestee was NOT FROM BRIMFIELD. Meth cooks and other criminal types, a word of directional advice from me, your personal GPS, Internet sensation, eccentric Chief Oliver: There are two state routes bordering Brimfield. There are plenty of alternate routes around Brimfield. Take one of those routes.

DAYSHIFT . . . Officers Pettit and Diehl with two arrests from Kohl's. The alert loss-prevention person there likes catching people as much as we do. Two females arrested. They walked into the store thin and walked out much "thicker." We are thinking it was the additional shirts and "booty" shorts they put on under their own clothing. Their "booties" and the rest of them were taken to the bed and breakfast . . . where the shorts are longer . . . and so are the days.

More letters from the elementary school

You guys are very nice to have and if we did not have you it would not be good. People would be bad and speed and do all that. Also, that was the best field trip EVER.

Love, Alyssa

Thanks for the walking field trip. The most awesome part was seeing the tank. Remember to let me borrow it for the zombie apocalypse.

Natalie

Thank-you a lot for letting us pet Havoc. I don't have a dog so it's fun to pet him. I know Havoc likes being petted because he wags his tail all of the time.

Colin

Dear Brimfield Police,

Thank you sooooooo much. I honestly can't tell you how much I thank you. I can't say it in words. I love all of the police dogs. Thank you for letting us see all of the cells. The only time I have seen cells is on old westerns. I can't thank you enough on this card.

Sincerely, Mckenna

Thank you for all of your hard work, you thief catchers.

Kyle

Dear Police Department,

Thank-you for risking your life for us and taking up your family time for us. That is very generous of you. You are always there for us.

Love, MaKenna

Dear Chief Oliver,

Thanks for saving us from the mean and evil people. I never ever had anyone nicer than you. You are the best in the whole world.

Mason

Dear Brimfield Police,

Thank-you for your help. Thank-you for saving us from bad people and thank you for making me laugh.

Sincerely, Taylor

Dear Brimfield Police,

I am happy to come to school and right when I come in I am safe and sound at school. I really appreciate all you have done for us. I love it when Chief Oliver gives us hi five when we walk in. I just wanted to say thanks.

Yours Truly, Kaitlyn

WEEKEND REPORT . . . Three were arrested at Kohl's on Saturday for attempting to utilize a "five-finger discount," which is not accepted at Brimfield stores. We are not a participating location. Officers also recovered numerous stolen items from stores not located in our fine community.

ON THE BOSTON BOMBING . . . Our hearts, prayers and thoughts go out to the people of Boston and everyone in attendance at the marathon yesterday. In addition to the victims, we are thinking about the police, fire and also civilians who acted quickly to aid others. I am proud to be in law enforcement today, as always. Out of our 39,000+ friends, many are from the Commonwealth or the Boston area. We are here for you folks. We are America. We ALWAYS get back on the horse . . . so, here we go. Giddy-up. Be strong today . . . we are the good guys.

"The gap in our economy is between what we have and what we think we ought to have—and that is a moral problem, not an economic one."

—Paul Heyne

On my island

Many of you have heard me use the phrase "on my island." My island would be called The Isle of Common Sense. Here are some of the highlights of living on Common Sense . . .

- Anyone who hurts a child, female or senior citizen would be taken to the beach and told to start walking into the ocean. Strong swimming skills are a must for mopes on the Isle of Common Sense.
- No one would receive any monetary benefits unless they worked. If needed, neighbors would help neighbors, but not to the point of enabling. If you don't work, you will not be permitted to have an iPhone. That's just logic. We would take care of the disabled or infirm. Able-bodied people must carry the water or swim. It's called tough love.
- No drugs on Common Sense. We get high from living life. If you have drugs, have strong swimming skills.
- The police officers would have no need to carry guns. We would all be trained in Judo, similar to the skills learned by Deputy Barney Fife from the Judo School in Mount Pilot. Our hands would be lethal weapons. Chuck Norris would be our training officer.
- Loud, floral patterned shirts would be very acceptable, in spite of Mrs. Chief and the chief children insisting that I not wear them. It's my island.
- Elected people would not get paid. The only mandatory meeting for them would be to plan the yearly festival. They would also count on only themselves to get elected. No political commercials or special interest groups. It muddles everyone's thoughts.
- Police cars would be those dune-buggy type vehicles. I have always wanted to drive a dune buggy.
- We would all still meet on Facebook. Common Sense would still have Internet sensations.
- If you steal on Common Sense, you have to work in the store or for the person you stole from to work off the offense. If you steal again, you swim.

- You could sleep with your doors and windows open on Common Sense. If someone violated your space, we would judo chop them . . . Chuck Norris style.
- Daughters could only date after the age of 25. Their date would have to have a college degree, a job and a house.
- There will be no baggy pants on the Isle of Common Sense. We do not want to see your underwear.
- Hugging will replace handshakes as the routine form of greeting.

Welcome to the Isle of Common Sense.

MIDNIGHTS . . . Two felony arrests last night . . .

It seems two females from Akron decided to go on a late-night shopping trip to Walmart. As the items were scanned and bagged, one of the females pushed a full cart of merchandise out of the store . . . the other female ran out after her. A witness snapped some pictures on his smart phone, which is always great when the suspects give us the old "that wasn't me" speech.

The females got away for a minute. We visited them at their house in Akron. The Akron Police Department showed up with us . . . we love networking. APD and BPD recovered over $1,300 worth of stolen merchandise.

Oh . . . and a little-known risk of the job: the house was infested with bed bugs and lice. The double whammy of itchy. Officers are decontaminating and the evidence has been treated and triple-bagged.

Great job to my midnight shift. Thank you Akron PD for the assist. Also thanks to the witness and his smart phone. Boo to the female arrestees for stealing and having the cooties. Ladies, enjoy the decontamination at the bed and breakfast. Enjoy the orange jumpsuits and anti-skid slippers. Send us a postcard.

"As the family goes, so goes the nation and so goes the whole world in which we live."

—Pope John Paul II

Dear Mopes in Training,

Sorry to bother you again. I know Officer Gyoker bothered you last night also. Here's the deal: You and your friends were called in because of your suspicious vehicle. You were sitting in your vehicle outside the "casino." Those locations sometimes get robbed. We are the police. We respond to crimes or potential crimes, so when the call came, in came the cavalry.

I do have to speak with you about your response, though. See, you do not live in Brimfield. We could not even remotely waste YOUR tax dollars. So while we appreciate your being such a stellar watchdog for how YOUR tax dollars are being spent (although we do not know for sure you have actually paid any taxes, ever), please refrain from the older-than-dirt statement, "I pay your salary" . . . because you don't. I am also reasonably confident that the people who do pay us would like us to figure out why you are here, just "hanging out."

—Chief

K-9 NEWS . . . Brimfield residents, county residents . . . friends, Romans and countrymen . . . oh, and Facebook friends . . . It is my true pleasure to announce that K-9 Nitro is now a fully state-certified and recognized explosives detection K-9!

K-9 Nitro and his human (mostly) handler, Officer Putnam, took their state certification exam this morning. Nitro is now state certified and is the first explosives-detection K-9 in the history of the BPD . . . and the only one in Portage County.

I would like to thank Officer Putnam for his dedication and hard work; and K-9 Nitro for tolerating Officer Putnam. Officer Eric Stanbro from the Canton, Ohio, Police Department helped Officer Putnam and Nitro above and beyond what we hoped.

STORY TIME . . . Gather around gang, Uncle Chief is declaring story time.

Once upon a time there was a thief. He was a big fella, with lots of artwork affixed to his body. The artwork was of devils and naked ladies and such. Nice artwork; menacing fella. His background included escapes from law officers, being armed and dangerous . . . and sometimes socking a police officer. Oh . . . and lots of incidents of taking things that do not belong to him. So many of those, in fact, that two other counties have active warrants for his arrest. Yes, boys and girls, he is in the mope stage of his life.

On this day, the thief decided to work his job in "The Brimfield Triangle." A non-scientifically researched hypothesis tells us that criminals have been coming to Brimfield for years and . . . disappearing . . . only to turn up later, unharmed, in another part of the county . . . in the bed and breakfast. Yikes!

The thief arrived at Walmart and filled his shopping cart with lots of items. Battery chargers, electronics and . . . lots of $39 flea collars. (Chief shrugs shoulders, gives blank stare.) The thief had no intention of paying for the items, and bolted from the store at a quick pace, cart and all.

Do not fear, lovers of justice. Officer Paul Gramlich was outside of the store in the parking lot, patrolling the area. The thief exited the store . . . and will turn up shortly at the county bed and breakfast. And two other counties have already made reservations for his stay.

And we all lived happily ever after.

Great proactive policing, Officer Gramlich. You are a MOPE MAGNET.

IN THE SCHOOLS . . . If you are out and about in our area today and see what appears to be a very young police force . . . no worries. Today is job-shadow day for the middle school. We are humbled and proud to say that more students than EVER have chosen to shadow our police officers. Some even requested specific officers. We had to turn some away, so we are making arrangements to get them in during summer break. We are teaching them the time-honored skills of "mope hunting" (with a safe view of the prey).

On friends stopping by

During a shift change yesterday, one of the officers said that some of our Facebook friends stopped by the department on Sunday. The family, from out of the county, admitted to following us on Facebook and wanted to visit the department and meet officers. The officers greeted them and gave them a tour, and I believe they left with some parting gifts. Detective Lance added to the conversation by telling the officers he had personally given four separate tours of the department during yesterday's dayshift. The conversation stuck in my head as I was giving a tour to a mom and her children this morning.

The officers in the conversation were Gyoker, Gramlich and Lance. I was sort of a facilitator, or instigator. The idea came up to start a "wall of visitors." Then we recalled the old Chi-Chi's restaurant and the birthday celebration you could have there. The staff would place a big sombrero on your head and sing a lively song. The officers tossed around a similar idea, involving an eight-point hat (our standard hat, which the ladies LOVE) for our visiting friends to wear. The officer would pose for a picture with the visitor and we could hang the pictures on the wall of the department. We also thought about having a guest registry in the front foyer. Ideas were flying all over the room.

After that conversation, and this morning, I thought of the fact that we were talking about doing this at a POLICE department. This is not a restaurant or store. It, using logic, should not be a place which people want to visit, take pictures and hug the occupants. But then again, logic began to change when we started our Facebook page. I believe this is the new logic, the new way of thinking, at least for one small department in a small corner of the world. I also believe that if what we do begins to catch on and other police departments begin a strong, constant and positive interaction with their own communities, things will change all over. We have to be a team (minus the mopes) in order to have any positive results. In cannot be a "them and us" attitude from either side of the badge.

We strongly encourage our friends to stop by anytime they are in our area. No matter where you are from, stop in and see us.

Welcome to the Graceland of police work. Cue up "Burning Love" and hand me my cape.

IN THE COMMUNITY . . . We may have lost our minds here. Some of my officers believe it is a great idea for us to hold a car wash. Proceeds from the car wash would go to our "Back-to-School Shop-with-a-Cop" program. The back-to-school program involves officers partnering up with students for some back-to-school shopping . . . for pants, shirts, socks, shoes and book bags.

I think it is a great idea. So the BPD will be having a car wash, here at Mope Central, on Saturday from 10 a.m. until 2 p.m. Officers will make your vehicle shine, in exchange for your donation to our Summer Shop-with-a-Cop program. There is no set price on this fantastic wash . . . give what you can.

We will not wear hula skirts and tube tops . . . or white t-shirts.

IN THE SCHOOLS . . . First graders are awesome. Sgt. Knarr, K-9 Havoc and Officer Sonagere have been on a "walking field trip" with the first-grade classes this morning. The students have played with Havoc, sat in the police cars (sirens were going off like mad), toured the fire trucks and learned some important safety tips. Officers refused to let any children "see the TASER." (We get asked that a lot.)

PERSONAL NOTE . . . The Powerball jackpot is going to be a bazillion dollars on Saturday. If I won it, I would come to work on Monday . . . and the rest of the week too. I would not quit my job. I like it far too much. I would likely have to fly somewhere to see Mrs. Chief, though. Probably Tuscany. That's okay . . . I like flying.

NOTICE . . . A reminder for those who live in the area . . . Our OVI checkpoint is tonight from 10 p.m. until after bar closing. It will be held on SR43 at Brimfield Drive, north of I-76. If you are a sober driver and do not want to be slightly delayed, please avoid the area. We strongly encourage all intoxicated drivers to continue on to the checkpoint. We have a special night planned for you. All intoxicated drivers will receive a personalized autograph from one of the "Internet sensation" crew: a free ride in a police car, a tour of your very own holding cell at Mope Central . . . and a commemorative photo of your special night. ***Disclaimer*** You MUST provide your own ride home . . . your car stays with us. We can't have you driving home all star-gazed.

If you drive intoxicated in Brimfield, you will be stopped and arrested. We are tired of taking that long walk to the front door, telling a loved one of a tragedy you have caused.

Don't be selfish and ignorant . . . have a sober driver.

I want a Batmobile

Det. Lance recently watched some story about the original Batmobile, from the Adam West "Batman" TV show. He told me about it, because he knows I am a fan. I want a Batmobile. I told Det. Lance I want one. He believes it would be perfectly normal for me to cruise around town in the Batmobile. I believe that is a compliment. "I think it would fit right in with your personality," said the wise detective. I'm still going with compliment.

Speaking of Batman . . . In the 1960s movie, Batman carried shark repellent on his utility belt. And a Bat-A-Rang. NO police store I have found carries either one. In the off chance there is a shark in Brimfield Lake or Mogadore Reservoir, I will have to wing it. "We're gonna need a bigger boat" comes to mind.

Speaking of sharks . . . if the Senate and Congress were our kids, they would be in a time out and go to bed without supper. They fight like six year-olds. Hey folks, it's about America. Keep your eyes on the ball.

Speaking of America . . . the parade registration is parade@brimfieldpolice.com. If you are a veteran or would like to walk in the parade, send us an email. It's September 21 and I invited all 48,000+ of you. I think some people are getting nervous. I'm not. I am as cool as the other side of the pillow. I like big gatherings, especially when there are lots of veterans. It's like walking amongst superheroes.

Speaking of superheroes . . . in addition to the Batmobile, I would like the Bat Utility Belt. It had a grappling hook, Bat Knock-Out Spray and smoke bombs. These smoke bombs are nothing like the ones that went off on my neighbor's porch when I was a kid. I stand by my story on that little incident.

"Life is like a ten-speed bicycle. Most of us have gears we never use."

—Charles Schulz

LAST NIGHT . . . The OVI checkpoint netted seven arrests, six of which were for OVI. The seventh was for an intoxicated person who had issues following instructions concerning staying put and not having an open container. Officers also recovered a loaded .380 handgun from one of the passengers being driven by an intoxicated driver. The owner did not have a CCW permit. Even with all of the advanced notice, bright lights and "warning" signs on the roadway, some people still made the choice to drive drunk and drive through an OVI checkpoint. Some people are awfully selfish.

IN THE SCHOOLS . . . I would like to squash a rumor or two. The rumor I have been signing yearbooks for the elementary school students is true. The rumor that selling that yearbook (containing the signature of a certain "Internet sensation") on eBay to cover the cost of your child's college is . . . false. (Humor alert.) Seriously, our officers have LOTS of requests to sign yearbooks. We will be in the schools regularly. If your child misses his or her favorite officer, stop by the department.

FACEBOOK . . . We passed 43,000 "likes" today . . . are you kidding me? Everyone pay attention. ATTENTION PLEASE! This is a police department Facebook Page . . . in the case you didn't see the officers, dogs, police cars, mopes and the "chief" references. We are not one of those bands playing that evil rock and roll music. If we were a band, we would be bluegrass . . . or polka. Chicks love polka music . . . and dancing.

DAYSHIFT . . . Officers just made an arrest. The person had a warrant for failing to show up for court. Appointments are a must. Be prompt for court and don't let your underwear show. It's a courtroom, not a strip club. Oh . . . and take a shower, and brush your teeth. Make a good first impression. I would breakdance to MC Hammer's "Can't Touch This" while wearing a Dallas Cowboys Cheerleader uniform if it meant not going to prison.

"We are what we repeatedly do. Excellence, therefore, is not an act but a habit."

—Aristotle

The coolest police chief in existence

I'm getting performance anxiety. The Huffington Post said it: I am the "coolest police chief in existence." Existence! I've been locked in my office all day, afraid to see if there are crowds of people outside . . . or paparazzi. I thought about getting a disguise. I thought maybe I would dress up like Wyatt Earp, John Wayne or Elvis. I am sure looking like any of those three would allow me to move around society without the paparazzi snapping pictures and trying to catch me buying sunflower seeds and bottled water at Speedway.

While we are honored and appreciate the kind words, we are still doing what we have always been doing. This recipe has never changed. A few times a day we get together and exchange some information with 46,000 or so friends. We have some laughs, maybe cry a little, frustrate the mopes and laugh some more. The number keeps growing, so the atmosphere must be good, we think.

We have people from Australia, England, Ireland . . . all 50 states, 29 countries and Brimfield, Ohio.

I don't believe I am "cool." Actually, I don't care if I am "cool," just like I didn't care when I was 12. What I care about is doing the best possible job, informing as many people as possible about police work, and having some laughs. I care deeply for this community and my staff. Without my staff, we would do none of the programs we do, or stop nearly as much mopery. You could make a trade of one department for another, and the BPD would not be the same. These officers love each other, look out for each other and as a collective group do more to serve the community than any group I have ever seen. This may shock you . . . I am not an easy guy to work for. I have expectations. My staff understands the mission and our vision and is constantly moving to get things accomplished. They help lost dogs, hand out ice cream tickets, visit our senior residents and chase bad guys. They are the Swiss Army knives of police work.

As always, thanks to all of you for being here. While we appreciate the kind words and attention from various media sources, we are just doing what we have been doing for the last couple of years . . . sitting around and chatting with some friends.

FACEBOOK . . .

The International Association of Chiefs of Police has a Social Media Center. That organization is usually on the cutting edge of leadership issues. Recently they tallied the Facebook "likes" for police departments, compiling a list based on how many officers each department had. The list is from the first of May.

For us, because of all of you, the number of police officers we have here (15) is sort of irrelevant. I am absolutely amazed and humbled by the results . . . check this out:

New York City: 169,720 "likes"

Boston: 85,285 "likes"

Philadelphia: 53,707 "likes"

Brimfield: 41,526 "likes"

Houston: 35,490 "likes"

Obviously, in the time since this was submitted by the IACP, we have already passed 43,000 "likes." Holy smokes.

On behalf of all of my officers and staff . . . we thank you for being here and for caring about what direction we (society) are heading. Without you, there is no "us."

And besides, you all may be more "touched" than me, which makes this awfully fun.

The Brimfield Police Department Reaches 44,000 "Likes"

Ranking #4 in police department Facebook "likes" in the United States, people who follow New York, Boston and Philadelphia police are all asking the same question . . . "Where the hell is Brimfield?"

Dear Hunters and Varmint Killers,

Before you start to vapor lock, I am a gun advocate. I am an NRA Life Member, and was raised around firearms. I have carried one nearly every day for the past 20 years. The point of telling you that is so you don't start whining when you read the next couple of paragraphs.

The time to NOT shoot critters, when you live reasonably close to a school building, is in the morning, when kids are coming to school. We know you shoot safely; that's not the issue. The issue is the loud boom a gun makes when you are sending varmints to critter heaven. When you rip off four or five shots at 7:30 in the morning and you live near a school, 911 rings off the hook and police officers experience what is known as the "pucker factor." That factor has something to do with constipation, and that's as far as I will go with an explanation on puckering.

So use your head when you live within sound distance of a school. Yes, that area is rural. Yes, you have a right to shoot. You also have a responsibility to not cause officers to run to the school, prepared to defend the students. It gets the officers all hyped up, and then I am left with officers who are all hyped up for the rest of day. They get talkative.

In closing, if you have been on planet Earth during the last two decades, you understand why I get a little edgy when shots are heard near a school. This isn't about your specific right to bear arms. I will always defend that right. Like I have said before, rights come with responsibilities and also should be exercised with common sense.

—Chief

Frequently Asked Questions

Hey folks . . . "Cheap Otter" here. I thought I would answer some questions sent via message . . .

- A mope is a person who leeches off us and usually is engaged in criminal activity.
- Yes, Brimfield is a great community, with great people. The population is 10,400. Yes, we are aware we have five times that number of likes on our page. We smell good. And we are honest.
- Brimfield is about 23 square miles. We have lots of open space, farms that have become houses, farms that are now stores, farms that are still farms . . . and very little mopery from people who live here. We catch the criminals as they drive through town. It's like a welcome wagon, with handcuffs.
- We do not believe everyone who has ever committed a crime is a mope. People change. I am the unofficial spokesperson for turning it around. I was sort of wild in my younger days. I was not a criminal, but I lacked some character. Mrs. Chief changed all of that, because she is no-nonsense. Shenanigans are fine. Nonsense is not. The point is as I have said before . . . once a mope, not always a mope. If you are a reformed mope, welcome.
- The "it's not my birthday" on the morning posts is all about reading things carefully. I once wished someone a happy birthday, and several posts later people were wishing ME happy birthday. So, everyday I have to tell everyone it is not my birthday. Ice cream cake is no good after an extended time in the freezer.
- I am not an elected guy. I was appointed as chief of police in 2004. I believe my bosses were having a weak moment due to my great skills for looking sad.
- No, I cannot come to (insert city) and be the chief. I promised my bosses I was staying here when I signed a contract. Unlike professional athletes, I believe a contract is your word.

- No . . . I will not be cloned. As wonderful as Mrs. Chief is, I am not one to try my luck. Gambling is great if it's not your money.

I think that covers it for now . . . I have about 400 messages and emails to go.

AFTERNOON SHIFT . . . Officers were called to one of the gas stations at SR43 and I-76 because "the employees are smoking weed." When Officers entered the building, the comparison to a Cheech and Chong movie could be made. Officers confiscated the wacky-tabacky and issued the two an autographed and personalized ticket for their transgression. Also, we are told, the owner of the business sent them packing. It is unknown if the potato chip inventory is off.

Weed is still illegal. We enforce the laws, we don't make them. So, please . . . tell someone else how great it is.

BPD POLICY . . . Well, some of you have been waiting on me to go back on my word. It has happened. All of you have heard me say many, many times that I do not care about tickets. However, I have changed my mind.

Effective next week, my officers will have a quota for tickets: at least one per shift. We are going to be profiling, too. We will target a specific group, with the express purpose of writing as many tickets as possible. I am strongly encouraging my officers to write as many as they can, every shift, every day. It is called Operation Safe Summer.

When Operation Safe Summer kicks off next week, officers will hit the streets looking for our target group: kids 12 and under. If a child 12 or under is observed wearing his or her helmet while biking . . . the child will be stopped and issued a ticket . . . for a free ice cream cone from Frank's Drive-in, located on SR43.

This is the kind of ticket-writing I REALLY enjoy.

The Brimfield Police Department Reaches 45,000 "Likes"

The "Floyd's Barbershop of Facebook" may have to add a few more chairs . . .

FACEBOOK . . . We passed 46,000 "likes" yesterday. For those of you who missed it, we awarded several door prizes, including the Rhinestone & Stud Setter by Ronco . . . and the wonderful 8-track tape from K-tel titled "GIRLS GIRLS GIRLS." You can't miss big milestones around here . . . the gifts and potential cameo appearances are just too stellar.

BPD POLICY UPDATE . . . We think Officer Diehl will be on Fox 8 News tonight. A reporter rode around with him for an hour or so. He was issuing tickets to children like his job depended on it. (I am such a hard person to work for . . . Muuuhahahah.) We think Officer Diehl is leading the shift with five tickets so far. We sure are generating a lot of . . . happiness. All tickets are for FREE ICE CREAM and are issued to children who are riding their bikes with helmets on. Afternoon shift will be out on the hunt also, so . . . BEWARE.

INTERNET CELEBRITY . . . A friend of mine texted me to tell me we were on a site called Gawker. I asked him a simple question: "What in tarnation is Gawker?" He then felt the obligation to tell me about the history of the Internet . . . and here I thought I was doing great. I guess being on Gawker is a big deal. He said it was even bigger than the Mayberry Gazette.

AFTERNOON SHIFT . . . Sgt. McCarty's shift continues to be in the soup most days. Officers were called to Old Forge Road for some sort of disturbance inside of a vehicle. It turned out to be a domestic situation. When officers arrived, the female passenger bailed out of the car and attempted to morph into an Olympic sprinter. There are reasons sprinters do not use street drugs . . . and those reasons were highly evident. She was quickly caught and arrested for drug possession. The driver was arrested for OVI. Again, mopes . . . the object of the game is to NOT GET CAUGHT. If you are going to be stoned out of your mind and in possession of drugs . . . don't punch each other in the face. It draws attention and attention brings the law dogs.

"If Columbus had an advisory committee he would probably still be at the dock."

—Arthur Goldberg

IN THE COMMUNITY . . . We received information from a confidential informant today. The snitch told us that these two young'ns were out and about, riding their bikes with helmets on. I ordered officers to the area. Officer Diehl caught up with the offenders and promptly issued both of them tickets . . . for a free ice cream cone at Frank's Drive-In, for wearing their helmets while biking. We would like to thank Frank's and also our anonymous sources for providing us some fun today.

Officer Diehl issuing tickets . . . for free ice cream.

FACEBOOK . . . The FB page may have taken another unexpected turn. Yesterday I received a letter from the president of a publishing company. This person had heard of us and "several" people have asked him about getting in contact with me . . . so, he did just that. I found him to be very pleasant.

The letter was inquiring about my interest in writing a book. I was floored. Seriously. It is one of the first times in my life I have ever wondered if I had been drinking (I have never had a drop in my life). Talk about being humbled.

In the next week or so, we will be having a meeting. We will discuss what is expected, what direction we are going and if it can be done. I have declared that a portion of any profit will be directed back to the BPD community programs. Mrs. Chief and I will also be forming a non-profit organization, to help clothe children, buy books to read and help out however we can with kids who need a little help. In spite of all of the hullabaloo, I am a public servant. I enjoy what I do. I will retire from this profession at this department and then . . . go fishing.

I will keep you informed . . . because that's how we roll . . . Chief Oliver

The Brimfield Police Department Reaches 47,000 "Likes"

As people (including newborn babies) seeking hugs pile through the front doors of the Brimfield Police Department . . . Philadelphia PD now sees us in the Facebook rear-view mirror . . .

To the spectator who was kicked out of a middle school basketball tournament,

I wasn't at the school today, but one of my sergeants and an officer were. They were called to escort you from the property. I would like to answer the "insightful" question you asked them. Since you are not from our community, I will explain how we work . . .

Yes, we have better things to do than deal with you. These things are also way more important. We are fighting a war on drugs. We have heroin overdoses at an alarming rate. We have thefts and burglaries due to drug use and poor parenting. We have drunk drivers, sexual predators and other criminals we are trying to catch.

Instead of dealing with those more important things, we were called to the school by officials because you decided to act like an ass, in front of a gym full of impressionable young athletes and other onlookers . . . at a MIDDLE SCHOOL basketball tournament. Please do us all a favor and explain to your children that the way you acted is NOT proper. Don't blame the refs, the coaches or the weather. Tell your child that life sometimes doesn't get the "call right," and we deal with it and move on. Otherwise, we or other law enforcement officers will be dealing with him in the future . . .

And stop using the "Don't you guys have better things to do?" nonsense. Of course we have better things to do. You stopped us from doing them and had our undivided attention . . . at a game played by and for children.

The car wash

I think the Facebook page finally dawned on me today. I mean . . . I know that it is unusual to have so many friends or "likes" on a police page. It may not be unusual for the big cities like NYC, which has a population of 8 million. But for us, with a population of 10,500, it's sort of awesome. What got me today was the outpouring of love and affection from all of you who showed up to get your car washed by professional law enforcers. Let's face it, we are not known for our car wash prowess.

Today, a police department in the Midwest U.S. was a destination. The people coming there were not coming to pick up arrested friends or relatives. They weren't coming to pick up police reports for traffic crashes or other incidents. The people were also not coming to have their cars washed because of our stellar reputation as car detailing experts. They came to see us . . . cops . . . the police. Not the "Every Breath You Take" Police, but the badge wearing, gun toting type. YIKES!

Today we hugged what we believe to be most of the population of the United States. Officers gave tours, posed for pictures and spent the time laughing and having fun. People asked to meet specific officers, including the funniest line . . . "Is that the Meth Whisperer?" We gave out mope stickers, badges, stuffed animals and spoke with so many people about the appreciation they have for us and the Facebook page.

Today I saw the impact we are having and the difference that can be made when agencies drop egos and agendas and just do what is right and proper . . . and it was fantastic.

We raised over $2,500 today for children in our community. These children are a lot like some of you were as kids. They are definitely like I was. They need some help with clothes and shoes for the start of the school year, and thanks to you; we will be there for them. No red tape, no agenda-driven politics . . . just a helping hand.

Thank you to all of you who attended today. We heard lots of "I can't start my mornings without you" and also "You are doing great things." We appreciate all of that, but just remember . . . without all of you, it does not happen. We have a 49,000-member team here. We have Republicans, Democrats, men and women . . . all shapes, sizes, religions and other "labels." It is living proof that when people

aren't agenda-driven or pot-stirring, things can be accomplished. Great things.

We honor our relationship and love all of you. Thanks for being here.

IN THE COMMUNITY . . . There is a nice story behind this picture (taken by Timothy Sainte-Hilaire of the Record-Courier).

A young boy named Matthew wanted to bring his police car to the car wash we held Saturday. For you new folks, we washed some cars to raise the money to take some of our school-aged residents on a little back-to-school shopping trip. We are going to buy them some new pants, socks, shoes and other items . . . so they return to school looking spiffy.

Matthew, who is at the younger-person speech age, wanted his car washed, so Officers Pettit, Diehl and Casterline made it shine. We also gave him a badge and "No Mopes" sticker for the car.

The young man refers to me by my new name, known by 2-year-olds all over the world: "Cheap Otter."

I am Cheap Otter.

Meth 101

The subject today is Meth 101. We have had some emails and messages on what exactly a person should be looking for when being on the lookout for meth mopes. We offer this, for your educational pleasure. Please, you sensitive types, do NOT bombard me with nasty-grams about "teaching people to make meth on a police FB page." That's not the case, so pipe down.

- The main ingredient for any batch of meth is ephedrine or pseudoephedrine. Although there is a restriction on sales in Ohio, that little charade is sort of like plugging a dam with your finger. Ten people may buy one box each and then take it to the cook. With as much of this product that is sold, America should have no sinus issues for the duration of all of our lives.
- Other ingredients include acetone, lye (drain cleaner), red phosphorus (usually from matchbook striker plates), denatured alcohol, Heet (gas treatment), camp-stove fuel, lithium batteries (they strip the lithium) and anhydrous ammonia, which is used to "gas" the final product by creating a chemical steam. All or some of these are mixed at various stages to get us our end result . . . meth.
- Equipment associated with making meth includes tubing (think fish aquarium), glass dishes or jars, 2-liter bottles, a heat source (camping stove, hot plate, a torch), coffee filters and sometimes measuring cups/glasses. There may also be masks, gloves, duct tape (for sealing the bottles during gassing) and empty pseudoephedrine blister packs.

So if you see a person going through the check-out with camping fuel, coffee filters, acetone and drain cleaner, he or she may not be working as a handy man/woman. He or she may be a mope.

Look out for that collection of chemicals along with 2-liter bottles, blister packs of pseudoephedrine and that "I have been up for five straight days look," and you have a Yahtzee.

Professor Oliver . . . Out.

AFTERNOON SHIFT . . . The shift has been pretty busy, mostly because Officer Gramlich has become the BPD "Meth Whisperer." It seems as though every fourth car he stops has meth, chemicals for meth or a meth lab. His fellow officers were poking a little fun with him this evening . . .

Chief: "Gramlich . . . no meth lab yet today?"

Sgt. McCarty: "We are trying to get caught up on paperwork, chief."

Gramlich: "They let the air out of my tires, chief."

Putnam: "We didn't let the air out of his tires . . . we clubbed his car. It's not leaving the lot."

So, the other officers have resorted to disabling Officer Gramlich's police car, so everyone can get caught up on paperwork—which looked like a pile about two feet high.

Never fear . . . Officers Allen and Dumont just stopped a suspended driver. He's getting arrested, as is his passenger . . . who has several warrants, including a felony warrant for dangerous drugs.

The beat goes on.

ANIMALS . . . We would like to smack the person who tossed the kitty out of his truck today near I-76 and SR43. You, sir . . . are a moron. Thank you to the passerby who brought the kitty to us. We will get it some help.

PERSONAL NOTE . . . I would like to thank the person who first mixed peanut butter with jelly and put them on bread. You are a genius . . . and if you were here, I would hug you. Brilliant.

The Brimfield Police Department Reaches 48,000 "Likes"

Like "Throwback Jerseys" and "Throwback Mountain Dew" . . . The BPD Attempts to Coin the Phrase "Throwback Common Sense"

Civility

Webster's defines the word "civil" in a few ways. The particular use of the word I was looking for was the second definition; "adequate in courtesy and politeness." Adequate is defined as "barely sufficient or satisfactory." So, the idea of being civil is basically being polite and courteous . . . at a minimum level.

I am beginning to believe some of us cannot even accomplish that.

I think we have lost some civility in our culture. Some would say we are no longer even a "civilized" society. I would not go that far, but I believe we are in the infancy stages of that predicament. If you need examples, scroll back a few posts and read the anger, emotion and insults on a few of our posts, starting with the Rottweiler post . . . YIKES!

Somewhere along the way, likely with the emergence of computers, threads, blogs and keyboards, we have become a tad uncivilized. Whereas in prior times the individual person perhaps did not have a loud voice, or maybe did not have the platform to have that voice heard, that is not where we are now. Today, everyone has an opinion and come hell or high water, they are going to tell you what they think.

Now to the meat and potatoes of this post . . . We need to be more civil to each other. Remember, it is the minimum we can do. The minimum. You and I may disagree on politics, social issues, or the redeeming qualities of singing "Suspicious Minds" while in the shower. That's okay; however, we need to do it with civility. There is no need for swearing, threats or YELLING. You make your point, I'll make mine and we move forward. If our views are something which need settled in order to move ahead, then we find common ground and move. It really is simple, as long as we are civil. When we add swearing, anger and exaggerations, we fail. If you need an example, look at Washington D.C.

On this page, as long as I am here (and that will be a while), we will act with decorum and be civil. If you swear, are vulgar or make threats, see you later. I like a variety of views and opinions, because those allow me to check my own views for validity. That's huge for me, because I am always willing to learn. If there is a view different from yours, counter it with civility: the minimum politeness.

Now, just so you are all aware . . . Calling a criminal a "mope" is very civil for me, personally. It is the minimum in civility and much better than what I REALLY want to call them.

Thanks for reading.

AFTERNOON SHIFT . . . Officer Gramlich, AKA "The Meth Whisperer," did it again yesterday. He traffic-stopped a vehicle and recovered the ingredients for a meth lab. Two subjects were arrested and charged with assembly of the chemicals to manufacture meth. A third subject got lost inside of Walmart. We will find him, soon. None of the subject are from here or live here.

While officers were looking for the lost meth man, another brain surgeon attempted to push a cartload of merchandise out of the store . . . without displaying the proper social etiquette of PAYING for the items. He happened to push it out directly into our officers . . . which goes to prove the theory of timing in life being very, very important. He first stated he had lost his receipt and then changed his mind and admitted to being a mope. He was arrested for theft and also had a warrant for his arrest from another police agency. Criminals . . . please remember . . . one of the goals of your career choice involves not getting caught. Walmart . . . Part 3 . . . Officers were called back for subjects stealing items, including a large TV. That place is like slow-motion looting. Officers arrived to find the subjects loading their car with the stolen items. The suspects saw the officers . . . and suddenly wanted to be considered for the 2014 Olympic sprint team. Officer Sonagere and others gave pursuit on foot . . . and then it dawned on us that the bad guys forgot their car. When the video picture of a suspect stealing a TV matches his driver's license photo . . . we get giddy. We towed his car and have him identified. He will have warrants for his arrest sometime soon.

The Brimfield Police Department Reaches 49,000 "Likes"

New York City, Boston, Philadelphia, Brimfield and Houston . . . The top five local law enforcement agencies for Facebook "likes." We will not tell the other four it is because of our cologne . . . and manly physiques . . .

The AP story

The Associated Press did a nice job covering what we are doing here, for the most part. The story was written after the car wash and some of the other things we are doing. It is nice to have someone notice . . . other than all of us here.

The main thing I want to convey this morning . . . Some of you have been getting upset over some of the comments posted on the various sites running the story. Don't let it bother you. I don't read the comments, because most are written by Internet trolls who are miserable with their own lives. They have keyboard courage. I used to answer them and try to have some dialogue when they posted here, but I have found they all usually have the same personality . . . angry and very passive/aggressive. Let's look at their most common posts to our page . . .

- "You're wasting taxpayer dollars." . . . I work lots of hours every day. I do something related to this job seven days per week. I post here, post at home and once posted about a lost dog while cutting my lawn. Our taxpayers get their money's worth, I guarantee it.
- "You're fat. (you can't chase people, get off Facebook etc., etc., etc.)" . . . Why yes, I am a portly fella. I make up for it with stellar good looks, a charming personality and good personal hygiene. Actually, I'm just short for my weight. I don't need to chase people. We have four K-9 units, I hire very fast officers, and I have a car. Besides, if I choose to, I can lose weight. You can't lose ignorance.
- "A police chief should not say the things you say." . . . Well, someone needs to. We have become this touchy feely bunch of sissified victims. Criminals are no longer responsible for what they do because of their "rough childhood" or "circumstances." Everyone has an excuse. My belief is that we ALL are accountable for our actions. We all have free will. If your free will involves you selling drugs, raping, robbing or otherwise creating victims, you need to be locked down in an adult timeout. When you go to timeout, we can't be the pushover parents who get tired of hearing you cry and let you out early. Do

the crime, do the time. If we ever tried it, I bet it would work.

My advice is . . . if you do not like the page, don't come here. We have been doing this for three years now. We have withstood lots of challenges. I am not changing how I conduct business, no matter what type of tantrum you throw.

And that's the way it is.

AFTERNOON SHIFT . . . Officers were called for a subject walking down Mogadore Road; an anonymous caller told us the person had an active arrest warrant. We made contact and . . . surprise, the subject gave us a false name. It is very important, when giving a false name and date of birth, to have some basic math skills. For example, if you were born in 1988, you are not 43 years old. The subject was identified and did have an active warrant. Anonymous callers are pretty smart sometimes.

IN THE COMMUNITY . . . We are gearing up for the 2013 BPD Car Wash. All proceeds go to our children's programs, particularly to buy back-to-school clothes, shoes and bookbags for some of our little friends. We start making the cars shine at 10 a.m.

Update: We raised $1,000 in the first hour of the car wash . . . You all are very, very amazing people.

Update 2: The BPD Car Wash two-hour total: $1,390. We are starting to slow down some. We have three wash stations, so the wait time is minimal; if you are in the area, stop and see us. Thank you to all who have been here. There is a lot of hugging going on!

Update 3: Car wash total, hour 3 . . . We are over the $2,000 mark! We are humbled by all of you and we thank you.

The Brimfield Police Department Reaches 55,000 "Likes"

Will the person who entered the door as the 55,000th friend please claim your prizes . . . We have a Robo Stir, A Gyro Bowl and the Partridge Family's Greatest Hits . . .

Meth 102

Being the great students you are, we are certain you remember Meth 101, which covered the red phosphorus/anhydrous ammonia method of making meth. In today's class, we will cover the "One-Pot" or "Shake and Bake" (with all regards to Ricky Bobby) method of making the nasty drug known as meth.

The shake-and-bake method has made meth far easier and faster to manufacture. The downside is that the danger of explosion has increased. The ingredients include our old friend pseudoephedrine; lithium strips, taken from batteries; drain cleaner (sodium hydroxide), cold packs or fertilizer, which is used for the ammonium nitrate content; and camping-stove fuel such as Coleman or another brand. The one-pot method uses far less pseudoephedrine and can be cooked pretty quickly, which results in the drug being cooked in cars, hotel rooms and even bathroom stalls.

These fine ingredients are mixed together to make the final product . . . meth. All of this can be and is usually done in a two-liter pop (soda) bottle. The reactions inside the bottle can be very unpredictable and thus are dangerous. It can result in things going boom. Boom may not be a scientific word, but if you ever been around a boom, you know what I mean. This also makes larger labs unnecessary, because more people are making meth for themselves to sell some and use some. If you see:
- Pseudoephedrine
- Cold Packs (the ones we crush and put in a cooler)
- Fertilizer
- Lithium Batteries
- Drain Cleaner
- Camping Stove Fuel
- Two Liter Bottles
- Coffee Filters . . .

You likely have a one-pot meth lab. Do NOT move or tamper with it. The labs, when done cooking, are usually discarded in ditches, trash bins and other locations. Call police and stay back. Class dismissed.

Dear Drug Dealers, Users and Manufacturers,

I have assembled a great crew of officers and K-9 units. We have the most recent training, policies and methods in place. Our dogs love to work. We are relentless in the pursuit of YOU. We can write search warrants with our eyes closed. We will use all legal means at our disposal to drive you from this community—likely resulting in you being driven to the county bed and breakfast in the back of a Brimfield Police vehicle.

We never sleep, ever.

If you sell, manufacture or use drugs in Brimfield, we will catch you. You will be charged with the appropriate felony. You will have to hire an attorney, make court appearances and likely lose your job (the legal and illegal ones) and the confidence of those who love you. It is a dead-end road.

If you are a user who needs help, call me. I will get you help. Fair warning: we do not discern between addicts and sellers—both are part of the problem keeping us from having a decent quality of life. Your way of life brings shame to your family and our community, and you must change. I will help you, but you must help yourself first—before we help you with a prison sentence.

We are not going away, and as long as I call the shots, we will be relentless and unyielding. If you sell drugs here, we will be coming through a door near you soon.

—Chief

FACEBOOK . . . We would like to congratulate all of you for helping us become the THIRD most popular local law enforcement page in the United States of America. The Brimfield Police Department has passed Philadelphia. The ranking is now New York City, Boston and . . . Brimfield.

We will be providing light refreshments and a short concert from a special guest . . . Vanilla Ice. I may join him for a rendition of "Ice Ice Baby" . . . "With the ragtop down so my hair can blow . . . "

As always, thanks for being here. The BPD and all of you make a great team. And the team concept is what police work is all about.

MIDNIGHTS . . . Officers Atha and Allen (and K-9 Drogen) were called to a house on Old Forge for . . . we'll call it an unwanted guest. An intoxicated female and one of her BFF's went to the house for a myriad of reasons, depending on who you asked and what time you asked them. When officers arrived on scene, the BFF took off running . . . although she had done nothing wrong that we knew of. We get that result sometimes . . . either people want to hug us or run from us; both of those results are based on our reputations as huggers and law enforcers.

Officer Atha thought perhaps there was a reason the female had boogied from our presence. He walked around in the back forty looking for her . . . and found her lying down in the grass and mud, kind of hiding in plain site. She told him she had no reason to take off running . . . and she truly didn't. Then she said, "This is going on Facebook, isn't it?" Officer Atha's response: "Yep."

A male staying at the house then chastised the entire group, telling them they could not "act like this" because they were not in another jurisdiction, they were in Brimfield. "I like reading the Facebook page . . . now I'm going to be ON the Facebook page." Officer Atha's response: "Yep."

The Brimfield Police Facebook page . . . it helps sober the intoxicated.

The Brimfield Police Department Reaches 58,000 "Likes"

Guest 58,000 to booking please; you have won Richard Simmons' "Sweatin' to the Oldies" and a FlowBee Complete Hair Care Set

On Field schools

Boy, am I hearing it this morning. I feel like the guy who stuck his head in a hornet's nest.

Good for me.

After I strongly recommended that everyone support the school levy, the comments have been plentiful. Most of the negatives have been from someone who heard from someone else. I figured you all should be informed.

I have heard I have no business commenting on the schools. That's hogwash. Education is definitely a police chief's business. I can show you numerous studies indicating the better the education, the less likely the person is be arrested and visit the state bed and breakfast. If the schools falter, so does the rest of the community. Property values plummet (more than they already have) and people lose confidence in the community as a whole. Outsiders look at the community as deficient and dysfunctional.

I have heard I was bashing teachers. That's "hogwash, part 2." I love teachers. I am where I am today because of teachers who looked past the poor kid in ratty clothes and pushed me hard.

I have also heard the school board is frustrated with me. Okay, I can't call hogwash on that one; I would be frustrated with me too. At least now we are frustrated with each other . . .

The education of the next generation is hanging on for dear life, in this district and numerous others. The proper answer is likely a restructuring of state and federal spending and a redirection of the money to local schools to offset local dollars. I have a better chance of winning the Mr. Universe swimsuit competition than any of us seeing that happen. There are too many hands in the bank at those levels and too many favors to return. For a while, we will be on our own . . . trying to figure out how to educate our kids while being fiscally responsible and sound along with having strong communications.

Here's the main point of the post . . . here is the message, reduced to the simplest form . . . It's time. It's time for leadership. It's time for leadership from everyone involved with the education of children. I am not talking about the actual education (classroom and teachers). I am talking about leadership of the process, the road leading to giving these children the best possible chance to succeed. It's time to put all personal feelings and agendas aside. It's time to put all special interests aside, meaning Tea Party, unions, government, and worrying about who drives the nicest car.

It's time to stop talking and start fixing the problems. It's time for dialogue. It's time to make sure the school district has enough money to succeed in its mission. It's time to stop complaining about what teachers' wages are or are not. No more envy . . . no more summers-off comments.

It's time to stop punishing local programs for the federal government's tax policies. It's time to stop hiding behind attorneys. It's time to handle the public's business in the public and not behind closed doors. It's time for REAL transparency and not just the buzzword. It's time for parents to be involved actively in the education process of their children. It's time. It's time to ensure that children have the best education mechanism in place.

If you are a leader in this district, now is your time. You campaigned for or accepted appointment to the job. It is time.

Why does the police chief care about the schools? What business is it of his? It is very simple: Education (along with strong parenting) leads in a path directly opposite of the path of mopery. In addition, I am awfully fond of these children.

The Brimfield Police Department Reaches 60,000 . . . uh . . . 61,000 "Likes"

Attention . . . Guests numbers 60,000 and 61,000 please report to the Chief's office for your prizes . . . You have won a Billy Big Bass Talking Fish . . . and Ray Stevens' Greatest Hits on 8-track, including the hit single "The Streak"

Happy Birthday, America

I love our country. I love the people, our ways of life and the sights, sounds and smells (most of them).

In my lifetime, I'm not sure I have seen us (all of us) fuss with each other as much as we do now. I rarely discuss politics; however, please keep this in mind: There are a lot of people, companies and interest groups that make LOADS of money keeping people stirred up.

Please take a moment out of your day today and read the Declaration of Independence. It will not take long and it is an enlightening document. Don't listen to what people say about it . . . read it. You will discover what brilliant minds were involved in forming our country, and how both sides of the aisle can distort the words. The founders wanted representation and used that as a foundation for where we are today . . . along with checks and balances adopted later, all put in place by a vote of the people.

As citizens of this great nation, we have a duty and obligation to be informed by UNBIASED sources. Not opinions, parties or dollar bills, but facts. One thing I truly believe about some of my fellow citizens . . . We rush to anger and judgment without all of the facts.

Lastly, thank you to all of the veterans from all walks of life and eras. I love every single one of you. You are the heroes in this country . . . not sports stars, singers or actors . . . you.

I am an American.

The Brimfield Police Department Reaches 64,000 "Likes"

From a secret location somewhere in MopeBusters Headquarters . . . McHale's Navy, Season 1, on Betamax is being readied for guest number 64,000 . . .

ANIMALS . . . There have been some black bear sightings in the southern portion of our great community. Saxe and Congress Lake, near the reservoir, seems to be a hot spot. The black bear is timid around people and will likely do everything possible to avoid you. If you are a female bear, you will not be avoided. This is probably a male bear, looking for a date. Don't try to make friends with him . . . just make some noise and he will move on. Don't poke the bear . . . for real.

MIDNIGHTS . . . Officers were called to a domestic incident at the same apartment building we arrested the meth cooks in last week. We are seeing a pattern at that location, so we will just drop by and be friendly every day or so . . .

The suspect assaulted his ex-girlfriend by striking her with a cue ball wrapped in a sock and also punched and kicked her. We would add the word allegedly . . . except the injuries are not alleged. This tough guy also held her against her will during the couple hours of on-and-off assaults.

She managed to escape and while running out of the house knocked a storage shelf into his path. He stole her car to skedaddle before we got there. While fleeing the scene, he crashed the car near the 700 block of Sandy Lake Road. After crashing the car, he did what most of us would do . . . he left the scene, went back home and hid in a closet. Officers Atha and Dumont coaxed him out of his hole and awarded him silver bracelets and a trip to the bed and breakfast. He is charged with felony domestic violence, kidnapping and theft. He hits women and attempts to exert control over them physically, likely because they are all far more intelligent.

Oh . . . and he is the father of the subject we arrested last week for cooking meth. Mopery is apparently the family business.

Great job, Officers Atha and Dumont.

The Brimfield Police Department Reaches 69,000 "Likes."

Guest number 69,000 . . . please come to mope central and claim your prizes . . . You have won a Ronco Bottle and Jar Cutter . . . and the K-Tel album "20 Great Truck Driving Songs" . . . from your besties at the BPD!

Gratuities

Since I was five years old I wanted to be a police officer. My best friend Andy and I used to play "cops and robbers" as kids. We were always the cops. Sometimes we were Batman and Robin . . . but we were ALWAYS the good guys. We are still friends today. That was during a time when kids could run around the neighborhood with toy guns and not create a Homeland Security meltdown.

When I became a police officer, I was shocked and sort of embarrassed at the "free stuff" available to police officers. As a rookie I was amazed at the discounts and free beverages heaped on officers. From the beginning I paid for my coffee and did not take discounts. It didn't feel right. At the risk of offending many of my police friends, it is NOT the right thing to do. I understand the concept, though. When a midnight officer walks into a convenience store, the workers feel safe. They also have someone to talk to, so many of the managers have made it a practice to "comp" coffee or pop. It encourages visits. I just have always believed that the cost is recovered somewhere. And we are paid to make them feel safe.

When I became chief, one of the first general orders I submitted was a "no gratuities" policy. We would take nothing without paying full price for it. We still do not. The first day of my tenure was memorable. I walked into one of our local shops here and poured a cup of coffee. I walked to the cashier and was greeted with "You guys don't pay for coffee." I had a line of seven or so people behind me, so I turned to all of them and said "Coffee is free today, people." I thought the clerk was going to pass out. She advised that it was only free for police. I politely told her if it was not free for construction workers, teachers, factory workers or others, it would not be free for us. She tried to tell me there was even a button on the cash register for "police coffee." I introduced myself as the new chief and requested the button be removed. It was.

As police officers, I believe we have enough issues with trust. (A very small percentage of the profession acts contrary to the oath the take, yet all of us pay the price.) We have to convey the message th our integrity is worth more than a 99-cent cup of coffee or three dol' off of a burger and fries. And it is about integrity, isn't it?

DAYSHIFT . . . Theft arrests at the Dollar General. We want to thank the employees there for doing a great job today. A male and female entered the store with their young baby and attempted the old "hide it in the diaper bag" routine. It didn't work out so well. They got arrested . . . the baby did not. (We never arrest babies, because of their cuteness.) Great job to Detective Lance (pinch-hitting on dayshift) and Officer Casterline.

FACEBOOK . . . Well, what a week. The Associated Press article kind of ignited a fire within the Facebook "likes" engine. The subsequent articles by the L.A. Times and others, and the various appearances on TV and radio, pushed it a long some. Now we are starting to slow down, so I figured this was a good time to catch up on some stats, via FB . . .

In the last seven days we have added 14,700 new likes. That is a pretty good pace. Additionally, in the last seven days, over 1.2 million people have read something on our page. Land sakes, that's a lot of people. It's a good thing I am an Internet sensation and refuse to suffer from performance anxiety. There is nothing worse than getting overly stressed and then getting the vapors.

In addition to the numbers, which are impressive, even for legends like us . . . we have received lots of emails and calls from other departments inquiring about our page, our school programs, ice cream tickets and other methods we use to engage our community. We even sent info about the ice cream citations to a department in Canada! We are pleased about the inquiries and the possible changes coming along for those communities.

If you are one of the zillions of emails or messages from the last week . . . be patient with us. We got a little . . . busy (overwhelmed?) with the calls and emails. I will attempt to send replies as soon as possible.

As always . . . thanks for being here and supporting our department . . . we are honored.

The Brimfield Police Department Reaches 70,000 "Likes"

All we can say is . . . thank you.

I am thankful

I am thankful all year. If you go back and read posts over the past two-plus years, I am always thanking someone. During Thanksgiving, I short-circuit. There are so many people I need to thank, I feel like an actor at the Academy Awards.

- My family. I have no idea where to even start. I am so thankful Mrs. Chief and the chief children love and support me. Sometimes I leave for work at 5 a.m. and sometimes I get home at 5 a.m. The phone rings non-stop on most days . . . my life is like a subway station in NYC. Being married to and having a dad as a cop are probably tougher jobs than being a cop.

- I am thankful for the opportunity to be in law enforcement. I love chasing bad guys.

- I am thankful for Mike Kostensky. He is one of my bosses. He, too, is eccentric, so he gets me. He is a huge supporter of us and, without question, I would not be the chief here if he did not take the risk. I have no idea what he was thinking. Sue Fields, another one of my bosses is great, also. She calls regularly to make sure I'm okay and not too stressed . . . she reminds me of a grandmother. She is also a huge supporter of the police department and great to work with.

- I am thankful for John Dalziel, our Township Fiscal Officer. John is the man when it comes to your tax dollars. He guards them like a human Fort Knox. He is a great friend and we have done great things financially for the police department.

- My officers are wonderful. So are their families. The officers are selfless and hustle. They work with and for me, regardless of my propensity to be a difficult boss. I am not even remotely easy to work for. I did not say I am mean . . . I am just hard to work for. We do have some laughs, but some days I would not want me as a boss. I am demanding and want problems solved. Thank you to all of my officers for your dedication.

- I am thankful for all of you. When we started the BPD Facebook page, I was hoping for 500 or so people to check in regularly. It was m' desire to communicate and have a TRULY "transparent" agency; ' agency interacting with the people we serve and also passing inforr tion in a timely manner. It has become so much more, because ' of you. I am grateful to all of you, more than you can imagine. 12,000+ people on this page was unimaginable when we started.

Thank you to all of you. I am humbled by all of the great people in my life.

IN THE COMMUNITY . . . We are told the Brimfield 5-6-year-old coach-pitch boys are playing for the championship trophy tonight at Gracie park in Rootstown. We want to wish the team good luck and great bat speed . . . take it to them, fellas.

AFTERNOON SHIFT . . . The Meth Whisperer was at it again . . . Officer Gramlich with a traffic stop and subsequent arrest of two females for possession of meth, assembly of the chemicals for manufacture and they also had a meth pipe. The arrestees, once again, are NOT from our community.

Life is often about which direction you travel. If you travel this direction with meth and chemicals to make more meth, life is about having lots of pen pals, money on your commissary account and making collect phone calls. Sad, but true.

A big thank-you and job well done to Sgt. McCarty, Officer Putnam and Officer Gramlich.

AFTERNOON SHIFT AND MIDNIGHTS . . . A big party was held by some college students in Brimfield tonight. Although we didn't receive official invitations, some of the neighbors believed we should make an appearance . . . likely because we are Internet sensations and generally the life of most parties . . . oh, and the drunk people in the street may have been a for calling us Johnny Law types.

The positive thing is that our invite came at shift change . . .

When we arrived, the intoxicated people in attendance were so awestruck by seeing famous officers, they began to run away. It looked like a cartoon. After the dust settled and all of the drunken 100-yard dash participants were rounded up . . . we counted 18 physical arrests, for various offenses.

Thank you to the afternoon shift for hanging over. Also, thank you to Kent PD for sending us a transport vehicle.

Great job, Sgt. McCarty and Officers Dumont, Putnam, Gramlich and Allen.

The heat

We had two of them today. I cringe when I hear about these calls. These aren't the earth shattering calls that give officers nightmares. These are the calls that annoy us to no end.

Hey, genius . . . leave your dog at HOME when you go shopping, please. We get these calls during the summer quite frequently. We had two so far today on afternoon shift. "Animal complaint . . . check for a canine left in a vehicle . . . " Seriously? Some people see no issue with leaving a dog in a car when the outside temperature is 88 degrees? So, what is the temp in the car . . . 648 degrees? We are all aware of the scientific fact that most dogs have fur, right?

Usually the officers pull up, get a plate number and find the person. Sometimes the pet owners are coming out as we are arriving. Most of them see nothing wrong with "running in for just a minute to grab something" while the car is off, the windows are "cracked to give him some air" and all is otherwise right in the world of someone who is not thinking ahead.

Fair warning . . . we are going to start looking at animal cruelty charges in these cases. It's not because we are jerks (you all know better), it's because it is wrong and we protect the defenseless. It was 85+ today on both calls. The dogs were panting like they had just chased a rabbit for the last 500 miles. It's just wrong, and that is common sense.

So, the next time you drive through a store parking lot and see someone in the back seat of their car, with their nose sticking out a "cracked window," don't give it a second thought. The officer and the dog will be in the store, visiting. The owner will be locked in the car, panting. I sure hope the officer and dog don't run into an old friend and start talking . . . yikes!

Owning a pet is a responsibility, not a status.

Over and out.

MIDNIGHTS . . . We received a call from a motorist traveling through Brimfield. The motorist reported seeing a vehicle driving down the road with a passenger "shooting up" another passenger with a hypodermic needle/syringe. Sgt. McCarty found the vehicle and stopped it at the Circle K Store. He was joined there by Officer Gramlich.

Shortly into the stop, a passenger tossed an active "shake and bake" meth lab, contained inside of a two-liter bottle, out of the window. One of the passengers also fought with officers while attempting to destroy items which we call evidence. No officers were hurt; however, one of the mope types did receive a few boo-boo's from the scuffle. You know us . . . we are NEVER excessive. My officers do have clear orders from me to defend themselves when needed. I will back them under those conditions every time.

The bottled meth lab rolled under the suspect's vehicle . . . which also had a slight fuel leak and was sitting on top of thousands of gallons of fuel. That's a GREAT situation to find yourself in; fighting with a carload of meth whack-a-doos while also trying to control a rolling bottle bomb. It was a great day in the Field of Brim.

Three suspects were eventually arrested. One of the people in the vehicle was a 16-year-old female. The lab was diffused on scene by the meth lab team and transported to a chemical facility by a disposal crew. Officers also recovered heroin, more meth and used needles from the vehicle.

I would also like to add something to this story. Some posters have commented about the amount of meth arrests we make here. Brimfield is NOT overrun with meth. I guarantee we do not have any more meth than most jurisdictions. There are a few differences. One is, I have some really great police officers. Our mission is to have an impact on crime. I have the officers' "buy-in" for that mission and they take it very seriously. They prepare by training, reading and working hard. The second difference is simple: I am letting everyone know what is going on here. I'll bet you one of my prized John Wayne movies that there were police agencies, close to where you live, that made four meth arrests last week. Some made that many in a day, depending on the size of the agency. The issue is . . . no one is talking about it. All of you and the BPD will talk about it, because of one simple reason: If you don't know there is a problem, you can't help us fix it.

If we all adopt the "anywhere but here" mindset, the criminals will have no shelter.

Small town police officers

Men and women who work in smaller police departments are at times the Rodney Dangerfield of police work. We get no respect . . . at times. Not all of the time, but enough to make us a little edgy on the topic. I hope to give you all some points to consider . . .

According to the Bureau of Justice Statistics, half of all local police departments employ fewer than 10 full-time officers. Almost 75% of police agencies in the U.S. serve a population of 15,000 people or less. So, mathematically speaking, most departments are "small town." Every once in while on our page, someone will rattle off the "small town cops" comment. I wear that one with pride. We are a small agency, no doubt. We serve a population of 10,400 with 13 full-time officers. Modern staffing methods point to the fact we are six officers short of "adequate staffing." Don't tell my officers that. Out of that total, 11 are in uniform and respond to calls, serve the public and enforce laws. These 11 officers answered 15,000+ calls for service and arrested 1,007 people in 2011. Like many other "small" agencies, we do not sit around watching a traffic light waiting on speeders, which is another big fallacy. Small town Brimfield and other police departments across the United States have handled some great and complex issues.

- In my first year as chief we handled four homicides; one included a rampage shooter. He's an ass and is on death row. No offense meant with the language . . . that's mild for how I feel about a guy who shoots and kills two women and a child. The other guy is in prison for life.

- We were one of the first agencies in Ohio to use the Safe Haven law. A few years back we had a newborn (less than an hour old) dropped off at the department . . . and I mean just handed to the on-duty officer. The law allows newborns to be delivered to a safe place within a certain time frame. The baby is safe and doing great, but what an odd thing for us.

- We have arrested and closed hundreds of burglary cases for multiple jurisdictions. One defendant committed 300 burglaries and break-ins in four counties. Our officers and detectives got him and we were able to assist eight agencies in three counties with solving numerous crimes.

I could go on and on with cases and incidents related to our community and other great small departments in the area. The purpose of this babble is not to draw attention; it is to give recognition. Small town officers face the same dangers, calls and issues that are faced by officers who work in 500- or 1,500- or 15,000-officer departments. A person who intends to shoot a police officer to aid an escape, or just out of malice, does not have a "small town" gun or "small town" bullet to use . . . the bullets are the same. The cars careening out of control on the dark roadway while an officer is out working a crash or arresting a drunk driver . . . same cars as in the "big city." The domestics are just as hairy and the drunks are just as intoxicated.

To all of my officers and the thousands of "small town" officers out there . . . thank you for your service. We often go the extra mile for our residents and develop great relationships, and THAT is one of the benefits of being small town "cop."

FACEBOOK . . . A gentle reminder for new folks, visitors and trolls . . . We honor your freedom of speech. We do not honor you using abusive language or having a potty mouth. This is a public location. There are ladies and children present, so we make our points without swearing or threats. We are on a mission to bring back good old-fashioned debate, without the nonsense.

If you act in this manner, you will be banished to some other cyber location . . . and then you can utilize your freedom of speech and right to assemble by holding up a "Chief Oliver is mean" protest sign while walking around outside of the police department.

I will bring you coffee.

The Brimfield Police Department Reaches 74,000 "Likes"

Guest 74,000, please report to the squad room. You have won some great prizes: A Ronco Pasta Maker and a great K-Tel album, "Disco Fever." We care enough to give you the VERY best . . . because we are the BPD.

DAYSHIFT . . . Well, the Facebook page may not be working very well. I know the criminal types watch the page. I have been told this. I'm not sure I am speaking proper mope language.

We just made two arrests at Walmart for theft. The two subjects have been visiting the store (and a few others in the region) for the last several days and pushing computers out the door. There are lots of cameras on the property. We usually catch the bad guys.

These two came in this morning and removed (stole) a computer. We had the plate of the vehicle and pictures and video of the suspects. We were hot on their trail . . . and then they decided to assist us by coming back this afternoon and stealing another computer.

Now, the catch to this whole thing came when I was talking to the suspect who stole the computer. I was jawing at him, telling him about how we do things here and about coming to Brimfield and committing crimes . . . and his reply was . . .

"I know, I read the BPD Facebook page."

So, heaven forbid this falls on deaf ears . . . Criminals, do not come here . . . we will catch you.

Two arrested and going to the bed and breakfast.

THE JUNE STATS ARE HERE . . . Officer Paul Gramlich, AKA "The Meth Whisperer," led the department in physical arrests by making a whopping 21 for the month, including at least nine meth-related offenses. We believe he really wanted this month's prize, which is a vintage Six Million Dollar Man action figure, with bionic eye and bionic grip. Great job, Officer Gramlich!

The Brimfield Police Department Reaches 76,000 "Likes"

Guest 76,000, please report to the front lobby . . . you have won a G.I. Joe with Kung-Fu Grip . . . and the great K-Tel album "K-Tel's Dynamite" featuring the single "Kung Fu Fighting," from the non-pugilists at the BPD.

AFTERNOON SHIFT . . . "The Meth Whisperer," Officer Gramlich, was at it again. Officer Gramlich traffic-stopped a vehicle and then called for a K-9. The doggie alerted to drugs in the vehicle . . . and officers recovered the chemicals for the manufacture of meth—including a bunch of pseudoephedrine, which a female decided to stuff down the front of her pants.

If I have a stuffy nose, I rarely keep my decongestants down the front of my drawers. It is strictly a hygiene thing for me. I usually ask for a bag at the checkout.

Three arrests, and none of the arrestees live here, as is the norm. They lost their bearings . . . got off course . . . and ended up in the Brimfield Triangle. They woke up this morning to loud voices, clanking and the smell of what is believed to be food . . . at the County Bed and Breakfast.

MIDNIGHTS . . . We had another great game of "Hide the pseudoephedrine."

Officer Dumont traffic-stopped a vehicle, and the game was on. The front male passengers handed the boxes of pseudoephedrine to the rear female passenger. She attempted to hide them. But we love the old "shell game," and Officers Dumont and Atha quickly figured it all out.

Three arrested and charged with assemble of the chemicals to make meth . . . and they are NOT residents of our fine community. They also had camping fuel and other fixins' for a batch . . . and now they are at the bed and breakfast, singing a giant rendition of "Folsom Prison Blues."

"I hear the train a comin' . . . "

If you drive through Brimfield with a meth lab or ingredients for one, you are making a mistake. If you come here to one of our stores to buy your supplies . . . you are making a mistake. We are not going away. We are here 24/7/365. We will be relentless.

Great job and hats off to Officers Dumont and Atha . . . keep taking it to them, fellas.

The Brimfield Police Department Reaches 80,000 "Likes"

Being the Police

I love my chosen profession. There is nothing I would rather be doing with my life, other than fishing (and I am not good enough to get paid for that). Law enforcement has one drawback . . . people at times want to hurt or kill us.

When police officers get dressed for work, they put on a bulletproof vest. Think about that for a minute. They are not in the desert, jungle or other front line battlefield. They are in a free country, among their own citizens. Yet they must take precautions against purposeful gunfire . . . for less money than an average autoworker makes per year. That is not a jab at my autoworker friends—it is just the truth.

To some, that fact is too much to handle and they move on and find another profession. For the rest of us, we hang out, do our jobs and spend some time ducking punches.

Here are some facts about police officers, courtesy of the National Law Enforcement Officers Memorial Fund . . .

There are more than 900,000 sworn law enforcement officers now serving in the United States. About 12 percent of those are female.

According to the FBI's Uniform Crime Reports, an estimated 1.3 million violent crimes occurred nationwide in 2010, a six percent decrease from 2009.

Crime fighting has taken its toll. Since the first recorded police death in 1791, there have been over 19,000 law enforcement officers killed in the line of duty. Currently, there are 19,660 names engraved on the walls of the National Law Enforcement Officers Memorial.

A total of 1,799 law enforcement officers died in the line of duty during the past 10 years, an average of one death every 56 hours or 156 per year. There were 163 law enforcement officers killed in 2011.

On average, over the last decade, there have been 58,261 assaults against law enforcement officers each year, resulting in 15,658 injuries.

Who in their right mind would sign up for such a job?

Police officers deal with things most do not or could not understand. I'm not being condescending with that statement; it is the truth. The police put on bulletproof vests, wear guns and are supposed to keep law abiding people safe from those who would make them victims. The police are screamed at, shot at, stabbed, spit on and assaulted . . . yet, we return every day for more. Police make a decision in less than a second, and people with law degrees and dreams of vacation houses in Maui take nine months to pick those decisions apart. Regardless of what we "signed up" for or are "trained" to do, trying to determine if the person in the woods at 2:30 in the morning, who won't show you his hands, is trying to kill you or not has to be a snap decision and it has to be right EVERY time . . . or the officer risks losing a house, job and more. I know some of you have met officers you didn't care for very much. I get that. I have met police officers, teachers, factory workers, lawyers and doctors I have not liked interacting with. Every profession has grumpy people. I choose to not judge an entire profession by one interaction. I hope you will do the same.

A majority of police officers love this job. They don't do it for the great pay. We make a good living and I am not complaining. Most, including me, do it because we have a servant's heart. We change tires, push cars, unlock locked doors and enforce laws which make this society a better place to live.

Many of you post about my habit of commending my officers on our page. That is huge for me. I have told all of you how I feel about my crew of crime fighters. They are the real deal. They are well trained, have developed great habits and have an unmatched work ethic. They come in early, leave late and in between that time they catch bad guys, interact with seniors and children and just serve people. I can't teach that. I can try to hire those skills, but cannot teach it. We can give them the tools, the training and other needed things to do police work, but I can't teach character.

I cannot write enough letters, send enough emails or post enough Facebook "atta-boys" to express my admiration for my officers.

*   *   *

To all police officers out there . . . and a bunch of you read our page . . . thank you for everything. Thanks for walking into that dark building at night, answering a burglar alarm with an open door and the hair on the back of your neck standing on end. Thank you for answering the call for the domestic dispute and the abuser who wants to assault you, too. Thanks for getting punched in the face while at work. Thanks for knowing you must have the exact proper backdrop before returning fire, while the criminal who is shooting at you can fire indiscriminately without a care in the world.

Thanks for hugging that child . . . the one who just watched a loved one die in a car crash. Thanks for taking time to speak with that other child . . . the one who has no positive role model to be found. Thanks for NOT kicking the life out of the pedophile. We must rise above the roadside justice. Thanks for answering the call for "cows in the road." Yes, we are wranglers, too. Thanks for completing your mountains of paperwork on time. We know the drunk driver is snug in his bed before your paperwork is done. Thanks for working all night and then making three court appearances . . . at 9 a.m., 11 a.m. and 1 in the afternoon. Thanks for watching our houses while we sleep. Thanks for working for the supervisor who probably should have retired 10 years ago. Thanks for working for those who do not support you. Thanks for the sacrifices. Thanks for working weekends, midnights, holidays and during the dance recital or baseball game. Thanks for working in the snow, rain or hot sun.

To the families who have lost a loved one in this job . . . my heart is broken for you. And to all who have died on this job . . . thank you for your sacrifice to the greatest profession on earth. We honor and love all of you.

And we will continue the watch.

Afterword

This may be the end of the book, but it is certainly not the end of the story. The Brimfield Police Department continues on, and so will the saga of mopes, a love for the community and the strong desire to serve and protect our residents. If you want to read more, join the conversation on Facebook at www.facebook.com/brimfieldpolice. I'm confident we'll have more to say.

All proceeds I receive from this book are being directed to The Chief Oliver Foundation. My wife, Lisa (Mrs. Chief), and I formed the foundation as a vehicle to give to those who need it. The foundation will distribute funds to police department charitable programs and assist juvenile survivors of sexual assault. We will strive to get these children into programs to help them move forward. For example, we will help these children by paying for dance, art and other programs . . . and sustain it long-term. I have always believed that the victims of crime are often forgotten when the wheels of justice complete all of their revolutions. We want to help change that. You can find us on Facebook at www.facebook.com/thechiefoliverfoundation or our website: www.thechiefoliverfoundation.org .

As always, a hearty thank-you and a chief hug to all of our thousands of cousins. Without you, we would surely not have as much fun.

Acknowledgments

I would like to acknowledge some very fine people for their assistance with my career and in my life travels.

To my officers and staff at the Brimfield Police Department . . . you are simply the best law enforcement people I could ask for. Thanks for your sacrifices to make this a better world.

Brimfield Trustees Mike Kostensky and Sue Fields . . . thanks for taking the chance on a loudmouth, inexperienced chief. And Mike . . . thanks for being the best boss ever.

John Dalziel, Brimfield Township Fiscal Officer . . . thanks for being honest, trustworthy and a good friend.

Lt. William Shanafelt (Ret), Western Portage Drug Task Force . . . Thanks for teaching me leadership. You were nutty; however, you were one heck of a leader.

Det. Paul Fafrak, Kent Police, Thanks for being a very good friend and a great partner during the "drug-unit days." You are one in a million and never fail to make me laugh. "They're cooking it up in bread pans!"

David Gray, Rob Lucas and the rest of the Gray & Company staff . . . you all are fantastic people. Thanks for this opportunity and for being one very professional and highly skilled team.

For biographies of active Brimfield Police Department stafff, please visit: **www.BrimfieldPolice.com**